BUILDING
THE
DREAM

BUILDING THE DREAM

A SOCIAL HISTORY OF HOUSING IN AMERICA

GWENDOLYN WRIGHT

The MIT Press
Cambridge, Massachusetts
London, England

Sixth printing, 1993

First MIT Press paperback edition, 1983

First published by Pantheon Books, a division of Random
House, Inc., New York

This book was printed and bound in the United States of America.

LIBRARY OF CONGRESS CATALOGING IN PUBLICATION DATA

Wright, Gwendolyn.
Building the dream.

Bibliography: p.
Includes index.
1. Housing—United States—History. 2. Architecture,
Domestic—Social aspects—United States—History.
I. Title.
HD7293.W74 1983   363.5'0973   82-24954
ISBN 0-262-73064-2 (pbk.)

Grateful acknowledgment is made to the following for
permission to reprint from previously published material: *The
University of Chicago Press:* Excerpts from *Moralism and the
Model Home* by Gwendolyn Wright. Copyright © 1980 by
The University of Chicago Press.

CONTENTS

LIST OF ILLUSTRATIONS

Appleton-Taylor-Manfield House, restored, Saugus, Massachusetts, ca. 1680 *(Photo by C. Parke Pressley, 1923. Courtesy of Society for the Preservation of New England Antiquities)*, p. 6

Parlor, restored, Appleton-Taylor-Manfield House, Saugus, Massachusetts, ca. 1680 *(Photo by William W. Owens, Jr., 1974)*, p. 13

Painting of a child, "Alice Mason, 1668" *(Courtesy of U.S. Department of the Interior, National Park Service, Adams Historic Site, Quincy, Massachusetts)*, p. 14

Francis Guy, painting of a winter scene in Brooklyn, New York, 1817–1820 *(Courtesy of Museum of the City of New York)*, p. 28

Row of artisans' brick houses on Aliceanna Street, Baltimore, ca. 1800 *(Courtesy of Historic American Building Survey [HABS], Library of Congress)*, p. 28

Thomas Carstairs's drawing of row-house floor plans and elevation, Philadelphia, built ca. 1801–1803 *(Courtesy of Library Company of Philadelphia)*, p. 29

Alfred Fredericks, "May-Day in the City," drawing published in *Harper's Weekly*, 1859 *(Courtesy of Museum of the City of New York)*, p. 30

ACKNOWLEDGMENTS

I HAVE BENEFITTED FROM THE ENCOURAGEMENT AND the suggestions of a large number of people in the time this book has been in the making. Three people deserve special thanks for their roles: Herbert G. Gutman, Dolores Hayden, and Robert N. Bellah. Each gave me support, both personal and professional, and the examples of their own impressive work, which I have tried to follow.

Many others have generously read and commented on parts of the manuscript, sharing their expertise in particular fields: James Deetz, David Gebhard, J. Brian Horrigan, J. B. Jackson, Kenneth T. Jackson, Michel Laguerre, Lawrence Levine, Leon Litwack, Roy Lubove, Roger Montgomery, Leland M. Roth, William Simmons, Kathryn Kish Sklar, William M. Sullivan, and Sally Woodbridge. I appreciate their suggestions and their challenges to my interpretations.

I would also like to acknowledge the help of the staffs of a number of libraries where I conducted research: the Library of Congress; the National Archives; the New York Public Library; the New-York Historical Society; the Boston Public Library; the Schlesinger Library of Radcliffe College; the Chicago Historical

Society; the Regenstein Library of the University of Chicago; the Newberry Library; the Seattle and Kings County Historical Society; the Los Angeles County Museum of Natural History; the Los Angeles Public Library; the California Historical Society; and the libraries of the University of California at Berkeley. In particular, Janet Parks of the Avery Library of Columbia University, Mary Ison of the prints and photographs department of the Library of Congress, Esther Bromberg of the Museum of the City of New York, and Arthur Waugh of the Environmental Design Library at the University of California at Berkeley were especially helpful. Marta Gutman and Ann Merrill were painstaking and often imaginative in helping with the research.

A generous fellowship from the Ford Foundation provided a year of writing and traveling. The questions I was asked by the foundation staff had an important influence in directing the course of my work.

For turning the experience into an unexpected delight, from beginning to end, my thanks to the many people at Pantheon who have been a part of this production—and especially to Nan Graham and Susan Gyarmati.

My husband, Paul Rabinow, has been supportive, lifting my spirits when they flagged and pulling me away when work became too encompassing. He has given me critical readings and productive impatience. Most of all, he has been the reason why I understood something more about what "home" can mean to people.

INTRODUCTION

FOR CENTURIES AMERICANS HAVE SEEN DOMESTIC architecture as a way of encouraging certain kinds of family and social life. Diverse contingents have asserted that our private architecture has a distinctly public side, and that domestic environments can reinforce certain character traits, promote family stability, and assure a good society. Those who sought a new social order, whether they were radical orators or enterprising capitalists, have argued that American culture was malleable, in part because the physical environment of previous generations was less of a constraint than it had been in other countries. They contended that new models for housing, even more than improved factories or institutional buildings, would provide the proper setting for a great nation. Others who sought to resist radical change or assimilation have also looked to the home as a reminder of their own cultural traditions and as a protected realm for private family life, presumably outside the larger society. As a consequence, Americans have been quite self-conscious about where they live and where their fellow citizens live as well.

Bearing these attitudes in mind, I have sought to characterize the controversies surrounding thirteen different kinds of dwellings at the time they were first adopted and then generally accepted. I am not offering a scholarly treatment of any period but rather an interpretative essay that attempts to raise certain issues about American housing, and that relates the various architectural and ideological models this country has adopted. At any point in the past when Americans had to consider housing for a particular group, they felt it was necessary to talk about much more than architecture. Discussions have involved hopes and fears about family stability, attitudes about community, and beliefs about social and economic equality. And these issues have influenced design.

By emphasizing certain themes, I do not want to suggest a consensus. More than one model for the home and family have usually co-existed, although seldom in harmony. The principal American type has been the detached rural or suburban single-family cottage for citizens "of the middling sort." But there have always been several kinds of specialized habitations for people who did not fit this mold. Such minorities have included city dwellers, both the poor and the wealthy, and various groups that chose to live collectively, with shared services and sometimes land held in common. Also, people whose lives were controlled by others had appropriate settings allocated to them. Several variations of industrial towns, designed by managers and professional planners, reflect ideas about control over and amelioration of factory workers. There is also a long lineage of slave housing in the South, some of which still stands, especially in rural areas. These two architectural traditions are now raising controversies as the descendants of worker and capitalist, black and white, consider historic preservation of the earlier buildings. Which memories, they ask, do we want to preserve?

Urban row houses, company towns, even residential suburbs, were usually planned in orderly rows of almost identical habitations. These planned communities form one persistent theme in American housing history, extending from the seventeenth-century New England township to the more recent townhouse development. A longstanding tension exists between the housing model based on communities of similar dwellings and a seemingly conflicting ideal of personalized, self-sufficient dwellings. Given the national tendency to endow domestic architecture with individual character traits and a social profile, these two patterns carry the weight of a social as well as an aesthetic dichotomy. Each of the four chronological parts of this book contrasts community planning with models for individualized houses. The ways in which planning has come to dominate every kind of housing in this country is a central theme. So too is the issue of homeownership, which has been so closely associated with detached dwellings.

This book is about ordinary houses—not all types of dwellings but only the kinds of "model homes" Americans built in great numbers, the housing prototypes they discussed with special intensity through the course of American history. It is a history of residential architecture but only rarely of professional architects. In this account, government officials, popular journalists, land speculators, reformers, and industrialists have been more important actors. It is also about the different kinds of people who lived in these houses, ranging from the New England household of the seventeenth century to the elderly women in a Chicago public-housing tower to the young couple in a townhouse condominium. What kinds of places did these people fashion for themselves, and what was proposed for them? How did they live in their homes, and how were they told they should live?

Housing inevitably involves a compromise between residents and groups of experts. Neither the way buildings look nor the way people live in them can be reduced to a formula dictated by architects, social scientists, or advertising companies. Particular households never fit a mold exactly or follow advice in magazines to the letter. Most Americans have strong opinions about their families, their communities, and their homes, and those stances are visible. Definite ethnic and class variations are recognizable, as are regional and personal variations.

However, the process of giving meaning to the home has not always been salutary. Slavery and racism, industrial exploitation, the segregation of classes, and a limited role for women have found expression in American patterns of residential architecture. The longstanding national tendency to view the home as the expression of the self has encouraged a staunch defense of social homogeneity on the one hand, and a cult of personalized decoration on the other. Yet, there is no necessary correlation between personalized architecture and a great range of character distinctions. In many cases, consumerism became institutionalized in home decoration as advertising promised new ways to promote family togetherness, social prestige, and self-expression. A preoccupation with the private dwelling has also encouraged a false sense of the family's self-sufficiency and a fear of others intruding. All too often, in suburbs and in cooperative apartments, community has meant the exclusion of those who are not like ourselves. These reactions, too, have a history.

Americans' passion for the home gives the history of housing a significance that goes beyond antiquarianism. Each debate about housing needs extended across class lines, although some groups have clearly had more power to implement their visions than have others. The assertion of a fundamental right to "a decent home" has been a basic tenet of the American way of life. Yet, the definition of "a decent home" raises difficult questions: What is the proper role of the family? What is a good balance between family privacy and community life, or between individual freedom of choice and governmental controls? Is the single-family detached house in the suburbs the only acceptable expression of the decent home, and the nuclear family the best living arrangement? Does democratic equality mean a right simply to shelter, or a right to dignity, choice, and acceptance by others?

Today, housing issues are important topics for numerous interest groups around the country. Rent control, racial integration, ethnic neighborhoods, zoning battles, the needs of elderly people, energy priorities, and the shortage of decent housing at affordable prices are the focus of diverse community-based organizations and special-interest lobbies on the right and the left. Books and conferences consider the future of the family and the scope of the current housing crisis. What does it mean, for example, when a pattern that, until recently, had been considered the "typical household"—the mother and young children at home and the father at work—now encompasses just over 10 percent of the American population? Many builders are troubled by the social and demographic changes, but in order to capture the potential markets, their designs must change according to changing living situations.

The current concern about a housing crisis, like the recognition of the diversity in American society, is overdue. However, both situations have created a sense of total discontinuity. It is as if, until now, life was stable, bountiful, homogeneous, and relatively unproblematic. The combined impact of a severe energy shortage, soaring prices, and social conflicts has left many Americans disheartened. They speak of the "end of the American Dream." They tend to connect that dream to certain kinds of houses —notably detached houses in the suburbs—and to the belief that those houses used to be available to anyone who worked hard enough. But this contemporary crisis is neither unprecedented nor as devastating as it seems. Many times in the past, Americans have had to find new housing alternatives in response to social, economic, and technological problems. This is not meant to downplay the current problems but to put them in a historical perspective, and to show that policies and attitudes of the past—ways of viewing conservation, the role of women, racial differences, or urban life—helped create the current housing crisis.

Ways of confronting problems also tend to be repeated. The sense of sudden crises, unrelated to past policies and requiring rigorously enforced solutions, occurs again and again. In this sense, housing is like other fields. People become involved in political or community action in response to social issues. They also tend to deny the complexity of the issues and the diversity of people who are affected. Then the activism is often short-lived.

Architectural structures cannot fully remedy inequalities or redress wrongs or solve problems. Yet houses and residential communities do point up a great deal about social values, in the past and in the present. The subject of housing stimulates debate and social action. The history of American houses shows how Americans have tried to embody social issues in domestic architecture, and how they have tried, at the same time, to use this imagery to escape a social reality that is always more complex and diverse than the symbols constructed to capture it.

—Gwendolyn Wright
February 1981

PART ONE

FOUNDATIONS FOR SOCIAL ORDER

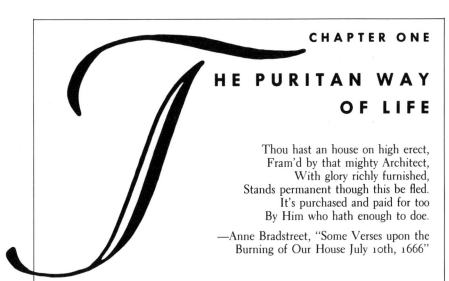

CHAPTER ONE

THE PURITAN WAY
OF LIFE

Thou hast an house on high erect,
Fram'd by that mighty Architect,
With glory richly furnished,
Stands permanent though this be fled.
It's purchased and paid for too
By Him who hath enough to doe.

—Anne Bradstreet, "Some Verses upon the
Burning of Our House July 10th, 1666"

THE PURITANS WHO SETTLED IN NEW ENGLAND IN the seventeenth century established a profoundly self-conscious way of life that extended to every aspect of each individual's existence: family, church, politics, work, landscape, and dwelling. This is not to say that everything they created during these years, from architecture to philosophy, was distinguishable from contemporary English traditions. The colonists brought with them an English cultural heritage. A continuity is evident in their writings, their laws, and their buildings. But the emigrants also had particular principles of religious and social life that were deeply opposed to Elizabethan standards. They wanted to create a society—and an environment—that reflected their own "purified" ideas of godliness. In New England, they altered many aspects of their common English heritage so that their lives would more accurately represent their particular values.

The Puritans soon came to see architecture and site planning as provocative didactic tools. Their dwellings and their towns were an original, non-European expression of their beliefs and fears. For the Puritans, architectural structures were a microcosm of God's exacting structure for the universe and a constant reminder of the way

He wanted them to live. This was an early instance of what would become a continuing American theme: the desire to give tangible expression to values, in part to celebrate self-confidence and pride, in part from fear of not being able to live up to one's ideals. The Puritans' goal in the New World, which governed all their activities, was "to manipulate material life for spiritual ends."[1]

To be sure, the English Calvinist heritage of the Puritans is not every contemporary American's background. Nor are these houses a legacy outside the small area where the Puritans erected their cities and towns. Yet many aspects of the Puritan ethic do color our broader American culture. Wealth was not necessarily considered a sign of God's favor, but most theologians believed that God rewarded his chosen with worldly success—and thereby also tempted them. Industriousness and respect for wealth as a sign of good work have become national virtues. The nostalgia so patent in colonial revival houses and quaint "New England village squares" of condominiums (often with false half-timber ornament) builds directly upon a common and vital image of what life was like in these seventeenth-century townships. The Puritan leaders established a system that linked most aspects of daily life with more abstract issues of religious sentiment, social order, and family bonds. In the process, they began a tradition of calculatedly symbolic dwelling forms, which has continued through many other American housing types. This history, therefore, begins with that early experiment.

The Puritans were the principal English group to settle in the New World, and the English were the largest group of Europeans to colonize North America. The Spanish, Britain's major rival, were more interested in founding missions and military *presidios* rather than *pueblos* for immigrants, despite their prototype colonial town laid down in the Laws of the Indies. These Englishmen and women had many reasons for their move. Some were husbandmen or unlanded farmers, either younger sons without claim to family land or men who had lost their holdings in the recent enclosure movement. Many were fervent Separatists in their religion who sought to purify the Church of England by creating a religious commonwealth that respected biblical injunctions and opposed what seemed the Anglican church's license. Critical of English society, the Separatists were persecuted in their homeland. As a result, numerous sects vowed to come to the colonies, there to create the kinds of religious communities they believed God favored and to raise their children in their own faith.

An important distinction sets apart one sect, the Puritans, ten thousand of whom settled in the Massachusetts Bay Colony between 1628 and 1634, armed with a charter to establish a holy commonwealth. Among them were commercial merchants and even members of the gentry, as well as artisans, farmers, husbandmen, and servants. Consequently, their project was endowed with more capital than other ventures. They rapidly became the largest and the most politically dominant colony.

Furthermore, these Puritans believed in the sanctity of the hierarchy that existed among them. God, they were convinced, had ordained certain people to be rich and poor, master and servant, according to a divine plan. From church to family, the Puritans lived in a highly structured, logically explained, and strictly enforced hierarchy. Yet, each of them had freely chosen to obey or, if necessary, to dissent, for God had given men and women the faculties of a rational soul. The tension of choice, on the one hand, and rigid laws and duties on the other, created a troublesome set of paradoxes.

The Puritans, in their constant self-doubt, their suspicion of their own senses and emotions, buttressed themselves with visible reminders of religious precepts and an image of how God expected the world to be. They carefully created an environment in which the houses and towns reflected their concepts about a divinely ordained structure for family relations and social life.

The opportunity to create such a world gave them great joy. Edward Johnson, a member of a contingent that set sail in 1630, acknowledged that they "forsooke a fruitfull Land, stately Buildings, goodly Gardens." In New England, "the onely encouragements were the laborious breaking up of bushy ground, with the continued toyl of erecting houses, for themselves and cattel, in this howling desert." Yet even the difficulties proved rewarding. The settlers worked "with much cheerfulness, that they might enjoy Christ and his Ordinances in their primitive purity."[2]

Conditions in New England were indeed primitive. Even with the benefits of money, provisions, and prestige, which brought the Massachusetts Bay Colony a remarkable amount of independence from the crown, there were innumerable hardships in their "errand into the wilderness." These would affect both social life and architecture. During the first winters at any new settlement, almost everyone suffered equally. The earliest habitations—dugouts, wigwams, huts of bent saplings covered with thatch or grass—provided minimal protection. One early inhabitant observed: "They burrow themselves in the Earth for their first shelter under some Hill side . . . yet in these poor Wigwames they sing Psalms, pray, and praise their God, till they can provide them houses."[3] These types of houses were partly adaptations of Indian dwellings, made from the same local materials. There was also an obvious carry-over from the crude, one-room windowless hut or "cottage" of wattle (interwoven twigs) and daub (a mixture of mud or clay, sometimes with hair or straw), used by poor English cotters in Yorkshire, Suffolk, or Lancashire.

Within a few years of the Great Migration of 1630, as the Puritan population steadily increased, the ministers, the governor, and the prominent merchants erected more permanent wooden frame houses. In a sense, they were laying out "company towns," with both an investment value and a symbolic expression of social hierarchy. Private domestic

· ·

The Appleton-Taylor-Manfield House at Saugus, Massachusetts, also called the Iron-works House, was built, ca. 1680, by a relatively wealthy manufacturer in the Massachusetts Bay Colony. His family and apprentices lived and worked there together.

architecture and public town planning worked as a unit to show the imprint of the Puritans' beliefs, and their concerns. By 1636, when Anne Hutchinson's Antinomian heresy contended that private revelations, rather than the public message of the ministers, were closest to God, the dominant interpretation of Puritan ideals could be widely seen in a massive house-building campaign throughout the Massachusetts Bay Colony.

What were these ideals? According to Puritan theology, every individual had to face his or her basically sinful nature and hope that God had the extraordinary beneficence to have granted salvation. They believed that this was a fairly arbitrary gesture on God's part, decided before each person's birth. A community that accepted this frighteningly peremptory relationship would then choose to come together in a covenant around a church and a minister. The covenant was a complex structure, one of the cores of Puritan dogma and experience. First was the Covenant of Grace between God and Abraham, in which God had provided all humans with the faith to believe in Him and with salvation for those He chose to redeem. God saved individuals, but He did not want people to live too independently of one another. The church covenant was the joining together, under a minister's guidance, of those who had experienced conversion and been accepted for baptism. These were the elite of the community, the only ones, until 1691, who were allowed to vote. (In 1691, property rather than sainthood became the basis for the franchise.) The state covenant nonetheless extended to the non-baptised in these religious communities. This was the God-given relationship of the governor and the governed in a cohesive political and social body. The family too was a covenant, with the father in the role of God's chosen governor.

An individual therefore existed only in a social context, in a network of relationships. No one was allowed to live alone. Bachelors and widows or widowers were placed with other families as servants or boarders (although widows usually remarried quickly, since women were in a minority). Everyone had to be part of the state covenant and part of a family government. The medieval sense of extended social bonds persisted: "a family is a little common wealth, and a common wealth is a greate family."[4]

The Puritans lived according to an innovative social contract. Relations of every sort were governed by an elaborately symmetrical system of logic. The principal text for Puritan theologians and scholars was Petrus Ramus's *Dialecticae* (1556), which described the inherent structure of all things in the universe as based on sets of dichotomies within a hierarchical order. God had determined the framework, and the minister's task was to make it visible. Within this order were husbands and wives, parents and children, masters and servants, governors and governed, each "relative" dependent on the other for its place in God's world. As it was explicated, the system worked against democratic restructurings. Once a person had chosen a spouse, or a group had chosen its minister or governor, they were bound to obey that person, unless he exceeded his office. In a celebrated oration at his 1645 impeachment trial, Governor John Winthrop declared that civil liberty was maintained only with subjection to authority. Yet there was room for active resistance; Winthrop was tried.

These orderly communities of church and state and family were not designed to persuade God to save anyone. That had already been decided. In fact, the moment at which God seemed to offer a vision of personal salvation was viewed with suspicion by the anxious Puritan. It could too easily be false self-assurance or the work of the Devil. Diaries, poems, and letters betray a constant, beleaguered self-examination of every thought and action. Good social conduct was, however, evidence of a person's being among the chosen, even if it was not proof. Only the "person of visible Sanctity" could have been granted salvation. Saintliness was a radiant quality, apparent in every gesture, word, and activity. Outward appearances and comportment were, therefore, always watched closely for signs.

The Puritans' sense of special status in God's eyes was deeply rooted. Governor Winthrop insisted upon the holiness of their expedition in his "Modell of Christian Charity," written as he crossed the Atlantic on the *Arbella* in 1630: "For wee must Consider that wee shall be as a Citty upon a Hill, the eies of all people are uppon us."[5] Winthrop's city was, foremost, a religious symbol. He and his followers saw themselves as the legacy of the primitive Christian church, the New Israel.

In Massachusetts, the holy commonwealth needed a definite form, a "visibility." The Puritans' mission required that they impose a defined order upon what must have seemed chaos. This seemed possible only among well-established and disciplined groups, in towns and cities, under the authority of a minister and a governor. A notable source for Puritan planning in New England is an anonymous document called "The Ordering of Towns." This model proposed a townscape of six concentric circles set within a square, six miles to a side. The meeting house at the center determined the size of the township, for no one was allowed to live more than one and a half miles away from it, in order to assure regular attendance. Town records provide numerous cases of people being required to move closer to the town center during the early generations. Even private property was, in theory, superseded by public order. The model town was intended to be an agricultural settlement with a tight core. Home lots were in the center of the village, together with the meeting house. Each family's strips of arable farmland, grazing pasture, and forest for wood, as well as the common fields, swamps, and rubbish waste ground, surrounded this nucleus of buildings.

The right to establish each new town derived from the Massachusetts Bay Colony General Court, which clearly followed this document in its calculations. Allotments were based on the position and wealth of a family within the community, so that the land divisions and the size of houses varied considerably. There were provisions to prohibit speculation: common practice in each new town required that a purchaser erect a house and enclose a certain amount of farmland within a given period in order to maintain the rights of private ownership. Finally, the prototype and the actual towns based on it were closed systems. Once land allocated for a township had been sold, newcomers had to find a minister and begin another community.

Within a few years of settlement, the elaborate structuring of the town had extended to architecture. The meeting house was always the first important building to be erected, and it was a consistent form from one settlement to another. Unlike Anglican churches, with their steeples and elegant Baroque ornament, the meeting house was an unpretentious structure, for the Puritans did not believe that human beings had the right to consecrate buildings. The church was the congregation, not the structure where they worshipped. In many ways, the meeting house looked like a large dwelling. Since religion extended to every aspect of life, and the building was not considered sacred, it was the site for many other public assemblies, and often for schools, in addition to religious services.

Next to the meeting house would be erected a house for the minister and homes for other prominent families. Farmers and artisans built dwellings nearby, where home lots had been allocated to them. In the early colonies houses were surprisingly varied in appearance, reflecting different regions in England and differing status in the New World. Archaeologists have discovered traces of several types dating from the 1630s. They include one-room framed cottages, sixteen to twenty feet square, with stone or brick fireplaces; houses with a kitchen lean-to added to the back, creating the familiar salt-box appearance; and ten feet by forty feet "long houses" with two hearths. In areas where field stone and lime for mortar were abundant (particularly in parts of Connecticut and Rhode Island), families built stone-ended houses and a few stone dwellings. Other structures of primitive "posthole" or bent-tree "cruck" construction, derived from English cottages and barns, were also scattered about. (However, since the sills were generally placed directly on the ground or laid on very thin stones, these have usually perished.) Over time, more and more families were able to construct wooden frame houses, although the amount of work and the large number of hands required for any house-raising still reinforced the social hierarchy. The Pilgrims, who first erected one-room or two-room thatched cottages, began erecting more substantial "faire and pleasant houses" of solid timber by the 1630s.[6] The first written account of a framed house for an artisan describes a simple story-and-a-half structure built for a Rhode Island weaver in 1640.

The most commonly constructed type of framed house in New England colonial towns was a two-room, or "hall-and-parlor," dwelling. The Fairbanks house at Dedham, Massachusetts (the oldest existing wooden frame building in the New World, built in 1636), is a good example of such a structure. A small receiving hall opens just behind the door, with stairs leading up to the loft bedrooms. A massive chimney (seven feet in breadth was quite common) dominates the entire space, as it dominated home life; here was the sole source of light, heat, and cooked food. A medieval sense of architectural planning is conspicuous. The two main rooms, to either side of the central hallway, are of almost equal size, generally each about sixteen square feet or one "bay." The door and windows are slightly asymmetrical as well. Likewise, the adjacent outbuildings, added as needs were apparent and time available, were neither placed on axis with, nor based on a module of, the principal structure.

While early-seventeenth-century houses may look like crude structures whose builders relied on different types of construction but showed no great thought for their appearance, many choices were being made in their design. There were important similarities among the houses in each Puritan settlement in New England. The carpenters did deviate from the English practices they had known, certainly rejecting the emerging Baroque fashions of Inigo Jones and Sir Christopher Wren, and adapting to the climate and materials of their new home. They also followed their own deeply felt religious and social beliefs.

Puritan ministers described a good sermon as being of the "plain style." They were aiming for a radically different effect from their Anglican counterparts. To their ear, metaphysical arguments and embroidered rhetoric were impious. Excessive ornamentation glorified the orator and played upon the passions rather than the mind of the listener. The Bible's use of "earthly Similitudes" was considered the most truthful and honest approach. Examples from other arts were frequently invoked to explain this attitude. Reverend Richard Baxter, in his definition of aesthetic standards, declared that "painted obscure sermons" were like "Painted Glass in the Windows that keep out the Light."[7] Theologians often employed such architectural metaphors to instruct congregations about God's intricate structure of the universe. The message was undoubtedly influential among the carpenters who erected houses in the holy commonwealth, for they were concerned about the world they were creating. During the first year in their new world, Francis Higginson had declared, "We that are setled at Salem make what haste we can to build Houses, so that within a short time we shall have a faire Town."[8] "Faire" implied square and regular, as well as handsome; the desire to create an orderly, attractive setting affected these Puritans deeply.

By the late 1630s, a type of domestic architecture particular to all the Puritan colonies in Massachusetts, Rhode Island, and Connecticut had begun to emerge. Because of the harsh winters and bountiful timber supply, it became almost universal practice to finish the exterior with clapboards, always laid horizontally and left unpainted. These clapboards were thinner and much more prevalent than the weatherboards occasionally found on English houses. Wood shingles replaced the English tradition of thatch for roof coverings, especially after several early fires. The "faire houses" were of a heavy, braced-timber frame, held together by mortise and tenon joints, stiffened by angle braces at the corners. Heavy oak interior beams buttressed the central chimney and ran the length of the house. As Samuel Symonds wrote of the 1638 house plans, "I would have the house stronge in timber, though plaine & well brased."[9] This type of construction was obviously labor-intensive. It was practical in the colonies, where wood was abundant. In England, however, a severe shortage of timber was transforming building practices in every village and city.

The structure of the larger houses—the braced frame, the wattle-and-daub or nogging (brick masonry) insulation set between half-timber diagonal infill—was based on familiar English building techniques. The infill of a house in the American colonies was then covered over, outside by clapboards and inside by lime plaster or, in elegant houses, by wide vertical wood paneling. In certain highly visible places, the frame structure was left exposed, contrasting sharply with the whitewash. In some houses color was used to emphasize the contrast: beams were covered with a thin coat of black, the summer beam and chimney girts in vermilion, or the posts in dark green. The example of the ministers' plain style suggests why the emphasis on visible structure within and naked simplicity without became so pervasive among Puritan carpenters and house painters.

The fortress-like appearance of the seventeenth-century colonial house also distinguished it from contemporary English dwellings. The door was a solid barrier, often of several layers studded with pieces of metal. Such heavy, defensive doors were unknown in England. Windows were few and small. Most families used only wooden shutters or oiled paper for protection, although a few later brought over small (about one-foot-square) English casements, leaded with diamond panes. The export of window glass to the colonies came under a high tax, so even a wealthy family could afford, at most, only two or three "lights." The windows were stationary, with the glass or oiled paper fixed in place, since night air was considered noxious. Even those who could afford casements often chose not to have many. Deputy-Governor Samuel Symonds, who could command what he wanted, specified for his house at Ipswich, "For windows, let them not be over large in any roome, & few as conceivably may be."[10] Such measures were in part efforts to conserve heat and ward off possible Indian attacks, and in part economies. They also reveal a particular stance toward the world outside the house, an attitude that would begin to alter dramatically in the next century. Nature was not considered a gentle, inspiring force to be courted, a teacher to instruct human beings about universal values. The wall of the house was decidedly a barrier to the outside; there was no thought of a continuity between interior and exterior domain.

Even more than the façade, the interior of a New England dwelling shows the distinctive architectural ideals of the Puritans. Here the family lived, according to the rules and duties of their covenants. Surveillance of one another was necessary. An individual promised God not only faith and good works for himself or herself, but a sanctified life for the entire group. As the Reverend John Cotton told his congregation, they were each responsible for "all under our reach, either by way of subordination or coordination."[11] If the family kept God's laws and lived harmoniously, then He would reward them, said the Scriptures, with peace and prosperity in this world; otherwise, He would smite them down like Sodom and Gomorrah.

Self-control had to be instilled in each individual, but it was enforced by the group. Composure and concord were especially difficult under the cramped living conditions that prevailed in all houses. Few families were composed of fewer than six people, with at least one servant or apprentice among their number. The average number of children was nine, although many died in infancy.[12] It was considered important to be together, all sharing the same space. The attributes most pleasing to God, in addition to virtuous living, were good work and industriousness.

• •

The restored parlor of the Appleton-Taylor-Manfield House shows the massive hearth and the exposed beams that dominated both downstairs rooms in a typical Puritan dwelling.

A painting of young Alice Mason, commissioned in 1668, shows a very serious, adultlike child. The checkered, canvas floor-cloth beneath her feet is an example of Puritan decorative liveliness.

Every hand should always be busy at a useful task. Children were especially prone to idle play, for they were closest to original sin. (As one minister wrote, God had reserved for them "the easiest room in Hell."[13]) The intensity with which Puritan parents sensed this need for rigor and hard work is summed up in the practice of "putting out children." If a son showed talent for a trade other than that of his father, or if the parents felt they were too permissive, they were encouraged to place the child in another family, sometimes in a distant town, sometimes for years at a time if he indeed became an apprentice.

Architecture aided the delicate duties of self-control and constant industriousness. In the seventeenth-century colonial house plan, there were rarely more than two downstairs rooms. The hall, or keeping room, was the center of the family's waking life: the place for cooking, eating, making soap and candles, spinning yarn and weaving homespun cloth, sewing shoes, repairing tools, keeping accounts, and reading Scripture. Women and men, children and servants, worked together, under each other's watchful eye. Even in larger estates, room-by-room probate inventories document the focus on the hall for all domestic production.

The parlor was the other downstairs room in a typical two-room house. Here bodies were laid in state, honored guests were received, and the family treasures, brought over from England, were proudly displayed. According to many seventeenth-century inventories, the parlor often contained the parents' bed. This particular room was actually a recent development in Britain, at least for those outside the aristocratic dwelling. Its appearance marks the emerging separation between public and private, intimacy and formality, which was just beginning to reshape the dwelling and the family's social life. For the first generation of New England settlement, this was a space in the house for certain formal domestic functions. It also allowed for parental privacy at night, but it was not a place where one could withdraw from the intensity and scrutiny of communal life and work. Such personal privacy was possible only in a diary.

Other small rooms for service and storage appeared quickly in New England Puritan houses, but they were not intended for individual retreat or social activities. The cellar, often simply a hole in the ground under part of the house, with sloping sides and dirt floor, provided a place to keep milk and potatoes from freezing. It was rare to dig out under one's house in England, but the New Englanders adopted the practice rapidly, adding other storage rooms as well. A buttery for cold storage of beer and other foods, a milkhouse for dairy products, even cheese lofts and cheese chambers were mentioned in inventories, although most storage was still incorporated into the commodious hall. Later in the century, the common solution to the storage problem was the lean-to, which often extended the entire length of the house at the rear, creating a salt-box profile. Eventually, the kitchen was fixed in the middle room of the lean-to, and the hall became a family sitting room and general workplace.

Most houses had upstairs chambers, which served as bedrooms and general storage areas. In one-room houses, there was a single upper chamber, which the children and servants reached by an extremely steep staircase between the entry and the central chimney. Around their simple bedding would be piled up all sorts of barrels, skins, bags of grain, yarn, spinning equipment, and "lumber," that archaic term for odds and ends.

This description of family life sounds frugal and austere, yet the Puritans were not as restrained and prim as they have often been portrayed. Though there were emphatic regulations governing display—notably the early law prohibiting the purchase or making of "slashed clothes," garments adorned with lace, silver, gold, or silk, ruffs or beaver hats—this was understandable in a community still trying to establish itself as a secure and sanctimonious institution. Overall, the issue was not self-expression but the "weaning of the affections"[14] from earthly goods and people to God. Human pleasures were supposed to make the individual love God more. Passionate love and sensual feelings were encouraged, even among those not yet married, as long as God was placed higher in one's affections. The letters of John and Margaret Winthrop were filled with powerful and beautifully expressed emotions. Anne Bradstreet's simple poem to her husband Simon began, "If ever two were one, then surely we./ If ever man were lov'd by wife, then thee" and ended correctly with the hope, "Then while we live, in love lets so persever,/ That when we live no more, we may live ever."[15] As long as the passions of the soul or the body were controlled by reason, they could lead men and women toward virtue.

Architecture duly revealed that spirit of joyful humility. Even on the austere, forbidding houses with their weathered clapboards and tiny windows, one could find adornment. Long before the delicate shapes and formal plan of the Georgian era became fashionable, the Puritans began to carve purely decorative forms into the frames of their houses. By the 1650s, curved brackets, carefully and gracefully incised, supported many overhangs. Handsome decorative drops or pendills in opulently rounded shapes hung from the corners. The houses of ministers, such as Parson Capen of Topsfield, showed that this sensual ornament was considered entirely proper. These details were purely decorative, signs of the carpenter's skill, a counterpoise to the boldly exposed structural elements.

Within the house appeared more signs of the Puritans' delight in display. The furnishings, while few, were often carved into elaborate rounded forms. Cupboards and chests were painted in vivid polychrome with the owners' names, surrounded by hearts, flowers, and geometrical designs. Even the walls could be brightly painted in red, green, and purple; sometimes dots of color were applied with a sponge, although this exuberant practice was more common after 1700. These decorations obviously derived from rural folk traditions, but the New England Puritans took great pleasure in them nonetheless. One Bostonian recorded the visit of a friend to his newly redecorated house. The friend "was much pleas'd with our painted shutters; in pleasancy said he thought he had been got into Paradise."[16]

Puritan houses, like their owners' lives, embraced both order and playfulness, solemnity and exuberance, delicate detail and forthright structure. Just as this group created an elaborate "morphology of conversion,"[17] in which each stage of God's grace was made visible and recognizable through a set of signs, so too the New England colonists leaned toward a literalness in the houses they built and the towns they planned. The forms revealed God's will; they also testified to human fallibility. The Puritans' desire to make their beliefs more substantial—in correct behavior, in the architecture of private homes, and in the larger community plan—encompassed a deep-seated doubt about their ability to act as they should without constant reminders. The combination of self-confidence and self-doubt, both made manifest in the built environment, would remain an important aspect of American culture for generations to come.

PART TWO

STRUCTURES OF AMERICAN NATIONALISM

WITH THE FOUNDING OF THE REPUBLIC, AND MOST emphatically after the War of 1812, the search for peculiarly American ways of doing things seemed to extend into every aspect of daily life, with demands for a national language, a national art, and an American approach to jurisprudence and child-rearing. Those who crusaded for cultural innovation based their appeals on pride and independence. An American culture, they contended, would unite diverse groups in the nation. It would represent and strengthen the country's political and social goals. Like the tariff, it would protect the national interest and encourage the self-sufficiency of the American people. Both the natural and the built environment could provide reminders of otherwise abstract national commitments to equality, individualism, and social order.

Accordingly, in 1785, Jefferson produced a system of land allotment, the National Survey, based on an infinitely expandable grid of square sections and quarter-sections, which he hoped would encourage the proliferation of equal, independent homesteads as the new nation expanded. In the decades that followed, hundreds of thousands of people moved westward, lured by the rhetoric that promised absolute freedom and total equality—and by the ease of buying land, another distinct benefit of this grid system.

Jefferson's survey, drawing upon a familiar Enlightenment concept, presupposed that the environment actually had a strong effect on human beings. For him, it took on the quality of an active force, a formative influence over the individual and the larger society. The right surroundings were considered one of the proper conditions that allow men and women to think clearly and behave rationally; they were a necessary part of a democratic republic.

Like Jefferson, other national spokesmen also claimed that certain fundamental social freedoms were necessary in a good society and that certain fundamental institutions had to be protected in order to balance individual autonomy. One of the most important institutions was the family, for it was considered the source of public virtue as well as the haven of private well-being and stability. In 1778, John Adams wrote that "the foundations of national Morality must be laid in private families."[1] The English and Puritan ideal of the home as a "little common wealth" and the state as a collective representation of individual households remained a cornerstone for the new nation. But if Americans were, in fact, to create an ideal commonwealth, it seemed essential that this concept have tangible form.

One task of America's new leaders, in addition to shaping a political system, was to adapt the ideal of a model home and family to the realities of an expanding frontier and a mobile population. A flexible framework would allow "the foundations of national Morality" to extend into diverse sections of the country, across the western territories, into free states and slave, into both rural and manufacturing areas, and still remain intact. The home environment could, it was hoped, abate the potential conflicts between different groups and remind even settlers on the frontier of their civic responsibilities. More than ever, the way to assure public virtue through the family was to consider the setting where the family would live. This may seem overly rhetorical; yet statesmen like Jefferson and Hamilton, theologians like Timothy Dwight, as well as writers, painters, and industrialists in every region, emphasized again and again the potential importance of the dwellings that would house American citizens—and even American slaves.

Homogeneity of dwellings, representing a shared set of values, would be the evidence of a pattern one recent immigrant, the Frenchman Hector St. John de Crèvecoeur, lauded as America's "pleasing uniformity of decent competence."[2] Nonetheless, as most of these enthusiasts were aware, the idea of a typical American family and a matching model dwelling for every household was, from the beginning, a strained concept. Even at the end of the eighteenth century, there were distinctly different social and economic classes, ethnic and racial groups, regional and urban-rural conflicts. For every five freeholders in the new nation, five adult males fit other descriptions: two were slaves; two, servants or propertyless tenant farmers; and one was employed in trade or manufacturing.[3] The supposedly typical small cottage for the farmer and his household was actually the last of four national housing types to be publicized during the early decades of the republic. Soon after independence, an urban tradition of plain, uniform row houses, based on models in builders' books, became an established form. In the early nineteenth century, enterprising mill owners erected towns near sources of water power, with boardinghouses and tiny cottages for their employees. Promoters insisted that both these types of habitations, although quite different from the rural cottage for the farmer, provided settings that were just as "distinctly American" and as beneficent in their influence. During this same period, southern planters refined their practices of building slave quarters. Even before they recognized the symbolic impact of grand, colonnaded mansions, slaveholders were convinced that their system of building slave cabins would stabilize plantation society and provide for the blacks—according to the way their white owners understood them to live.

Each of these distinct patterns of dwelling, family, and associated values took hold in a particular region, although they also occasionally overlapped in cities. Each was designed to provide for a particular conception of family and community life; and together, they represent the major variations on the generalized idea of a model dwelling which would form a good American.

CHAPTER TWO

ROW UPON ROW IN THE COMMERCIAL CITY

The taste for the fine arts when it shall become
a national taste, will be as permanent
as the national language. It will not be a
fashion set by a Charles, or a Louis XIV.

—Benjamin H. Latrobe, Oration to the
Society of Artists
of the United States, 1811

IN AMERICAN CITIES, AS IN SMALL TOWNS AND IN
the countryside, the choice of architectural style for housing acquired a weighty social significance. Urban Americans wanted their
dwellings to embody a new aesthetic for a new social order. The
artful copying of established European styles was insufficient,
though designers were expected to be familiar with this precedent.
Carpenters and builders insisted that an emphasis on native practicality and economy should balance the art and grace of classical
forms. Writers and public orators repeatedly evoked the need for
the symbolic presentation of republican values. This was a rather
vague challenge, inadequately met by capitals in the shape of corn
and tobacco, or plaster rosettes depicting indigenous fruits and
flowers. Public-mindedness in design was more to the point. "I do
not mean that the public has a legal right to control the tastes of
the citizen," explained a character in James Fenimore Cooper's
Home as Found (1838), "but in a republican government, you
undoubtedly understand, Miss Eve, it will rule in all things."[1]

Daniel Webster, in an 1836 address to Boston's Society for the
Diffusion of Useful Knowledge, tried to specify the definition of
republican art. He criticized extravagant architecture and furnish-

ings as unpatriotic indulgences. In contrast, Webster declared, industrially produced building materials and simple, useful objects were truly democratic, for they would be widely available to all citizens. Industrial technology, good craftsmanship, and a plain aesthetic advanced the republic, for

> the unquestionable operation of all these things has been not only to increase property, but to equalize it, to diffuse it, to scatter its advantages among the many, and to give content, cheerfulness, and animation to all classes of the social system.[2]

For Webster, an avowedly simple and rational way of living was the essence of democratic virtue; and urban houses should show this self-conscious restraint. The editors of the *North American Review* echoed this opinion when they exhorted "all house-builders to 'fling away ambition'; to contrive their houses with a view to comfort rather than show; and to take special care that the proportions be not so great, and the cost so extravagant, as to gain for their edifices the unenviable name of 'Follies.' "[3]

There was by no means universal agreement on what constituted republican design. An essay, written in 1790, began with the assertion that the tenets of American government required that every citizen protect the public happiness. The author then suggested that true patriots would build their houses only of brick, because such dwellings, "in which more money has been spent and more of the refined taste gratified," would increase popular affection for the soil and, hence, for property. "A habit of thought arises, favorable to the population," the essayist continued. "Emigration would be less easy and not so common were a finer spirit of building to prevail."[4] Yet the pressure for restraint dominated appeals for the adornment of private property, at least through the 1830s. In theory, in classless America, all dwellings would embody the same principles and would therefore look alike.

The repetition of simple forms in housing was taken as visible evidence of equality of station in society. Equality was a goal that engendered constraints, tensions, and symbolic responses from the beginning of the republic. Most citizens did not actually believe in full equality; they believed in conditions for individual freedom, which theoretically allowed for an equalizing process, and in social practices that outlawed aristocratic privilege. They had hopes for a society in which the public good would be a shared concern, so long as it did not interfere excessively with personal freedom. What emerged as a solution of sorts was the "fabrick of Freedom," a visible structure that embodied both common good and personal gain.[5] An important thread in that fabric was the built environment, representing private property and public commonweal. A smooth, uniform environment was considered a sign that Americans had resolved some of their deepest conflicts.

In practice, at least in the early years of the republic, many houses for clerks and artisans did resemble, both inside and out, the more modest residences of the merchant and professional classes. The row-house designs and theories of American architect Charles Bulfinch or builder Asher Benjamin influenced housewrights and carpenters who engaged in less pretentious practices. Throughout the first half of the nineteenth century, the relatively homogeneous appearance of urban houses corroborated a widely held impression that almost every American family could own their own home. For a decade after the Revolution, many artisans were, in fact, able to purchase single lots in the sale of confiscated loyalist estates.

But soon investors began acquiring much larger tracts, forcing prices up. One historian estimates that the value of land in Manhattan alone rose by nearly 750 percent between 1785 and 1815.[6] By then, more than half of the homes in the nation's larger cities were rented, mostly by the families of artisans and unskilled laborers.[7] They could seldom raise the capital for a down payment; and since loans were not amortized over time, they risked losing their home on the date the mortgage fell due. Even in the 1790s and the early 1800s, journeymen staged protests against the increasing cost of living, and especially the high cost of housing. They did not contest the symbolic idea that well-built, simple, uniform houses represented an egalitarian society, only the fact that the order was illusory if they had no place in it. As the architectural imagery of egalitarianism took form, the actual economic conditions in American cities became more stratified.

Carpenters and housewrights of the early republic saw their jobs as part of a nationalistic mission to build good American dwellings for all classes of citizens. They were as conscious of this ideal as they were of the economic and political barriers to its being realized. The earliest American guides on construction and design, notably Owen Biddle's *The Young Carpenter's Assistant* (1805) and Asher Benjamin's *The American Builder's Companion* (1806), claimed to inaugurate a new, republican course for American architecture in their aesthetic and in their commitment to economy and utilitarian concerns. The authors were interested in the issues of everyday life. They also taught the principles of English architectural forms and provided elegant neoclassical details for doors and mantels. But style was often secondary to practical considerations. Benjamin in particular committed himself to reducing the expense of labor and materials in his designs. While uniformity was the essence of beauty, he explained, "the convenience and needs of the occupants" should always be the principal consideration for American residential design.[8]

Most builders took such dictums literally, designing for economy and simple comfort. Well into the nineteenth century, the average building craftsman worked in wood frame, except in cities like Philadelphia or New York, where nearby supplies of red sandstone or clay for bricks allowed these materials to be used inexpensively. Occasionally, officials insisted on the need for such substantial dwellings. In the nation's capital, for instance, federal commissioners specified that only brick houses were permissible. Other cities eventually passed fire ordinances prohibiting further frame construction in heavily populated downtown areas. Nonetheless, frame row houses predominated in Washington, as elsewhere, during the early years of the republic. The supply of housing was inadequate, especially for workers who lived in these areas with their families so that they could be close to their places of employment. Consequently, even with the regulations that governed new construction, inexpensive frame houses remained in downtown areas for many decades to come.

From the late eighteenth century into the early nineteenth, most dwellings for the families of urban skilled workers were small houses of one or two stories. Although small and closely set along narrow, winding streets, the dwellings were in fact detached, for they had been built at different times. Francis Guy painted a winter scene of Brooklyn between 1817 and 1820, when he lived in this separate town, a ferry ride away from Manhattan. Guy depicted the boisterous activity of tavern and "coffee room," slaughterhouse and store, mixed in with such small dwellings, all facing different directions. There were also a few examples of the more carefully planned and uniform row houses on some of the Brooklyn streets, for this was one of several American cities where builders had been erecting detached row houses since the mid-eighteenth century.

By 1800, the row house had become the established and predominant form for residential building in Providence, Baltimore, Annapolis, Philadelphia, and most other cities. Builders relied on standard row-house façades and plans, usually derived from details in builders' guides. The

A winter scene in Brooklyn, New York, 1817–1820, by Francis Guy, shows the variety of people, activities, and building types on a typical urban street in the early republic.

. . . .

A row of two-and-a-half story row houses for artisans, built on Baltimore's Aliceanna Street at the beginning of the nineteenth century, repeated the same roof height, dormer windows, shutters, and doors on each dwelling.

Boston Housewright Society officially endorsed Benjamin's *The American Builder's Companion*. The Carpenters Company of Philadelphia maintained an extensive library of such books, beginning in the early eighteenth century with English imports and expanding as American texts became available. Philadelphia's Library Company, founded by Benjamin Franklin, also offered its members the opportunity to study English and American guides and to examine the plans of their fellow builders.

Most builders simply copied from existing houses, perhaps introducing slight modifications. Professional architects criticized this method, but to no avail. James Gallier condemned the builders' predilection to work without drawing up plans, for it created monotonous vistas. William Ross faulted the "general sameness of design (or rather want of design), in the street fronts" of New York.[9] Yet, this aesthetic was

• •

Thomas Carstairs's floor plans and elevation for a block of middle-class row houses, built ca. 1801–1803 in Philadelphia, documents the house builder's attention to precise uniformity.

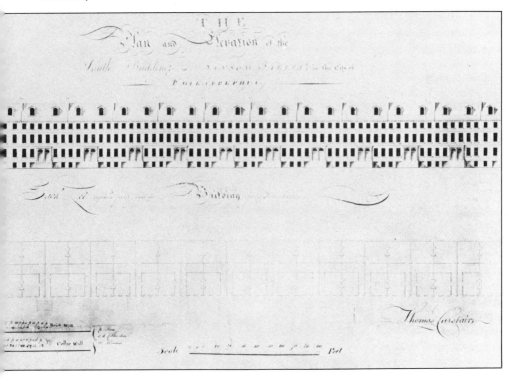

prized, in part because it supposedly referred to egalitarian values. More-over, for most families, it was easier and much less expensive to buy directly from a builder who had constructed a number of similar houses at affordable prices. He would have timed construction (an average of one and a half years) to be finished by the first of May, which was generally moving day in most cities. (figure 7) He usually built on speculation, rarely on commission for particular clients. The idea of the personalized dwelling had not yet taken hold among—or been sold to —the American middle classes. When it did, in the years after the Civil War, it was a predominantly suburban fantasy, although urban row houses too would boast elaborate decoration, inside and out.

In early-nineteenth-century cities, a speculator often sold several lots to a housewright or an independent building tradesman—usually a car-penter, bricklayer, or shipwright—who put up one or two new houses

· ·

An engraving of "May Day in the City," ca. 1850, shows the boisterous street life that contrasted with the demure façades of urban row houses. Note the cast-iron balcony of the most recently built dwelling.

within a year and then sold them for the capital with which to begin a new venture. In other cases, investors underwrote a professional row-house builder's expenses to hire a crew and buy materials to build three or four dwellings, and then sold the finished structures. This pattern of investor's capital, construction by journeymen artisans, and a speculative market predominated in every American city, encouraging conservative construction techniques and a cautious attitude toward new architectural fashions.

Even when several different builders took on the adjoining houses of a block, a common desire for simplicity and uniformity prevailed. The height of roof lines, the placing of cornices and string courses between floors, the height of basements and of the steps or stoops leading up to the first floor, even the window treatment from floor to floor and house to house, were consistent. Flat planes, repeated openings, and judiciously

· ·

The Andrew Ross Tenant Houses, built as rental property in 1810–1811 in Georgetown, District of Columbia, are an excellent example of Federal-period detailing. Slightly different ornament distinguished the doorways, offsetting the uniformity. The archway led to a service alley for coal and deliveries behind the row of houses.

simple ornament characterized the Federal style. This simplicity and uniformity were based on aesthetics, not on economy. It required time-consuming attention to line up the doors and cornices and to maintain the same window sizes, especially when filling in between existing dwellings. The decisions were not based on stock door or window sizes either, since carpenters still made every door and window frame to order on the site. Municipal regulations governed building materials because of the extreme fire hazard, but they said nothing about the size of openings or the distance between a house and the street.

English visitors clearly recognized the distinctiveness of the housing and street patterns in American cities, and understood the reasoning behind the cultural stereotype. Frances Trollope complained of the dreary insistence on homogeneity. "The great defect in the houses is their extreme uniformity—when you have seen one, you have seen all," she contended.[10] Others praised the "regularity and neatness which everywhere prevail."[11] Even Mrs. Trollope recognized that the Americans took great pride in their row houses and straight, tree-lined streets, especially in Philadelphia, still the political and intellectual center of the country. After the Revolution there had been a visible increase in social and economic differences, "Europeanism" to these republicans, and a visible uniform environment seemed a way to curb that tendency.

Yet, European splendor was still tempting to many Americans. Thus, by the early 1800s, each eastern seaboard city boasted a few examples of stately residential architecture on a scale of size and grandeur found along the avenues of London or Paris. These rows did not disrupt the aesthetic of uniform quality, but the caliber of materials, ornament, and size was obviously unattainable for most Americans. The vogue for the majestic row commenced in 1794, when architect Charles Bulfinch, recently returned from studies in Europe, convinced a group of prominent Boston businessmen to join him in a type of investment called a tontine, in order to build a version of the English residential square. He completed only half of the elliptical Tontine Crescent, erecting a curved block of sixteen neoclassical houses grouped within eight identical porches. Then the venture failed. The backers insisted that the other group of dwellings, facing the central park, be detached houses set in a straight line. Bulfinch himself went bankrupt as a result of his shares in the tontine.

Despite Bulfinch's financial failure, examples of similarly grandiose projects soon appeared in other American cities. Robert Mills built Baltimore's prestigious Waterloo Row, a terrace of twelve houses, in

1815. New Yorkers took special pride in Colonnade Row, also called Layfayette Terrace, a four-story expanse of marble front and continuous colonnade, where each finished unit sold for an astounding $25,000–$32,000.[12] The idea proved so popular that smaller versions of the monumental terrace appeared in other neighborhoods, where builders replaced the marble, brick, or stone with less expensive wooden colonnades.

Architecture had a strong symbolic function in these colonnaded terraces, as it had in the simpler row houses and detached dwellings. Greek columns and pediments appeared on all kinds of American architecture between 1820 and 1840, both public and private buildings, urban and rural, as an expression of affinity with the ancient Greek democratic city-states and sympathy with the plight of contemporary Greece. The widespread acceptance of the Greek style also shows how shallow this desire for visual expression could become. The irony is that the same classical white porticoes were taken as the manifestation of civic virtue and social reform in the East, simple ways and democratic strength in the West, and the heritage of slavery and aristocratic leadership in the South. Political and social differences were harbored in the very image of unity.

Though row-house builders followed much the same format from one city to another, style and construction nonetheless drew from local traditions and different market conditions. The streets gave a traveler a distinct sense of which city he or she was visiting. The houses of Boston tended to be larger than those of New York, while those in and around Philadelphia were noticeably more cramped and severe. The New York row house had a distinctive high stoop for its entrance. (The word derived from the Dutch *stoep,* a flight of stairs that had served to keep the dwelling above Holland's recurring flood waters.) The typical New York pattern of a tiny front service yard and storage vault to serve the kitchen—which opened on this lower-level yard—also contrasted with the façades of residences in other cities. There, rear alleys met the need for delivery space, although covered bins for coal often protruded onto the sidewalks.

Materials also differed somewhat from place to place. New Yorkers used the local red sandstone, also known as brownstone, for lintels and basements, where more elegant granite or marble would be too expensive. Bostonians and Philadelphians began to rely almost exclusively on brick by 1830, when a deep-red pressed brick of high quality became available. In every city, builders and housewrights usually painted the bricks a more intense red or reddish brown than the original clay. Some gave them a totally different hue. Frame detailing was even more bold. Colors ranged from blue, green, and yellow to a brilliant scarlet. Doors were usually shiny white. Roofs, in general, were more subtle hues of slate, or tin plate painted to simulate slate or copper. Small dormer windows in the roof lit the attic floor, where the servants lived in a middle-class household, or where the children and boarders lived among the working class. Despite the liveliness of the colors, the overall mood of these streets was quite sober, given the rigorous uniformity and re-strained ornament.

The average urban row house was narrow, usually only fifteen to twenty feet across, extending back for about thirty to forty feet. Behind the dwelling the family had room for a garden, a few chickens and a pig, a well or a cistern for collecting rainwater, and a privy, placed directly over the cesspool. Sometimes a covered walkway protected the path between the house and the privy. In the workers' blocks, other one-story or two-story dwellings were soon erected in the back, between the privy and the alley, and the backyard facilities had to be shared by several households. Crowding in the cities became so bad, and rents so high, that basements were rented out to the very poor. While the façades of middle-class dwellings still followed the same formal rules as those of artisans' row houses, the rooms were used quite differently.

Floor plans of all row houses were simple and homogeneous. A long, narrow side hall usually led from the entry along the entire length of the dwelling. At the back of the house was a narrow flight of stairs, and behind it stood the door to the yard or alley. A working-class house often consisted of only a single room on each of the two or two and a half floors, in which case the hall was omitted. The middle-class row house had two identical square rooms on each of three or three and a half floors. In most cases, the kitchen took up the back half of the basement, and a combination family dining room/sitting room/nursery occupied the front of that floor, although sometimes the kitchen and laundry stood in a separate, connected structure at the back of the house. One New Yorker of the 1830s commented that the family generally lived in the basement, except when company came.[13] Then they moved up to the formal first floor, with its front parlor and more elegant dining room for entertaining.

Entertaining was not that common, however, except among the upper classes. English visitors were surprised by the American predilection for all-male business dinners; the women, in contrast, paid social calls during the day. Contemporary paintings depict women sitting at the parlor table chatting, or a larger dinner party of men in a fancy urban dining room. When mixed gatherings did occur, they were generally informal afternoon tea parties, small dinners, or dances. The unpretentious row houses accommodated this social life quite well. As James Fenimore

. . . .

Henry Sargent's "The Dinner Party," painted in Boston in 1820, possibly showing the artist's own house, depicts a dinner of business colleagues in a fashionable Beacon Hill row house. The scale is somewhat misleading, however, for even in upper-class row houses such rooms were typically 25 feet by 14 feet, and the gentlemen would have been rather crowded.

Cooper noted of those in New York, the modest façades "convey a proper idea of the more substantial comforts, and of the neatness that predominated within."[14]

The simple floor plans divided up the activities and the inhabitants of the row house, at least in a perfunctory manner. Family bedrooms were on the second floor, and on the third as well in larger houses. A craftsman's apprentices or the servants in a middle-class household lived in the attic. This provided rather cold quarters in the winter, since few houses had furnaces, and a fireplace was seldom considered necessary for the top floor. Few households could afford imported glass panes (especially since the excise tax was three times their cost), so shutters were used. These kept out the cold or rain to some extent, but the smells and insects of hot summers entered freely. A large proportion of women's work—spinning cloth, sewing clothes, dipping candles, and the countless other tasks of daily life—was relegated to the open, unpartitioned attic. During the day, the servant, as well as the housewife and daughters, also spent a great deal of time in the basement kitchen, a room with only a seven-foot-high ceiling, but the heat and confinement often became so uncomfortable that the women moved to the adjacent family sitting room.

Folding or sliding doors appeared on the principal living floors in many row houses by the 1820s, and soon became a mainstay. Opening up the doors allowed the two rooms to be used as one large area for a party or a dance. In the heyday of the Greek Revival, in the 1830s, carved columns and friezes often graced these openings. Many dwellings had built-in cupboards, or "pantries," around the slots in the wall where the doors would fit. These added general storage space. On the upper floors, closets for clothes, washbasins, and chamberpots were usually built in between the bedrooms. In the basement, large stone or brick rubble vaults at the entrance allowed for cold storage and dry firewood.

By the 1830s, subtle changes were instituted to accommodate a more elegant social life and greater wealth among urban middle-class families. The standard of living of the journeyman and his family was declining, while that of the professional and his family was rising. Since the lot size was fixed—especially in New York, where the Plan of 1811 had firmly established a gridiron for all streets—spaces had to be used differently within each new house. Dwellings rose three and four stories above the basement. A more elegant door announced the entrance. It was placed in the center of the dwelling, flanked with Greek pilasters and a pressed-glass fanlight above. In especially elegant homes, an oval staircase, with overhead skylight and galleries, replaced the narrow stairs and the pinched, unfurnished side hall. Rooms took on fanciful shapes, almost always asymmetrical, sometimes featuring an undulating curve around a bow window or elliptical staircase. In Boston the fashion for swelling bow-window fronts spread through many of the better neighborhoods. The work of the house was relegated to the basement kitchen and nursery and to the large open space on the top floor. In between was openness, elegance, and opulent display.

Romanticism began to make itself felt in urban row houses as well as in country cottages. Tall porches or intricate cast-iron balconies extending across the row-house front appeared throughout New York, Pennsylvania, and Ohio in the 1840s. Cast iron became even more prevalent and fanciful in the southern cities, especially Charleston, Savannah, Mobile, and New Orleans, as well as St. Louis, which retained some French influence. Materials for the façade changed, too, in accordance with romantic ideas about beauty. In New York, dark, deeply incised brownstone fronts, which offered greater possibilities for dramatic shadows and coloring, replaced brick and the lighter stones. By the mid-1850s, these would be capped with high mansard roofs and then by the heavy brackets of the Italian Renaissance *palazzo*. As the builders and architects of urban row houses experimented with more "natural" shapes, colors, and materials, they created more lavish dwellings. For small-town and rural Americans, these romantic styles of architecture were intimately tied to an idealized image of the nuclear family, but for urbanites the associations of fashion and social status were dominant.

Economic pressures in these years were such that many workers' houses, originally designed for one-family occupancy, were subdivided and shared by several families or a family and boarders. The phenomenon extended to other classes, too, where economic hardship was not an issue. By the 1830s, boardinghouse life had become rather prevalent among well-to-do young men and women in American cities. Newly married couples often chose to forsake the demands of supervising their own households and the difficulties of procuring good servants. Among the middle class, the trend took off with Boston's acclaimed Tremont House, which advertised special facilities for permanent residents beginning in 1829. The Astor House and Franklin House in New York soon became well known. Elsewhere, the residences simply took on the name of the proprietress, who was usually a widow, for few widows owned property outright. Boarders, young and old, male and female, mixed with travelers in the dining room at meals and in the parlor during the day.

The "fashionable boarding house" raised many eyebrows among matrons and foreign visitors; but despite the complaints that they were improper, that they encouraged transience and discouraged domesticity, boardinghouses extended throughout all classes in American urban society.

The mix of plain, unpretentious row houses and boardinghouses accentuated the appearance of equality in early-nineteenth-century American cities. Merchants and butchers, lawyers and carpenters, some of the wealthiest families and some of the simplest, lived in such dwellings. Yet, despite the homogeneity of façades, the location of houses announced the class of their occupants. The tendency toward economic and social bases of segregation became increasingly explicit after 1820, extending to many vocations and ethnic groups. Sometimes legislation restricted racial minorities' rights to own property. The high cost of land, especially

· ·

"Scene in a Fashionable Boarding House," a lithograph from the 1840s, depicts the types of persons who might be found at such a residence, ranging from the newly married couple and some young dandies to an elderly retired gentleman.

in prestigious neighborhoods, meant that economic and social classes were, in fact, separated. Blacks and the very poor were relegated to particular districts, often on the outskirts of cities, which the middle classes shunned as dangerous, "vicious" areas. Cottages and row houses of well-established clerical workers, shopkeepers, and professionals stood in clearly defined neighborhoods. The homes of the elite—whether mansions, row houses, or fashionable boardinghouses—were grouped together. While there was relative consensus about architectural style, which was evident in different classes of houses, and a widely shared idea that this style symbolized republican values, the actual conditions of social, economic, and environmental inequality were present from the start and grew more accentuated.

This early pattern of segregation of populations should be distinguished from zoning, which was a much later phenomenon. In almost every urban neighborhood—except the most fashionable and (more problematically) the extremely poor—patterns of mixed residential, commercial, and light industrial use dominated the early "walking cities." The first floor of many small houses functioned as a workshop or a store. Large multiple-pane windows let in more light and encouraged passersby to enter a shop. Master craftsmen housed apprentices in the top floors of their buildings, maintaining their shops on the first floor or next door to their own living quarters. Increasingly, though, the craftsmen's wives protested against the extra demands and the loss of family privacy; after the 1820s, many apprentices and journeymen began to rent single rooms in lodging houses or dormitories near their work. Taverns and coffee houses proliferated throughout every city and every neighborhood. Shops, markets, and street peddlers' stalls provided gathering places outside the home for urban women. While some husbands maintained the eighteenth-century practice of doing the family marketing, shopping was increasingly a female activity. This was especially the case for women who had no servants and kept their own boardinghouses or private homes. Living quarters were generally cramped in the cities of the early republic, so everyone spent time in the streets and shops.

The early-nineteenth-century city had its unpleasant aspects as well. Fires occurred an average of once a night in a large metropolis. Police protection was minimal. Mud, open sewers, fetid refuse and garbage, together with cacaphonous noise, made for unhealthy conditions in every quarter. Stables were found in almost every neighborhood, and manure piled up high behind them. Sanitation remained a private duty, for there were no municipal services, except in Philadelphia. Pigs were protected as scavangers and roamed the streets, but they could consume only a small proportion of the debris. Few engravings of early American cities acknowledged these conditions.

The familiar portrait of harmonious, restrained residential architecture in ante-bellum American cities was exactly the image that the residents wanted to achieve. It can be deceptively engaging. The current romance with Federal townhouses disregards the less pleasant sides of this past, taking the architecture at its original symbolic level. There was, in fact, a deepening tension between the orderly dwellings and the uncontrolled problems of epidemics, poverty, garbage, and overcrowding. The fact that buildings appeared uniform belied the growing economic segregation and social inequality. Many observers worried about the lack of stabilizing family influence over the numerous young single men who worked in the cities and lived alone. Few public amenities or municipal services—parks, public baths, schools, cultural institutions, municipal sanitation—kept apace of the fast-growing urban populations, although American towns were generally more advanced than their European counterparts. For the majority of urban Americans, the practicality and pleasing uniformity of their houses seemed sufficient. These dwellings formalized and systematized the society they hoped to create.

CHAPTER THREE

THE "BIG HOUSE" AND THE SLAVE QUARTERS

This world is not my home,
This world is not my home,
This world's a howling wilderness,
This world is not my home.

—Southern black spiritual

BEFORE THE ESTABLISHMENT OF THE REPUBLIC, SOON
followed by the introduction of new agricultural methods, dealings
with slaves and slave quarters were somewhat casual. Not all large
plantations used slaves; and on those that did, the slaves were
allowed to build their dwellings as they wished, following African
ideas of a tightly clustered, asymmetrical village compound. (This
same pattern also characterized the plantations of the former
French and British colonies in the West Indies.) Before rotation
of crops, when soil became depleted, the entire household—including the planter's dwelling and the slaves' simple huts—were peri-
odically moved to a new location on the plantation. Many slaves
never built houses but simply lived in the lofts of barns or in storage
rooms.

With the invention of the cotton gin in 1793, higher profits
stimulated the rapid spread of cotton plantations and larger holdings of both land and slaves. Tax lists began to identify "Negro
quarters" as permanent. By the early nineteenth century, plantation slavery was deeply entrenched in the South. In 1810, the
southern slave population numbered more than a million. In some
parts of the Black Belt, slaves outnumbered whites by more than

two to one. The slave population then quadrupled to about 3 million in 1850 and 4 million on the eve of the Civil War.[1] During these ante-bellum decades, slaveowners, especially the wealthy planters, developed a more architectural, more symbolic, and, at the same time, more calculated way of regulating slave life. While the extent of control varied according to the wealth, education, and conscience of the individual owner, a distinct pattern emerged, defining first the slave quarters and then the architecture of the big houses.

Even with the cotton boom in the lower South, slavery did not figure directly in the majority of southern households. Only about a quarter of the white families ever owned slaves, and only 12 percent owned as many as twenty. By 1860, one tenth of the planter community of 385,000 slaveholders owned half of the South's slaves; only three thousand individuals through the entire ante-bellum period owned a hundred bondsmen or more, and there were some who owned thousands.[2] This group dominated the South's economy and political life, and it also defined the pattern of accommodations for the great majority of black men, women, and children in the United States.

Even the non-slaveowning independent farmers and poor white tenant farmers supported the system of slavery. Poor white farmers could not themselves duplicate the graceful, if distorted, world of the planters —travelers' accounts testify to the meanness of their homes and their manners—yet they could take a certain pride in the image of a region of gentility, hospitality, and leisure, which depended on slaves. More importantly, southern whites feared a slave insurrection and an ensuing massacre of whites, especially after the Haitian uprising of 1791 and Nat Turner's insurrection of 1831. And they believed in the fundamental inferiority of black people. Whether or not they owned slaves, they usually defended their "peculiar institution" fervently.

The defense for paternalistic slavery posited that because blacks had such a different physiology, they did not suffer pain, whether from childbirth, disease, or beatings, as did whites. Supposedly, blacks did not appreciate the pleasures or responsibilities of domesticity—as defined by genteel white ante-bellum society. In line with these arguments, most slaveowners made certain decisions concerning the slaves' work routines, their social activities, their home and family life, each of which the owners believed needed close supervision but not much indulgence or sentimentality. It seems highly probable that many slaveholders used their ideas about black culture—the assertions that blacks were inevitably dirty and promiscuous, undeveloped morally and socially, impervious to many diseases and to education—to justify the exceedingly poor quality of the housing built for slaves. Arguments in favor of the institution allowed—almost required—whites to accept the overcrowding, the dilapidation, and the control they exercised over their slaves' quarters.

Every planter, and especially the owner of a large plantation, had to consider the physical layout of his property with care. Slaveholders certainly wanted to maintain tight control over their property: keeping an eye out for trouble or slothfulness, protecting the overall health of their slaves, presenting a reasonably favorable picture to visiting foreigners and northerners. In addition, by the late eighteenth century, many educated planters dabbled in architecture as one of a "gentleman's pursuits." By the beginning of the next century, their taste for neoclassicism was evident in the arrangement of slave quarters, even before it appeared in the colonnaded Greek Revival mansions of the 1830s. When a young man added significantly to his holdings in land and slaves, he rebuilt the quarters so as to make them more acceptable, at least in relative terms. Evidence of authority, a desire for formal architectural order, and an attempt to regulate slave living conditions pervaded even the most spartan of slave quarters on the larger plantations.

In general, by the early nineteenth century, cabins for the principal slave quarters were set off at some distance from the big house. Sometimes the cabins were visible; sometimes they were not. The quarters were usually downwind from the big house so that smells could be avoided, and behind the house, so that the planter's family had a pleasant vista. On a large plantation, groups of field slaves might still build huts in compounds, which followed an eighteenth-century Afro-American pattern, but the supervision exercised by the owner over the main quarters, which were closer to his residence, was unmistakable.

The regularity of the rows of slave cabins or barracks, housing several groups of slaves in one building, suggests the degree of the owner's control. A former slave described the quarters on a Virginia plantation: "They were log cabins. Some had one room and some had two rooms, and board floors. Our master was a rich man. He had a store and a sawmill on the creek. The cabins were covered with boards, nailed on, and had stick-and-mud chimneys. . . . The cabins were built in two rows not very far from the misses big house."[3] Frederick Law Olmsted, touring the South in the 1850s for *The New York Times,* described a smaller Virginia farm that had much the same pattern: "Their 'quarters' lined the approach-road to the mansion, and were well-made and comfortable log cabins, about thirty feet long by twenty wide, and eight feet tall, with a high loft and shingle roof. Each, divided in the middle, and having a brick chimney outside the wall at each end, was intended to be occupied by two families."[4] Other descriptions and site plans from the ante-bellum decades present a similar layout. The rows of houses might be arranged in straight lines or arcs. Often regularly spaced trees lined the road that could be seen from the big house or the entry drive.

On most nineteenth-century plantations, the size of slave habitations was uniform, unlike the earlier slave compounds, although the dimensions and the type of construction varied from one plantation to another. The most common sizes ranged from a ten-foot square to a slightly larger rectangle, although there were even rare cases of conical habitations. Most cabins consisted of a single room, perhaps with a sleeping loft

· ·

A row of double houses for slaves on the Hermitage Plantation, St. Catherine's Island, South Carolina, all built of pisé (rammed earth) with wooden shutters, shows the emphasis on order that characterized ante-bellum plantation slave quarters.

above. The larger two-room cabins generally housed two separate family groups.

On large plantations especially, when dimensions varied from one cabin to another, it was because the owner wanted to achieve a certain effect. At the Couper Plantation on St. Simons Island, part of the Georgia Sea Islands, the overseer's cabin dominated the row of slave dwellings, in both size and position. Its detached kitchen was slightly larger than the entire area of a single slave cabin. At the Evergreen Plantation in Wallace, Louisiana, the middle two cabins in each row of eighteen were slightly larger than the others. The Kingsley Plantation, built as a slave-importing station on St. George Island, Florida, in 1813, had two arcs of sixteen cabins, with the first and last in each arc notice-

. . . .

On the Evergreen Plantation at Wallace, Louisiana, the exacting construction of the quarters is almost sculptural. The careful ordering of this environment, laid out shortly before 1830, extended to an alley of oak trees planted in front of the cabins.

ably larger than the others. These are clear examples of the owner imposing a classical order on the plan for the quarters, as on the rest of the plantation, by creating a heavier central point or a defined emphasis at the ends of his composition. The larger cabins also reinforced his hierarchy, for they would be given to the overseer, to favored slaves, or to those with special skills. Architectural considerations and planned social stratification dictated the differences in an otherwise uniform row of slave quarters. The evidence, in either case, points to the slaveholder, as amateur architect or warden, extending his control over every detail of his plantation.

The tension between a slave's desire to maintain some vestige of an African heritage and a slaveowner's desire to assert his control occasionally led to direct confrontation. A few slaves undertook the construction of dwellings that were forthrightly African. A former slave from St. Simons Island remembered the cabin built by a friend named Okra in the early nineteenth century: it was an African hut with a dirt floor, wattle-and-daub walls, and a conical thatch roof. "But Massa make 'im pull it down," recounted the former slave. "He say he ain' want no African hut on he place."[5] Thus, while slaves might indeed have tried to bring some reminders of their past into their homes, by the nineteenth century the masters considered this a potentially dangerous act.

In the ante-bellum decades, few Afro-American slave quarters suggested evidence of such a distinctly African imprint. There was almost no ornamentation, even though West African dwellings would have been decorated with paint, carving, shards, and carefully arranged thatch roofs. The starkness of the cabin was not simply a matter of insufficient time or inadequate tools. The skill of black craftsmen and women is recognizable in musical instruments, fabrics, boats, baskets, tools, grave markings, and numerous other objects that were elaborately carved, colored, and adorned. The fact that the houses do not display the same sense of exuberant artistry suggests the owners' strong disinclination to allow houses to be a major part of black culture, as well as the slaves' sense of greater autonomy in other areas of daily life and artistic expression.

Most slave houses, built of hewn logs and daubed with the red clay or mud of the region, looked fittingly primitive to whites. A few houses were constructed of rough brick or rammed earth (a technique known as pisé, which derived from Africa). Descriptions and excavations suggest that many interiors were plastered and whitewashed, sometimes as a yearly sanitary measure. But other accounts, such as that of the former slave Louis Hughes, say that "no attempt was made to give them [the quarters] a neat appearance."[6] Chimneys were of crude brick or, in less substantial cabins, a combination of sticks and clay. The chimneys and the grease lights or burning pine knots often caused devastating fires in the closely set wooden cabins. Log barrels of rainwater were dispersed around the quarters in case of fire. Often the wobbly look of a chimney leaning away from the house reflected an intentional effort to keep sparks off the roof.

In general, ventilation was extremely poor. Cold air circulated freely through the chinks in the wall, while smoke from the fireplace blackened everything inside. As John Brown complained: "The wind and rain will come in and the smoke will not go out."[7] If there was a window—and many cabins had none—it was small and seldom had a pane. Instead, shutters might be used to keep out the rain. In some instances, the doorway provided the only fresh air. This raised a conflict for the inhabitants, who had to choose between letting in a breeze and protecting themselves from snakes, animals, and intruders. The unpleasant, often unseemly aspects of slave housing corresponded to the prevailing white attitudes about blacks, and especially their opinion of black domestic life. In appearances, at least, the only order came from the slaveowners.

The owners' desire for authority extended to slave family life as well as to architecture. Owners frequently renamed their slaves, forbidding the use of African names or black family names. For records, a slave might be identified as Lloyd's Sarah or simply given the owner's paterfamilias. Although many couples did have wedding ceremonies conducted by a black preacher or a white clergyman, slave marriages did not exist under civil law, since slaves were legally property and not persons. Owners were free to make or sever these unions, and slave families were often broken by the sale of one or more members. This happened in approximately 32 percent of all recorded slave marriages.[8] The mother-child biological bond was considered primary to the husband-wife tie, yet children could also lose both parents, by sale as well as by death. While some owners encouraged stable family life, others viewed family bonds as potentially subversive. As one visitor put it: "To encourage and protect their homes generally would be in effect to put an end to slavery as it is."[9]

The slaves did develop ways of resisting this authoritarianism. When families were broken, a relative or a close family group would take the child in. This practice, together with the pattern of children learning to address older slaves unrelated to them by either blood or marriage as "aunt" and "uncle," created a particular, rather diffuse kinship structure. According to Herbert Gutman's research, the slaves invested symbolic meaning and social obligations in non-kin relations and in their community as a whole. Despite the injunctions and forced separations, slaves passed down family names, but kinship ties often had to be kept relatively covert.

In a similar fashion, slave artisans hid their efforts to create homes—rather than simply crude shelters—for slave families, homes that would reveal pride in craftsmanship and an Afro-American artistic tradition distinct from the owner's architectural control. Certain underlying construction details, rather than obvious ornament for a dwelling, were likely to receive close attention from the black carpenter. Usually, these would be hidden by the outside wall. On most plantations, the slaves handframed and pinned their own houses. Nails were rare, and it was time-consuming to cut them by hand, although they were used in building the big houses. Few nails are found in existing slave quarters or on excavations of pre–1840 sites. The façades of rough shingles or split logs were certainly nothing like the clay or bulk-earth of a typical West African dwelling; yet beneath the façade, the framework of hand-joined wood and wedged-in stones closely resembled traditional West African construction, which was based on poles lashed together and daubed with mud or clay. Even the floors, which usually consisted only of tamped earth, were evidence of a hidden African tradition: slaves cooked clay over a fire, mixing in ox blood or cow dung, and then poured it in place to make hard dirt floors, almost like asphalt. The slave narratives, gathered by WPA writers during the depression, tell of the slaves' great pride in construction skill. In slave houses, in contrast to other crafts, these signs of skill and tradition would then be covered over. This is not to say that the use of Afro-American construction techniques assured a strong sense of an independent culture or made the house a secret weapon of active resistance to white domination. Yet, domestic architecture did mediate between two very different ways of viewing black culture in the South.

Even in their crowded, spartan cabins, blacks maintained a sense of family bonds, community ties, and privacy. A slave household often contained eight or ten people, children and adults of all ages living together in a single room or a room and an upstairs loft. The group generally included extended family relations, as well as the nuclear family. There were relatively few old people, for the life expectancy of slaves was much lower than that of the white population. The cabin itself

The remains of a freed slave's cabin, built at Island Creek, Maryland, a few years after the Civil War, reveals the elaborate construction techniques of the typical Afro-American habitation, both before and after emancipation. Clapboards covered the underlying structure of wood frame, hewn logs, and oval stones between the layers of wood.

offered little more than cramped sleeping space. Most slaves slept on blankets or straw mats on the floor, or on narrow wood pallets softened with moss. Yet these single-room dwellings functioned as complex spaces for family living, eating, cooking, entertaining, and intimacy.

When a couple decided to live together or to marry under slave rituals, they were allocated a section of a cabin and moved out from the quarters they had previously shared with their own parents or the adults who had raised them. On a large plantation with numerous slaves, this cabin was often shared for some time with another family group. Slave couples hung up old clothes or quilts to establish boundaries; others built more substantial partitions from scrap wood. Parents also sought to establish some sexual privacy from their children. A few ex-slaves described modified trundle beds designed to hide parental love-making; in other cases, the children climbed up the ladder to the loft. In "shotgun" houses, with a row of rooms, adults slept at one end of the house and children at the other, with the boys on one side of the room and the girls on the other. Even in the one-room cabins, sexual segregation was carefully organized. Although any kind of privacy proved difficult to attain, it was clearly a central concern in the quarters.

Each cabin also provided a place for family meals. Most plantations rationed out food staples: hominy, cornmeal, fatback, and salt pork. From these, the women would provide their family's dinners, usually one-pot stews made over the open fire or cornmeal mush served in wooden trenchers, with the leftovers eaten cold and hastily on the way to the fields in the morning. Fish or wild game, caught by the men and the boys, and vegetables grown near the cabins supplemented the sparse rations. The adults drank liquor, distilled in the woods. On a few of the large plantations, older slave women cooked for the entire field slave population. However, even under this centralized system, families ate their meals together in their own homes.

There were few means a slave could use to achieve some degree of security. A conjurer's horseshoe or some other magical object on the door barred evil spirits and persons from entering, and a conjuring gourd lay just within reach inside for the same purpose. Such efforts to exert some control over one's life through magic balanced the extreme absence of power that the slave experienced in most situations. Because most slave-owners contended that the blacks had no sense of private domesticity or sexual morality, the people against whom conjuring mechanisms were least effective were the white masters seeking sexual adventures in the quarters. The whites insisted that black women were by nature promiscuous, and punished those who fought back.

The dwelling was therefore not a haven for the black family. Many activities took place outside the cabins, and many social ties were based on extended family or friendship bonds. Men usually hunted or fished together, collected firewood from the swamp, grew vegetables and made liquor together. Women sewed clothing for their families and occasionally cooked together. The brief time after sundown and the evening meal, and the day of rest on Sunday, offered the only opportunities for such activities. A few owners locked the doors of their slave cabins at eight o'clock and set out night patrols, worried that carousing would slow the following day's work, but most slaves were left to their own devices, as long as they were not remiss in their work.

Because the cabins were so tiny, dancing, singing, storytelling, and religious meetings usually took place on front porches or in the "street" behind the row of slave cabins. Slave churches were the scene of regular festivities that formed an integral part of black Christianity. In addition, late at night, men, women, and children would steal away to their "hush-harbor," a secret church site in the woods. Here, with the sounds of singing and chanting muffled by wet blankets hung from the trees and such magical devices as an iron pot turned upside down to absorb the noise, they communicated with African spirits and with a Christian God who truly loved them as his children, and interspersed the joyous sounds with bitter tales of wrongdoing. Whereas the white preachers and even many black ministers insisted that the Bible condoned slavery and required the slaves' absolute obedience, this secret church offered a more rewarding vision of a sacred world in the present and in the heavenly future.

Most slaves went out to the fields to work from sunup to sunset, with a break at midday in the hottest part of the summer. Several groups did not fit into this pattern, and special accommodations had to be made for them. Old people, too feeble to toil in the fields, and people who were disabled or recovering from the numerous diseases that plagued them, reported to one of a group of outbuildings between the quarters and the big house. The men gardened, cleaned the stables, tended the animals. Older women cooked for the other slaves, washed and mended clothes, or spun and wove the coarse cotton for these clothes in the loom house. Slave hospitals on many of the larger plantations—with slave doctors, herbalists, midwives, and visiting white doctors in attendance—provided a place for those who were too ill to work. Fanny Kemble and other visitors described slave hospitals with unglazed windows, dirt floors, and swarms of insects, suggestive of the discomforts many ailing slaves must have suffered.[10]

The larger plantations also had nurseries, usually a double-size cabin, where older slave women cared for the young black children. Because mothers were generally sent back to the fields a few days after they delivered, there was rarely time for nurturing or even for nursing. As "quarter hands" and then "half hands," the "children's squad" trained for a life of toil: pulling weeds, hoeing, cleaning the yards, and then going to the fields part-time alongside their mothers.

Certain adult slaves received special attention throughout their lives. The skilled craftsmen on a plantation—slaves trained as engineers, coop-

Slaves spent much of their free time in the "street" behind the quarters, as in this watercolor of a South Carolina plantation in the 1790s. Here they sang, danced, played music, told stories, and courted.

ers, carpenters, stone masons, weavers, millers, blacksmiths, gardeners—
were the "slaves of significance," enjoying higher status and better hours
than ordinary field slaves.[11] Although they lived in the same quarters,
these prized slaves were often given larger houses and other privileges.

Domestic servants frequently lived apart from the other slaves. Those
with families, even husbands or wives, could be separated for weeks or
months. While they sometimes had special quarters closer to the big
house, many house servants had no private living space at all. Louis
Hughes described sleeping on the dining room floor in the big house as
a young boy. Valets or seamstresses were often required to sleep in the
hallway or in the bedroom of their master or mistress, especially if
someone was sick, or rising early, or had any special needs. House
servants did enjoy relatively greater privileges. They dressed well, ate
well, and occasionally could speak back to their mistresses. Nonetheless,
their positions were not necessarily more desirable than those of slaves
in the rest of the community. The never-ceasing range of chores and the
open-ended hours meant that this work was, in many ways, more demanding and consuming than field labor. Equally important was the
effort to cut house servants off from their families and friends in the
quarters. In the white mythology of slavery, personified by "Uncle Tom"
and the black "Mammy," the domestic servants were more loyal to the
white family than to their own black families. Household slaves had to
act out those roles.

The difference between slave life on the plantation and slave life in
southern cities was even greater. For those who knew the pleasures of
urban life, unless they left their families behind on the plantation, the
preference was clear. In his 1845 autobiography, Frederick Douglass
described his impressions as a young boy:

> I had resided but a short time in Baltimore before I observed a marked
> difference, in the treatment of slaves, from that which I had witnessed
> in the country. A city slave is almost a freedman, compared with a
> slave on the plantation. He is much better fed and clothed, and enjoys
> privileges altogether unknown to the slave on the plantation.[12]

The southern cities provided the opportunity for extensive interrelations
between black slaves and whites and, at the same time, the greatest
autonomy for the blacks. Urban slaves accounted for only 5 percent of

the total southern slave population, but they comprised at least 20 percent of the population in cities like New Orleans, Mobile, Baltimore, and Savannah, and outnumbered the whites in Charleston.[13] These urban slaves and free blacks—mostly mulattos with a white parent or grandparent—represented a significant variation in the general pattern of a slaveholder's extraordinary control and license over black housing and home life.

Three characteristics distinguished southern urban blacks. First, the shortage of men—they were usually sold to planters who needed field laborers—led to a different structure for family life. Second, urban blacks lived in a cultural milieu far removed from that of the plantation. They usually dressed in relative finery, often learned to read and write, and mixed with a variety of people, black and white, free and slave. Young women who became the concubines of wealthy white men sometimes traveled to Europe. Under New Orleans's *plaçage* system, which institutionalized common-law marriages between white men and black women, a man promised the woman's family to provide her with a house and a stipend for each of their children. Third, while owners and municipal governments tried to restrict the slaves' activity, many urban slaves went about the city rather freely, sometimes even living outside their masters' supervision.

Southerners' reliance on slaves for arduous labor made blacks indispensable in the cities. Slaves did most of the construction work (except for fine architectural finish work), city maintenance, and even industrial labor. (This was especially prevalent in shipyards, tobacco and iron factories, mills, and on the railroads.) By hiring out his slaves, an owner received the 25 cents–50 cents per day his slave would earn by cleaning gutters, grading and paving streets, building bridges, and digging sewers for the municipality or for another white. Few overseers chained the slaves or patrolled their coming and going from these jobs, so slaves could move through the city as they wished. Legal mechanisms such as badges for hired-out slaves and fines for owners whose slaves were picked up on the streets, while seldom effective controls, testify to the whites' fears that urban blacks had too great a liberty.

Clear evidence of this incongruity between control and autonomy was the prohibition on slaves "living out" away from their masters and thereby evading supervision. Some slaves rented a room or a house, often with their husband or wife, sometimes using money supplied by their owners. In most southern cities, laws prohibiting living out were on the books since the mid-eighteenth century, but they were rarely enforced.

The words describing such black housing—"shanties," "sheds," "hovels," "shacks," "dens," and "huts"—suggest the state of dilapidation and overcrowding that prevailed, yet these dwellings did provide some relief from white dominance over the black slave. Even the multistoried wood or brick "tenements" for ten to fifty, even a hundred young male slaves working in industry offered a certain degree of autonomy. Occasionally, bondsmen who lived out simply disappeared into the free black neighborhoods on the outskirts of the larger cities.

All the same, both the smooth-talking black, dressed in fancy duds, moving in many social circles, and the independent accommodations were unusual among city slaves. Many industrial slaves were not permitted to leave the walls of the hemp factory or the sugar mill where they labored. Most urban slaves worked as domestics, and most owners were determined to maintain control over their property. The predominant pattern was the construction of slave quarters adjacent to the dwelling of the master and mistress. On a small city lot, the quarters typically stood behind the main house and yard, easily visible at all times. Given their proximity to the big house, urban slave accommodations tended to be of a better quality than the plantation quarters, especially those for field slaves. But these too comprised a definite part of the system of slavery.

The most conspicuous aspect of urban quarters was the high protective brick wall built behind them, often a foot thick, sometimes sixteen feet or even twenty feet high. In principle, the only way into and out of the residential compound could always be watched. Alleys were rare in most southern cities, again because these minor thoroughfares allowed an area for slave activity outside of white surveillance. Yet Savannah's pattern of lanes, established by James Oglethorpe in 1733, later enabled the slave to slip out through the rear stables and sheds into a relatively independent back-street life; in other cities as well, the blacks came round to the side streets for their social life.

The first floor of the quarters contained the kitchen, storerooms, and sometimes the stables, so that unpleasant smells and heat could be isolated from the white household. Sleeping rooms were on the second floor. If an owner had more than a few slaves, they shared rooms, usually ten feet by fifteen feet. Many slaves slept on the floor. The peak of pressure on space occurred in the 1830s, when the southern cities were growing especially rapidly and before the urban black population had begun to decline—only to rise dramatically during the Reconstruction decades. Yet conditions were scarcely comfortable in the decades

Slaveowners in the southern cities wanted surveillance and economy, but the close proximity of the quarters to the "big house" led many of them to add some architectural ornament, as in this elegant example from New Orleans, built in 1854.

preceding the Civil War. One physician in Charleston put the blame for the 1857 yellow fever epidemic on slave houses, "crowded, or rather packed, from basement to attic with human beings."[14]

Owners gave little attention to conditions in the slaves' housing, despite the unpleasant climate in southern cities. In contrast, an elaborate regional architecture accommodated white families who lived or summered in the cities. Charleston houses had multistory "galleries," positioned so as to take advantage of cooling breezes off the ocean; in New Orleans, a light parasol roof, tall ceilings, large door and window openings, patios, loggias, and the doorway jalousie maximized ventilation and privacy. These innovations were built, and perhaps sometimes designed, by black artisans, although only houses for whites incorporated the improvements into their structure.

The patterns of ante-bellum plantation quarters and urban slave housing survived in the South well into the twentieth century. W. E. B. DuBois, describing Georgia's Black Belt in his 1903 publication, *The Souls of Black Folk,* noted that some blacks lived in the self-same cabins of their slave ancestors, while others built similar crude structures on the sites of slave habitations that had fallen apart. "The general character and arrangement of these dwellings remains on the whole unaltered," DuBois observed.[15] The reasons for that continuity are, for the most part, the infamous legacy of racism. These structures had first appeared in response to the institution of slavery, and they endured after emancipation. The cabins were inexpensive; they represented dominant white attitudes about black domesticity, black sexuality, and black standards of character and cleanliness; the houses were seen by the whites as an expression of the fundamental differences that legitimated segregation policies.

At the same time, even the least substantial of these cabins suggests a desire for cultural continuity among the blacks themselves. Both the rural cabin and the small city dwellings say something about their occupants' family life, the carpenters' building skills, and the severe limitations placed on these people. We know very little about what that culture was really like or how these houses were really used. Today, however, with the awareness of the creative dynamics of black culture, the complex human dimensions of these dwellings, both rural and urban, and the social life that took place around them are gradually coming to light.

CHAPTER FOUR

HOUSING FACTORY WORKERS

> [The] transition from mother and daughter
> power to water and steam-power is a great one,
> greater by far than many as yet have begun to
> conceive—one that is to carry with it a
> complete revolution of domestic life
> and social manners.
>
> —Horace Bushnell,
> "The Age of Homespun" (1851)

AS THE COUNTRY EXPANDED ITS ECONOMY TO BUILD
factories for American products, such as guns, locks, shoes, and
cotton cloth, Americans, given their commitment to an egalitarian
society, had to decide what to do with industrial workers. Industrialists sought to convince others, as well as themselves, that a shift
from the farm to the factory would not create a permanent proletariat class. Such a class would undermine egalitarianism; and, even
more dangerous, at least in the eyes of many observers, demands
for wages would threaten property and order. Rural homesteaders
and urban property owners feared riot and rebellion from a class
condemned to perpetual poverty. De Tocqueville and other political commentators considered this country's urban poor "a rabble
even more formidable than the populace of European towns."[1]

Early American factory owners therefore claimed that while
industry would surely flourish, industrial work would be only a
temporary condition for those who took it on. Transience offered
a remedy to manufacturers, as well as an opportunity to the workers
themselves. One Massachusetts industrialist, Nathan Appleton,
pointed to the opportunities of the West, where a factory worker
could eventually move on to establish a home and an independent

livelihood as a farmer, after putting away a necessary sum for land and tools. While this panacea had enormous appeal to factory owners and managers and to many hopeful employees, the problems of meager pay and the lack of a practical agricultural training among most industrial workers posed major obstacles. The other favored approach to the issue was to stress that factories would concentrate on workers of a certain age; after their period of employment, it was assumed they would leave factory life to make their own livings on farms or in small towns.

There was a general consensus that the principal blame for industrial problems should be placed upon the cities. The Society for the Encouragement of Domestic Manufactures declared that American factories would be located outside urban areas, "on chosen sites, by the fall of waters and the running stream, the seats of health and cheerfulness, where good instruction will secure the morals of the young and good regulations will promote, in all, order, cleanliness, and the exercise of civil duties."[2] The message was clear. Closeness to nature would encourage virtuous living for both workers and their overseers. Of course, it was essential that early factories be in rural locations for more technical reasons too. American machinery ran by water power, usually a waterfall or a canal dug alongside a fast-moving river to create a similar drop where a water wheel could be placed.

Growth was often rapid once a large company or several related mills established themselves in a given hamlet. The towns of Lowell, Lawrence, Manchester, or Paterson were urban within a very short time. Nonetheless, industrialists emphatically denied that these enterprises were anything but villages. When Alexander Hamilton and the Society for Establishing Useful Manufactures founded a model "national manufactory" at Paterson, New Jersey, in 1791 (Congress had refused to allocate funds to make this a part of Hamilton's larger plan to centralize and modernize the national economy), it was the corporation—not the city—that received a charter. Designs for the industrial area and residential section of Paterson, undertaken by Major Pierre L'Enfant, the engineer-architect who had laid out the national capital, were formal conceptions for an ideal corporation; there was no political mandate for municipal self-government. After a slow period brought on by the Panic of 1792, boom times followed the War of 1812. The architect Peter Banner designed workers' housing for employees in the city's several large factories. For a century, Paterson was the fastest-growing city on the East Coast. Yet it was not until 1831 that a township charter passed. Likewise, the managers of Lowell, Massachusetts, relied on the idyllic vision of bucolic surroundings for several decades, even as workers spoke of Lowell as the "City of Spindles."

Denying city status to industrial centers was a strategy for portraying them as fundamentally rural settings with unnaturally large but still-transient populations. Just as parks and "rural cemeteries" alleviated the crowding in commercial cities during these decades of rapid growth, nature comforted the eye in industrial towns. As they surveyed the picturesque settings, the flower gardens and trees of mill towns, George Washington, and later Charles Dickens and Andrew Jackson, could disregard the fact that few factory workers owned their own homes or took much satisfaction in their labor. A twofold argument for the mill towns contended that pastoral surroundings would temper in-

· ·

In an engraving of Lowell, Massachusetts, ca. 1850, well-dressed visitors are enjoying the view of an industrial city they could still regard as charming and bucolic, despite its size and its factory pollution.

dustrial ugliness, while industry made the beautiful landscape useful.

Living places for workers were an immediate concern to the industrialists. When a manufacturer established a mill in a rural area or a tiny hamlet, he had to provide some accommodations to attract a work force. Housing involved a moral issue, too, at least in the manufacturers' publicity. After all, many Americans believed that the home determined individual character and national character as well. A sign of this pervasive assumption was the mill owners' eagerness to make some special provision for workers' housing and to advertise such efforts quite prominently. George S. White's tribute to Samuel Slater and the early American factory system, published in 1836, devoted an entire chapter to demonstrating the "Moral Influence of Manufacturing Establishments" through decent housing and industrious habits in the factories. In such company-built housing, two solutions prevailed, each adapted to a different system of manufacturing: the row of boardinghouses and the row of tiny cottages or tenements. Both were built and owned by the employer, and rented out to workers, supposedly for a brief period of tenure. According to the industrialists, factory conditions were less at issue than housing, which would continue to have an influence over the workers' families after they had left the industrial town.

In the United States, as in England, textile manufacture was the first craft to be taken from the home into the factory, although for several decades the various processes of carding, spinning, and weaving were kept separate, and some "putting out" of tasks to families on a piecework basis continued. This was the branch of industrial production that laid the foundation for American patterns of economic growth and American ideas of the social effects of factory life. The person responsible for initiating the shift was Samuel Slater, whom Andrew Jackson later called "the father of the American factory system."[3] In his youth, Slater had worked as an indentured apprentice in the English cotton mill of Jedidiah Strutt and Richard Arkwright. Arkwright had an ingenious system, comprised of a mill with fast-moving spinning frames run by water power and housing for the large families who provided workers in nearby "Arkwright villages." British authorities banned the export of manufacturing devices like the frame, and even tried to prevent the immigration of factory workers, in an effort to hold on to their monopoly on textile manufacturing. Slater memorized the technical plans and then slipped out on a ship bound for the United States. In 1789 he remodeled an old fulling mill in the Pawtucket Valley of Rhode Island. Four years later, with financial backing from two Providence merchants, he erected a new mill (which is still preserved as a museum) and housing for the mill employees.

Under the "Rhode Island system," as it was known, advertisements were posted in small towns and published in rural newspapers, encouraging whole families to come to a mill town. A father might work feeding cotton into the picker or tending a heavy spinning mule, while the mother was in the carding room or at a throstle twisting yarn, and various children wound bobbins, carried cans of cotton slivers, formed yarn into warps or balls, stirred vats of dye, or helped the adults tend the cumbersome machinery. Slater followed the English practice of employing mostly children under twelve years of age. By 1824, some 2,500 children between the ages of seven and fourteen worked in the Rhode Island textile mills.[4] They were agile and could be paid very little. This was what the American industrial class's pledge to prevent the formation of a permanent proletariat amounted to in practice.

Not all manufacturers provided housing, but those who did stipulated that a household had to furnish a minimum number of workers—usually between four and five—in order to rent. Private rooms were almost unheard-of. The nuclear family formed the basic living unit, to which were added relatives and other single men and women boarders. All children and unmarried adults lived in family groups. In the Rockdale manufacturing district, south of Philadelphia, 14 percent of the cottages were rented out to widows or other female heads of households whose children and boarders—usually extended family members—worked in the textile mills.[5] David Humphreys, who hired New York orphans as well as entire families, housed some three hundred people, mostly in rows of attached dwellings, near his Connecticut mill. Timothy Dwight, the Yankee theologian, visiting Humphreysville, praised the "delightfully romantic" setting, which was combined with a purely American inventiveness and industriousness in the factory.[6]

Most American industrialists set up factories in small villages or undeveloped areas where there were no local builders. Consequently, they had to provide housing for their employees. In Rhode Island and Connecticut, factory owners erected rows of almost identical cottages. The regularity and uniformity strengthened the image of an orderly, utopian industrial development in New England. Façades were chaste and conservative, in local stone or white painted clapboards. Cotton or woolen mill owners established the majority of these company towns, although other kinds of industrialists built housing along the same plans. Eli

Whitney, who was responsible for the idea that all parts of a product should be standardized in size and shape for easier repair and replacement, opened a factory at Mill Rock, Connecticut, in 1798, where he produced locks and guns for a government contract according to his "American system of manufacture." Whitney provided rows of identical small cottages for his workers, since the factory village, which came to be known as Whitneyville, was far off the beaten track of settlement.

Most of the houses in early industrial towns were for individual households—nuclear families and their boarders—but some were shared

William Giles Munson's painting of the Eli Whitney Gun Factory at Mill Rock, Connecticut, in 1826–1828, depicts both the neat rows of workers' cottages and the romantic natural surroundings of the ideal American factory town.

by two or three families. In North Carolina, when textile mills materialized in the mid-nineteenth century, rows of log cabins alternated with "long houses" of attached stone tenements. Such tenements had also appeared in New England and Pennsylvania mill towns by the 1830s, when factory work forces increased in size. In the Rockdale, Pennsylvania, manufacturing area, the tenements provided accommodations for different immigrant groups, each of which lived in a distinct area of the factory-town. This, however, did not represent an example of poor-quality housing for foreign workers. At this time, most of the immigrants housed by industrialists were English-speaking and relatively skilled. In Rockdale, they tended to be families with highly valued experience in the British mills.

In the better homes for skilled workers, there would be a tiny front parlor, as a gesture to formal social life, and a slightly larger combination sitting room/dining room/kitchen for most family activities. Young children played here, before attending a few years of public school and being gradually assimilated into factory employment. Their mothers watched over them while preparing meals, doing household chores, or working at some task that had been put out from the mill into the neighboring households. But factory pay was preferable to the rate for piecework, and many married women returned to the mills. A grandmother or aunt then looked after the small children; and, for a short time during the day, the houses did not seem so cramped.

By far, the greatest strain on space in the workers' houses occurred at night, after a thirteen- or fourteen-hour day at the mill for most of the occupants. Following the meal, the household would retire to sleeping quarters, which offered almost no privacy and little in the way of comfort. Many cottages had a single bedroom to the rear of the dwelling, and sometimes another in a cramped half-story above. A few cottages may have had as many as three designated sleeping areas, if they provided many workers to the mills, but even this was seldom sufficient. The kitchen and any other family room doubled as bedrooms; but with households of between six and ten people, including unmarried adult women, elderly relatives, and unrelated boarders, crowding was always a problem. Parents usually kept the younger children in their bedroom. The others then divided up by sex rather than by age or relation.

Inadequate sanitation facilities, poor ventilation, and dampness—most houses were built directly on the ground—meant that living conditions could be quite uncomfortable. The kitchen fire filled the room with smoke, and the single window could scarcely clear the air. The well and privy, usually shared by several families, were located in the backyard. This was a convenience only in that there was already so little space inside. Laundry hung out back to dry on washdays, and children played there. Some families constructed small kitchens in a backyard ell in order to make the living area more commodious.

Home was certainly better than the mills, however, where heat and humidity were overbearing. The overseers kept the windows shut and the furnaces running at high temperatures at all times, for they believed that this would protect the wool or cotton. The air was filled with floating particles of cotton and dust; and the stench of cotton wool, impregnated with oil from the machinery, was nauseating.

However crowded, impermanent, and constricted these various dwelling places might have been, they were the homes of working men, women, and children. After a long, trying day at a loom, the home provided a retreat. These places can therefore tell us something of their occupants' lives.

At the same time, mill owners went to great lengths to establish the moral influence of their enterprises through their control over both domestic and work environments. Slater and his followers insisted that they were overseeing the religious training, practical education, family bonds, and work habits of employees and their kin. "Multitudes of women and children have been kept out of vice," testified one industrialist, "simply by being employed."[7] Farm people learned modern schedules and skills. Children would be kept from idleness, women from gossip, and men from drinking. President Andrew Jackson congratulated Slater for creating a new population, "not ragged and oppressed . . . not sunken in profligacy and dissipation, but raised in intelligence and morals, as well as religious feelings, beyond the other parts of the states."[8]

The influence of the model cottages was considered especially useful in inculcating middle-class values. Smith Wilkinson, a mill director in Pomfret, Connecticut, reconciled the fact that he and his associates owned all the houses with the formerly "ignorant and vicious" state of his employees' morals. He described the changes in families who "must conform and be moral, to be accepted" in his village, but insisted that absolute control was always needed.[9] According to Anthony F. C. Wallace's excellent history of Rockdale, the industrialists publicized their housing programs, since this was the most effective way of attracting workers and winning the confidence of the middle-class public; but because of their low opinion of working-class parents, they actually anticipated that the church, the school, and the Sunday school would have a greater socializing influence over children.

The vision of orderly homes was sufficiently vivid that several accounts of life in mill towns insisted that most working men owned their own residences and land. In fact, homeownership predominated only in farming villages.[10] Whether families rented from the mill owner or from a local speculative investor (whose cottages were usually less desirable than those provided by the company, for he had little interest in publicity), they had only a temporary claim on their homes. If a family could not continue to furnish the hands they had agreed to provide, they faced eviction. In several towns, the average tenancy was only about a year. Many families simply moved from one mill and one rented cottage to another, but it looked as if the industrialists were preventing the creation of a permanent industrial proletariat.

Industry grew rapidly in New England. By 1810, 250 textile mills were scattered throughout the region. In 1820, the number of cotton mill workers was reported to be 12,000; a decade later there were 62,000. By this time, women employees outnumbered men by more than two to one, primarily because of the competing textile mills, with their own system of housing workers, that had grown up around Boston.[11]

Francis Cabot Lowell was responsible for this alternative industrial system. He had waited out the War of 1812 in England, traveling and visiting cotton mills. Upon his return, he joined with a number of friends from other Boston Brahmin families to establish a textile weaving company. The Boston Manufacturing Company (later the Lowell Associates) chose for their first site the town of Waltham, Massachusetts, nearby on the Charles River. This would soon be followed by their more famous town, named for Lowell. The venture was, from the start, more ambitious than the contemporary Rhode Island enterprises. An unprecedented amount of capital was invested; more land was purchased and platted; and more processes were brought together under one factory roof. The "Waltham system" centralized all the steps in making muslin, from cleaning the bales of cotton to weaving the sheeting. (In Europe, the traditions of village specialization still prevented this integrated approach, and other American firms had followed their precedent.) These mills needed a large number of laborers because of the increased production and the greater variety of skills involved. Since the looms had been made more efficient mechanically and were not so heavy as the machinery being used around Providence, Lowell reasoned that almost all the work could be undertaken by women operatives.

The proposition had its benevolent side. The life of young women on New England farms was usually isolated and filled with drudgery. The local soil was rocky and recalcitrant. Many farms needed the added income from a daughter's employment. The desire to put aside money for a dowry and a piece of land to share with an eventual husband, or the chance to buy new finery or an education, prompted many young women to go to the factories. As Sally Rice of Somerset, Vermont, wrote her parents in 1839: "I am most 19 years old. I must of course have something of my own before many more years have passed over my head. And where is that something coming from if I go home and earn nothing. . . ."[12]

Factory life provided young women with some independence and companionship with other women of the same age. In one large Lowell company, 95 percent of the women workers—the vast majority of employees—were native-born farm girls, and more than 80 percent were between fifteen and thirty years of age.[13] Although the schedule of factory life was more rigid than life on a farm, the labor and the hours were not necessarily more arduous. A young woman who lived on a family farm had to contend with strong patriarchal control over her earnings, activities, and social life. Many factory girls quickly learned to ridicule the rural accents, dowdy clothes, and homespun ambitions of newcomers—and even rejected many of their parents' values, preferring to marry mechanics or shopkeepers and stay in town. Fully a third would find the urban life of Lowell and other factory towns too alluring to return to their rural hamlets.[14] The rise of the New England mill in the early nineteenth century, especially the intense experience of female boardinghouses, helped shift the culture, as well as the economy, toward a more urbanized, industrialized way of life.

Lowell and his associates definitely benefitted from their system. They could not be accused of disrupting agricultural production if they hired mostly women. The traditional association of women with domestic textile production made this an unintrusive industrialism. Women could be paid less than men and presumably were more docile. Finally, women were supposedly transient. The Lowell Associates claimed that most operatives returned to their farms or married after a few years of employment.

Within a few years, the system had proven so successful that the

Boston Manufacturing Company purchased a larger site. Francis Lowell had recently died, and the new location farther up the Merrimack River, at the village of East Chelmsford, was named for him. The planning of Lowell was put under a former Boston merchant by the name of Kirk Boott. Boott laid out the factories first, taking maximum advantage of the falls and the canals he had constructed. The style of the first factory building was still conspicuously domestic, except for the clerestory windows in the roof monitor and the great expanse of the two-story brick edifice. Boott then platted out the rest of the town into a strict gridiron. The Lowell Associates owned almost all of the land, except for a few shops and cottages belonging to townspeople, and Boott divided it into four districts, each with a distinct type of housing.

The mansion of Kirk Boott commanded the entrance to the factory grounds. Its Greek portico and spacious yard differentiated it from every other building in the town. Nearby were the quarters for married workers: cottages for overseers and foremen, and double houses, called tenements, for clerical workers. The housing of the managerial class, while not as grand as Boott's mansion, boasted some architectural finery. The simple box shapes were distinguished by a Greek porch or later by Gothic window tracery. Thus, they looked like other ideal American cottages in other, less preordained towns. The two-story blocks of tenements were more austere and contained smaller apartments for their occupants.

Boardinghouses, either in pairs or in blocks of eight continuous buildings, were erected for the young women workers. It was these boardinghouses which marked the experiment, in both architectural and social terms. The typical house was wood frame, with a plain, unadorned façade. It had two or three stories and an attic, lit with dormer windows. In the early 1830s, twenty-five women might reside in one of these houses, sleeping four to six in each bedroom, two to a bed. The rooms provided no space for furniture other than the double beds and the women's trunks and bandboxes. Harriet Martineau was outraged at the lack of privacy in such an otherwise well-intentioned experiment: "In America, where space is of far less consequence, where the houses are large, where the factory girls can build churches, and buy libraries, and educate brothers for learned professions, these same girls have no private apartments. . . . It shows a want of inclination for solitude."[15]

The vast majority of the unmarried female employees at the mills lived in these boardinghouses; all others had to prove that they resided with their families. In the hours when they were not working in the factory, the residents read, wrote letters and poems, or visited with friends, either in their rooms or in the public rooms on the first floor. The parlor provided a place for receiving acceptable young men (with the approval of the house matron) or staging a lecture. The dining room, where three rather substantial meals were hurriedly eaten each day, also served as a social area. The house matron's rooms were by the front door, where she could watch every coming and going, and enforce the company's 10:00 P.M. curfew.

The Associates and their agents set the regulations for their female employees, at home and at work. The "respectable" housemothers enforced the required church attendance, hours of sleep, eating and visiting rules. They prohibited dancing, alcohol, and "improper conduct." They even checked to make sure that each girl was vaccinated and quarantined when she became ill. Henry Miles, a local Unitarian minister and an apologist for the mill owners, explained the policy: "Public morals and

· ·

An engraving of Dutton Street, Lowell, ca. 1848, contrasts the early wooden boarding-houses in the foreground with the monumental and far more crowded new brick blocks of boardinghouses that had just been completed. One of the Lowell mills is at the end of the vista.

private interests, identical in all places, are here seen to be linked in an indissoluble connection. Accordingly, the sagacity of self-interest, as well as more disinterested considerations, has led to the adoption of moral police."[16]

The widely known *Lowell Offering*, a publication of the young women's own poetry and prose, presented glowing accounts of industriousness and self-improvement realized through the extended influence of factory and boardinghouse life. Stories told of girls like Ellen, who complained: "Up before day, at the clang of the bell—and out of the mill by the clang of the bell—into the mill, and at work, in obedience to that ding-dong of a bell—just as though we were so many living machines." Her friend, Almira, then countered this argument with a reminder of the "dull, lifeless silence" of the farm.[17] In comparison, she explained, factory life was pleasurable and rewarding.

More critical descriptions were censored in the early years in order to bolster the image of rewarding labor as a preparation for earnest, hardworking home life. Yet resentment was expressed in songs and poems, which would later be published. The depression of 1837–1840 brought these complaints to the forefront. Many farmers lost their farms, and their daughters were no longer so free to return home. Working conditions worsened; the machinery was speeded up; the numbers of looms to be tended increased. The Lowell Female Reform Association took up the cry of neighboring women in the Lynn shoe factories. Both spontaneous and planned strikes, then called turn-outs, occurred more frequently. Young women spoke out before state legislative committees. Their new journals demolished the myth of the beauty of factory life. A millworker's description, printed in the *Voice of Industry*, gave a harsh characterization of life in Lowell: "And amidst the clashing noise and din/ Of the ever beating loom,/ Stood a fair young girl with throbbing brow/ Working her way to the tomb."[18]

Conditions in the houses also deteriorated. Money for room and board did not increase; and in order to make ends meet, matrons were forced to cut back on food and to crowd more girls into each room. Boardinghouses soon accommodated up to fifty or sixty residents, now sleeping eight or twelve to a room. The new blocks of houses were longer, stretching 250 feet. Built in dark-red brick and rising a story higher, they were monumental and austere habitations.

The "New Block" of 1848 was the last major addition to company housing in Lowell. The Associates had changed their hiring policies, retaliating against the operatives' demands by shifting over to Irish and

The *Lowell Offering* was the company magazine, which contained writings by the factory girls. The frontispiece of an 1845 issue depicts the manufacturers' allegory of the virtues of factory life: employees had time for reading and self-improvement, while they also learned the rewards of industriousness in the mills.

French-Canadian workers, whom they could pay even less than the native-born farm girls, and they now dropped their program of moral and environmental reform.

Even at the earliest and most idealized stage of the model industrial town, the Lowell Associates had not provided any accommodations for the immigrant laborers, mostly Irish, who had dug the canals and built the mills and the housing. Cast off to the outskirts of the city, these men, many with their families, had lived in tents and then in makeshift wooden huts of unfinished lumber, piling up sod on the sides for insulation. Conditions worsened with the increased immigration resulting from the Irish potato famine of the late 1840s; other "ideal" industrial towns, such as Lawrence, Fall River, and Amoskeag, also found themselves surrounded by shantytowns and impoverished immigrants. The "underground mud huts of the 'City of Cork,'" as a Lawrence newspaper editor called these areas, were wretched places.[19] Yet the men who planned the company towns, reluctant to admit that they fostered this class of worker, therefore averted their attention. When the immigrants were brought into the factories in the 1840s, the huts remained on the outskirts, and privately built tenements supplemented the large company-owned boardinghouses, most of which were sold to become more privately owned tenements. An 1849 observer found in Lowell 254 tenement buildings inhabited by 1,054 individuals, the vast majority of whom were immigrants who now worked in the mills.[20]

The illusion of a pure, moral environment in boardinghouses and textile mills was no longer an issue for industrialists or for the public. In fact, by 1850, the ideal of a rewarding factory environment seemed naïve. The depression of 1857 assured the end of this experiment in industrial and environmental control. By this time, too, the country had come to accept industrial growth as indisputably necessary. The same moral rationales were no longer needed. The quality of the products rather than the effect of the home environment on workers was the pride of American industry. Factories became larger and noisier, machinery faster and more dangerous. Few people took much notice. The ideology of industrialism no longer had to celebrate the image of an ideal community, preparing healthy young people for their futures as dutiful farmers and housewives. Industry existed to produce goods for the middle-class American home and to assure the continued prosperity of the national economy.

CHAPTER FIVE

INDEPENDENCE AND THE RURAL COTTAGE

We believe that every improvement in the abodes of men which renders them more neat, comfortable, and pleasing, contributes not only to physical enjoyment, but to mental and moral advancement.

—Henry William Cleaveland, *Village and Farm Cottages* (1854)

TO THE MAJORITY OF CITIZENS IN THE EARLY republic, the ideal American home was an independent homestead, attractive enough to encourage family pride yet unpretentious and economical. Itinerant artists, traveling across the countryside on horseback, specialized in paintings that portrayed these very qualities. Such artists decorated the interiors of homes with bright geometric patterns and näive murals, and often did a painting of the family dwelling or a portrait of the family members. Rural women and young schoolgirls took the home as a favorite subject for their needlework samplers, surrounding the image of the simple, productive house and garden with virtuous proverbs or biblical quotations.

The country's leaders were surprisingly attentive to American predilections in domestic architecture. A few, such as Thomas Jefferson, were distressed about the aesthetic disarray that could result from thousands of quickly built, untutored dwellings, occupied for only a short time by restless homesteaders. For those who feared attacks on private property, even the forms seemed an invitation to anarchy. Jefferson was troubled by the impermanent look of most of the simple wooden houses in his native state of Virginia.

He wanted to see an end to these "ugly, uncomfortable, and—happily —more perishable" dwellings.[1] A stable agrarian citizenry in substantial brick or stone houses would form a solid basis for the young nation's strength.

For Jefferson, and for many other civic leaders, there was a problem of guiding, but not regulating, domestic settings. How could Americans create an environment that protected the respect for order,

· ·

The ideal home was a favorite subject for needlework samplers. This 1808 embroidery by Mary Richards of Portland, Massachusetts, evokes many of the qualities ante-bellum American culture associated with the home: family self-sufficiency, Christian virtue, diligent work, and small-town community.

self-sufficiency, and spirituality they held in common, without imposing on the freedom of each individual and each family to live as they pleased? The answer was the concept of the model home. Some prototypes could be small and inexpensive; each would be ornamented, so that the family would recognize their home as a place of beauty, repose, and Christian virtue. There was also a mechanical image at work here, a notion of continuous improvements on a templet to make the product better and cheaper. Optimistic belief in inevitable progress encouraged the assumption that aesthetic, technological, and social breakthroughs would keep occurring. This would not be a legislated model, based on regulations or laws everyone had to follow. Instead, it would be a guide, an inspiration that each builder and each family would adapt to the circumstances at hand. Several kinds of dwellings were publicized as model homes during these years, but the greatest attention was bestowed on the detached cottage for the independent farmer and his family. This rural home, like the family for whom it was designed, was considered the basis for America's strength and progress.

By 1830, ministers, schoolteachers, physicians, poets, and jurists all over the country were instructing their fellow citizens about good homes. Writers noted the trappings of an interior and the style of a façade as indications of the character of residents. The popular lady novelists Lydia Sigourney and "Fanny Fern" often relied on architectural description to enliven their stories and their moral advice to readers. So, too, did Henry David Thoreau, Washington Irving, and James Fenimore Cooper, who was especially vehement against the "mushroom" appearance of Greek Revival cottages, which seemed to spring up out of nowhere, unplanned, like an infestation.[2] Soon Henry Ward Beecher and Horace Bushnell were preaching to their congregations about an ideal home on earth, for which they gave occasional detailed specifications. Beecher even advertised household products and later wrote a sentimental novel, Norwood (1867). Bushnell's Christian Nurture (1847) described how the home and family life could foster virtuous "habits," thereby encouraging the development of gentle Christian children. Regulation and love would build "domesticity of character."[3] The right home environments could help assure the blessed eternal peace of "home comforts" in heaven. These writers all wanted Americans to become more aware of the power of "influence" they attributed to the domestic setting. They hoped families would create better homes and thereby strengthen the bonds of family life.

The task of defining the American home was a national mission. The goal was a general idea of the optimum setting for "the typical American family"—still depicted as an independent yeoman farmer and his hard-working immediate kin. This representative national home would not be the stately mansion of the wealthy, as if the grandest structure stood for the aspirations of the entire population. It was an average house for a family "of the middling sort."

There was, as yet, relatively little emphasis on the home as a unique statement, an individualized setting for a particular family. Increasingly, though, home and "outside world" came to be posed as separate spheres. True, the familiar communal festivities of the barn-raising, the quilting bee, and other less formal gatherings took place in the homes of any small village. At the same time, the private home was becoming the locus of a sentimental search for meaning and security. Authors of domestic guides spread this concept. According to Lydia Sigourney, one of the best-known writers of the early nineteenth century, the woman was responsible for perfecting an alternative to the commercial world where her husband and sons had to work:

> For she, with harmonizing will,
> Her pleasures in her duties found,
> And strove, with still advancing skill
> To make her home's secluded bound
> An Eden refuge, sweet and blest,
> When weary, he returned for rest.[4]

Duty to husband involved adorning the home in the image of a private haven, rich in simple beauty and her own homemade ornament.

Even more consummate was the woman's power as a mother. Around 1820, childhood suddenly became the focus of numerous books, sermons, and meetings. It was presented as a distinct period of development, quite separate from adult life yet critically determinant of later adult character. The Calvinist doctrine of the infant's inherent sinfulness gave way to a focus on the child's social nature and individual conscience, both of which were supposedly molded during the first few years of life. The family, in effect, created the child's personality and character. By 1830 child-rearing was seen as indisputably a female task, though not an innate skill. If a woman lived in a city, she might attend a maternal association, where women exchanged information. But for the most part, she had to rely on recently published books and magazines for advice. These described the awesome power of the mother and the home, and then intimated the course the mother should pursue in teaching her children values.

Increased attention to the individual, especially the individual child, and to the home as a place for moral education, encouraged a focus on private spaces within the home. Children who had misbehaved had to be isolated from their siblings for self-examination, Bushnell and other ministers explained. They should not be forced into a dark closet but into a small room for solitary reflection. A vigorous campaign against corporal punishment stressed the superior effect of the good home environment in the development of a strong personal conscience. While there was no thought given to the idea of private bedrooms for every child, the emphasis on increased privacy and greater specialization of rooms was evident.

Both Lydia Sigourney and Catharine Beecher, author of a *Treatise on Domestic Economy* (1843), insisted that each house needed separate areas for family social life, personal privacy, and household production. The kitchen and pantry were usually set off from the main body of the house in a rear wing. The frequent use of the phrase "work room" in guides and floor plans indicates that in most rural families, the wife and daughters spent much of their time here, making butter churns and curtains, soap and brooms, as well as preserving food, cooking, and washing clothes. In *Walden,* Thoreau lamented the tendency to isolate these activities architecturally, complaining that "there is as much secrecy about the cooking as if he [the host] had a desire to poison you"; but his protest went against the grain.[5]

Nomenclature announced the higher level of specialization in other areas as well. The "parlor" was the room where the family entertained visitors. The "sitting room" was for more intimate family gatherings in the evenings. A few larger houses contained both, but most designers had to choose the appropriate word, and they stressed its connection to a sociable or a family-centered domesticity.

Whichever word was used, the formal front room contained a great variety of pieces and styles, creating a rather festive air. In rural areas, it was common to paint stenciled decorations on the walls and to marbelize furniture in imitation of exotic woods. Machine-made rugs, geometric floor mosaics, and carefully swept arrangements of sand created a variety of patterns underfoot. Birdcages were common. With relatively little space allocated to storage in most houses, the walls were covered with hooks bearing hats, coats, framed pictures, farming and cooking utensils, and high shelves, where plates and platters were kept. By 1840, almost all New England women could read, and interest in education abounded throughout the country. Consequently, a bookshelf stood in most parlors. Since this room was the repository for "art," it usually contained family-made paper lace, landscape paintings, embroidery, and shadow boxes, together with the revered activity of such work in progress. This was the room for social events and daily family gatherings. The cover for the sheet music of an 1841 ballad entitled "My Mother's Bible" depicted a family gathered around the parlor table, while the father read by a kerosene light. A line from the song brought the setting and the sentiments together: "Again that little group is met within the

. . . .

John Lewis Krimmel's painting of a quilting party in 1813 shows the typical interior and the highly valued social life of an early-nineteenth-century farmhouse. The Chippendale clock, birdcage, books, and pictures suggest that many households paid careful attention to their domestic surroundings.

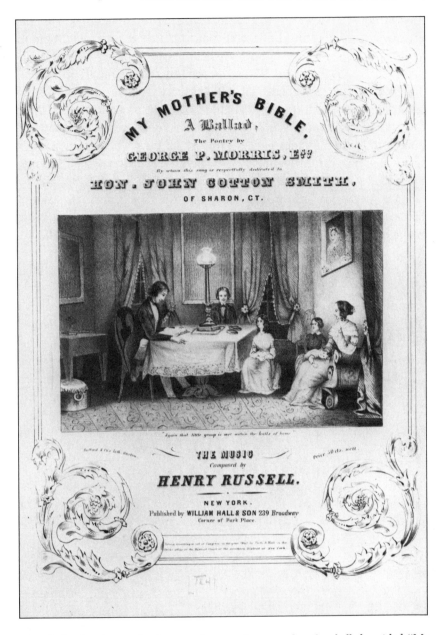

The idealized parlor on the sheet-music cover for a popular 1841 ballad entitled "My Mother's Bible" presents a more urbane and reserved household than Krimmel's painting. In a room with stylish Empire furniture, the family has gathered together to hear the father read the nightly Scripture.

halls of home." However, the idealized image has done away with the disarray and flamboyant decoration that would have been found in most homes.

In the 1840s, builders began to publish architectural books that brought together floor plans, details, perspective drawings, and empassioned texts, assuring readers that these house plans would enable them to create perfect homes. Many such "pattern books" contained specifications for all the buildings needed for a small town: a church, a school, a store, and a variety of houses, ranging from estimates of $200 to $20,000. In the titles of the books—Edward Shaw's *Rural Architecture* (1843), Alexander Jackson Davis's *Rural Residences* (1842), Andrew Jackson Downing's *Cottage Residences* (1842), or Calvert Vaux's *Villas and Cottages* (1854)—authors emphasized their variations of the authentic American rural cottage or farmhouse.

A typical proposal for a farmer's cottage showed four rooms—a parlor, family sitting room, workroom, and bedroom—as well as a hall, a porch, a pantry, and two closets, all squeezed into 525 square feet. In such a small area, rooms had to serve several functions. The sitting room doubled as a dining room and a children's bedroom. For larger houses, some designers included explanations of the newly defined spaces, proposing that an extra downstairs room could be used for an elderly relative's bedroom or for a sick child. Others suggested that a separate dining room would enhance domesticity. With this attention to use, the symmetrical placing of rooms was abandoned, even in the smallest cottage. The dwelling was evolving into a more intricate, specialized setting, with each room having a distinct shape.

Within the national prototype, builders presented ingenious variations of their model cottages. In *The Immigrant Builder* (1859), Charles Dwyer described inexpensive dwellings of sod blocks, rammed earth, adobe, and lightweight wood frame, so that a homesteader could use the cheapest materials of the region where he settled. Other authors showed more artistic variations, with the façades based on the myriad revival styles of nineteenth-century Europe. Each style corresponded to a particular terrain: a wooded hillside, a rocky seacoast, a plain, a town. There were still a number of Greek-style dwellings in these pattern books, but they seemed controlled and severe alongside the florid examples of Byzantine, Italianate, Gothic, Norman, Lombard, and Tudor styles. Davis boasted fourteen distinct styles in his book of house designs. Diversity had become fashionable.

Nineteenth-century builders actually spoke of "styles," not revivals,

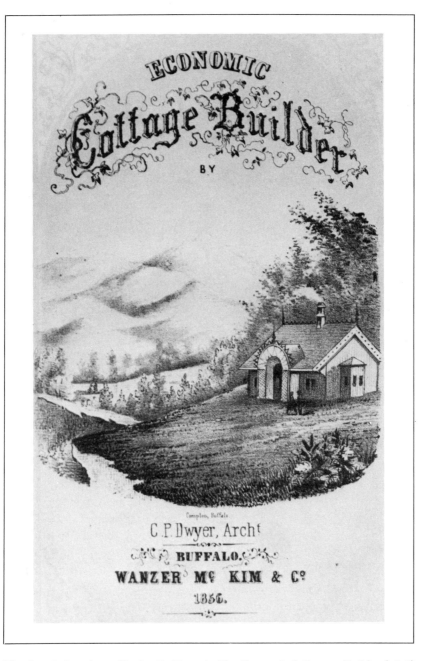

The frontispiece from Charles P. Dwyer's *The Economical Cottage Builder* (1856) shows a decorated dwelling in the frontier wilderness. The cottage combined the builder's concern for original American styles, symbolic architecture, and practicality.

the term we use today for historical references in architecture. They were interested in evoking a mood, using certain architectural motifs to set the stage, rather than in presenting a clear portrait of a particular historical period. The effect of the new range of styles was an informality, a license to play with composition and ornament. The box shape of the house was broken; bay windows and porches formed a more complex outline. Medieval-inspired ornament and a pointed gable roof were evidence of the Gothic style; square bays, a heavy extending roof supported by brackets, and a campanile-like tower were the basis of the Italianate. Soon the creative possibilities open to the carpenter expanded these definitions. The rich, flat carving under roof barge boards, over doors and windows, dripping from shutters and porch supports—described then and now as "gingerbread"—was, in general, impossible to classify.

As pattern-book images germinated, they spread to other forms of literature. A Philadelphia publisher, Louis Antoine Godey, and his editor, Sarah Josepha Hale, decided to promote an "own-your-own-home" movement by featuring American villa and cottage designs in their monthly women's fashion journal. Between 1846 and 1898, *Godey's Lady's Book* published some 450 model house designs—the basis, according to one report, for over four thousand houses built in a single decade.[6] Readers who wrote to the journal's office received a complete set of drawings for any model house. The marriage in *Godey's* of sentimental poetry and prose, delicate feminine fashions, and idealized American homes brought together several kinds of specialized literature into a new discourse on domesticity.

The pattern books of Andrew Jackson Downing, a widely respected Hudson River Valley landscape gardener, offer a systematic presentation of this period's code of domesticity. Like other ante-bellum home designers, Downing foresaw a far-reaching, pastoral landscape, dotted with pleasant houses, varied but always orderly, each one set in its own extensive, well-tended garden. In his books on rural and suburban residential design, and in his editorials for *The Horticulturist,* Downing outlined his rules and categories for all American homes. First, houses should fit with their surroundings, for only certain styles appeared appropriate in particular settings. Second, houses should look like houses and not like other structures. Here Downing relied on the theory of associations developed by eighteenth-century English aesthetic philosophers. The value of an object or a view depended on deeply rooted symbolic associations it evoked. However, Downing and other American pattern-book writers challenged the idea that all associations were based on highly educated perceptions, for this had decidedly elitist overtones; instead, they asserted that many architectural forms—and particularly those of domestic buildings—elicited universal responses. Therefore, all houses needed certain domestic symbols to articulate the feelings Anglo-American culture connected with the home. Downing called this "expression of purpose." Chimneys and overhanging roofs with high gables and deep eaves evoked home, as did the welcoming entry porch and the comfortable side piazza. Delicate ornament, such as Gothic trefoil tracery over a window or a carved Italianate bracket under the roof, reminded a viewer of the elegance and handiwork within. Gothic details also reinforced the religious ties of a Christian home.

• •

A Gothic-style cottage built at Easton, Pennsylvania, ca. 1840, followed pattern-book guidelines in every detail, providing a diminutive entry porch, a prominent chimney, and abundant architectural ornament.

According to Downing, who cited the English art critic John Ruskin, domestic architecture should express the owner's "condition" or class, his occupation and background. (The man of the household was specifically the reference in this iconography.) Downing catalogued three kinds of houses for three groups in the society: villas for "persons of competence," cottages for mechanics or working men, and farmhouses for farmers. He felt that distinctions were necessary and that no one should try to present a grander image than was appropriate. "But *unless there is something of the castle in the man,*" he wrote, "it is very likely, if it be like a real castle, to dwarf him to the stature of a mouse."[7] Every American deserved a good house, from the working man's undecorated cottage of rough wood to the wealthy man's Italian campanile tower. All the same, since no pattern-book designer could believe that anyone in America would remain either poor, a worker, or a servant for very long, they paid relatively little attention to the quality of housing for these classes.

Pattern-book designers considered themselves a critical component in the creation of a democratic republic. Their publications, which explained how to build good homes in the country, supposedly provided every citizen with the opportunity for independence. If all Americans had access to plans for orderly dwellings, adapted to every budget and region, then those who continued to live in rural hovels or crowded into unkempt urban tenements did so because they were less civilized, instinctively less drawn to the good models than were their neighbors. Henry Cleaveland, Charles Dwyer, and others considered this argument in some detail, positing a hierarchy that ran from animals to less-than-human savages (including poor whites) to a pinnacle of a virtuous, average American family living by Christian values in their own small cottage. Each included in his argument several examples of one-room and two-room cottages in rammed earth or rough logs to support the claim that a decent home was available to any American at almost no expense. There was no excuse for poverty.

Morality was central to Downing's vision and to that of most antebellum domestic designers. He called for "republican homes," comfortable and beautiful yet never so ostentatious as to belittle the neighbors or aggrandize the children's manners. Every American dwelling, he insisted, could be "a home of the virtuous citizen," if it were thoughtfully planned.[8] Downing posed domestic architecture as a counterforce to the "spirit of unrest" and the feverish pace of American life.[9] Yale theologian Timothy Dwight, writing of his travels through New England, had also worried about the power of the disorderly, unpleasant setting. "The habitation has not a little influence on the mode of living," he wrote, "and the mode of living sensibly affects the taste, manners, and even the morals, of the inhabitants. If a poor man builds a poor house, without any design or hope of possessing better, he will . . . conform his aims and expectations to the style of his house. His dress, his food, his manners, his taste, his sentiments, his education of his children, and their character as well as his own, will all be seriously affected by this ugly circumstance."[10] Downing's friend Nathaniel Willis (the brother of the novelist "Fanny Fern") wrote about the powerful symbolism of domesticity in his magazine, the *Home Monthly*. For Willis, too, morality was closely tied to control. He looked to "home associations" in architecture, landscaping, and literature to balance the franticness of "our plastic and rapidly maturing country."[11]

The cottages in pattern books were meant as family farmhouses, although many were erected in the small frontier towns that speculators built in promising locations. Despite the growing urban population, the nation was still overwhelmingly rural. Every writer on domestic life and architecture and every communitarian "social architect" insisted that true men and women could be raised only in the country. Nathaniel Willis was one of many who connected rural virtues to republican values: "[W]hile a family *in town* may be governed and held together mainly by money, there is a republic within the ring fence of a *country residence.*"[12] Anti-urban sentiment was widespread, and it extended beyond a fear of the poor. A book describing the homes of famous national authors captured the mood with its passing references to urban habitations, with their "dreary monotony of front, . . . houses which are mere parallelograms of air."[13] Rural Americans wanted diversity and symbolism, an Eden of interest and delights away from the city.

Given these sentiments, builders were quick to play up natural materials in domestic construction. Pattern books praised unpainted wood siding. Vertical board-and-batten was favored because it represented the simple wood studs of the structure beneath the sheathing. If paint were used, it was to be of a hue that would harmonize with the natural surroundings: russets, lichen greens, and grays replaced the white of Greek temples. Every pattern-book writer agreed that a house looked best when it was made of timber, stone, or clay found in the surrounding area rather than more expensive, fashionable materials transported from afar.

Insistence on local materials often translated into an attack on aristocratic luxury and a sentimental celebration of the homes of the rural poor. Writers warbled that the most beautiful paintings, which evoked the noblest sentiments in the observer, portrayed the humble farm rather than the mansion. In *Walden,* Thoreau called upon all suburbanites to remember this fact when choosing a house design, and to opt for the least pretentious style. (He went so far as to champion the model of the Indian community in which, he claimed, every family had a shelter as good as the best; simplicity was thus the key to equality as well as the mark of goodness and beauty.) Not even the impermanence and coarseness of the crudest frontier house could quell pride in American design. As one pattern-book author claimed: "[W]e are proud of the flimsy, unsubstantial structures, so sneered at by foreigners, which dot the whole face of the country. They are the homes of the people, who will by-and-by build and own better ones."[14] Homespun rusticity was an admirable aesthetic to these builders, who carefully cultivated the primitive in their drawings and in their rhetoric.

The cult of the ordinary and commonplace—what Emerson exalted in *The American Scholar* as "the common . . . the familiar, the low"—extended to a romance with the log cabin.[15] Such a construction type was actually a Scandinavian model, comparatively rare on the frontier; but by the late 1830s, writers of all national backgrounds claimed the rugged American log cabin as a common cultural heritage. The fad reached new proportions with the studied populism of Jacksonian Democrats. Supporters of Harrison's 1840 presidential campaign then took it up, passing out pamphlets and hard cider from makeshift log cabins, and proclaiming the cabin as a symbol of solid American frontier vigor. Catching the enthusiasm, pattern-book designers included idealized drawings of log cabins among their model houses, praising the supposedly indigenous forms and the visibly hardy strength of the materials.

Celebration of the natural and the ordinary was not particular to America, of course. Throughout Europe, the rise of romanticism brought a widespread fascination with the natural and the unspoiled, whether magnificent or commonplace. Appeals that the builder take the surrounding landscape into account—a general formula by 1840—cited eighteenth-century English theorists of the picturesque. American styles were also derivative. Even the Greek Revival, the symbol of national independence, took place after a classical revival in England and on the continent. The Gothic Revival, which followed, combined a glorification of the American landscape with architectural reminders of European history.

While acknowledging these influences, American builders, unlike most professionally trained architects, saw it as their duty to introduce originality. The theme of national unity through intense individualism and artistic creation ran through every pattern book. Stylistic inventiveness was lauded as a way to be fashionable and to assert cultural independence. By the 1850s, builders were mixing styles and playing with decorative motifs quite freely. They introduced daring "inventions"— hexagonal or circular dwellings, with rooms cut into unusual elliptical shapes or curious wedges. By far the most popular of these eccentricities was the octagon house. In *A Home for All* (1848), the phrenologist and spiritualist Orson Fowler claimed that the octagon was a 20 percent more efficient use of a given square-foot area, and intimated that it possessed certain mystical powers. For a decade, octagonal dwellings, schoolhouses, and other structures were erected from Natchez to San Francisco.

Fowler's functionalist argument echoed the self-praise of other builders who claimed that their housing models were "built to live in," based on "common sense," while those in rival books were too expensive and elitist, preoccupied with aesthetics at the expense of practicalities. The desire to use science and technology—or sometimes pseudo-science and gadgetry—for the common good of the society was another distinguishing feature of American romanticism.

In building, the most important technological innovation of the antebellum years was the balloon frame. This type of construction, first used in Chicago in 1839, radically transformed the work of building a house. The earlier method had relied on heavy pieces of lumber, connected by hand-cut pegs and mortise-and-tenon joints; an entire frame wall was fitted on the ground and lifted into place by a crew of men. The balloon frame, as its name implies, was based on much lighter, pre-cut pieces of lumber, held together with nails. It required fewer workers, and much less time and expense. The factory production of nails and the mill cutting of standardized sizes of lumber made the balloon frame available to carpenters and self-sufficient individual builders along any well-traveled route.

A keen interest in applied science and innovative home technology spurred the patenting of countless household conveniences at mid-century, including ice cutters, pie sectioners, cherry pitters, and lawn mowers. The word "gadget" (from the French *gachette,* a piece of machinery) entered the national vocabulary. Builders had at least one chapter on domestic technology in their guides, including instructions for an open wooden drainpipe to carry off waste water from the kitchen, a concrete cesspool, or a fresh-water cistern, with its charcoal and ash filter beneath a false floor. Because almost every household had to rely on its own system of water supply and its own provisions for waste disposal, these were also carefully described. Even in the large cities, except for Philadelphia, the provision of municipal reservoirs and waterworks was relatively recent, and there were no controls over the delivery of services by private companies. Household technology showed the need to ensure health on a private basis, as well as Yankee ingenuity.

Despite the interest in technological innovations and the homogenizing influence of pattern-book designs, the late colonial styles remained the basis for much of the construction that took place west of the Alleghenies throughout the first half of the century. American romanticism in architecture had a distinctly conservative side. Families from England brought with them the knowledge of how to construct a simple foursquare frame dwelling, its façade unadorned, save for symmetrically placed windows and doors. Dutch, Germans, or Scandinavians, who began to immigrate in large numbers after 1830, reproduced approximations of the houses they had known, with high brick or stone corbels on the side, plastered masonry, and small, asymmetrically placed windows. Dwellings of the western cities and rural areas were generally simpler than those in or near the established cities of the eastern seaboard. The nationally popular styles such as the Greek or Gothic appeared much later in the West. This was due in part to the hold of the immigrants' diverse cultural traditions and in part to a shortage of time and skilled labor. Yet Lexington or Cincinnati or Cleveland could boast merchants' houses as fashionable as any in Philadelphia or Boston. Stylistic constraint and simplicity of forms, especially in the early houses of frontier towns, was also an expression of many settlers' belief that they would soon be moving to a better house. A definite pattern was established early on. Seeking to escape the pressures of a limited land supply, Americans tied social mobility, as well as economic security, to property ownership.

The most conspicuous theme in American model cottages, as in actual homes of the mid-nineteenth century, was privatism. Each pattern-book drawing showed a single, isolated dwelling surrounded by a carefully tended garden. Occasional double houses appeared, but designers stressed separate entrances for each family and thick party walls. They also declared that these were transitional dwellings for families who would surely go on to their own private dwelling. As one commentator explained, Americans tended to enjoy associations with others in their politics but not in their homes.[16] The suspicion of urban row houses, communitarian settlements, and industrial boardinghouses was both political and architectural. In builders' guides and in other forms of popular literature, detached dwellings in the countryside were taken as the symbol of certain key national virtues. On an individual level, they represented personal independence. On a social level, they showed family pride and self-sufficiency. Politically, the architecture seemed an expression of democratic freedom of choice. And economically, it mirrored the pattern of private enterprise, rather than planning for the overall public good, which characterized American society.

· ·

The Colonel G. R. Howard House in Palestine, Texas, built in 1851, is a late example of the Greek style, which had passed out of fashion except in the frontier areas.

PART THREE

CCOMMODATIONS FOR AN INDUSTRIAL SOCIETY

IN THE DECADES FOLLOWING THE CIVIL WAR, AMERICANS tried to reconstruct their belief in inevitable progress and national destiny. But even enthusiasm for the higher level of industrialization that wartime had encouraged was tempered by an awareness of its social and environmental consequences. The differences among socioeconomic classes became the focus of journalistic exposés, social science studies, and varied reform campaigns. The urban poor were suddenly a source of shame and fear for the rest of the society. By the end of the century, the wasteful extravagance and lack of social conscience among some of the recently and extraordinarily wealthy capitalists came under attack. Middle-class men and women, while trying to imitate the well-to-do and isolate themselves from the poor, nonetheless recognized that class distinctions encompassed great differences in wealth, social pretense, and domestic habits.

Urban reform movements sought to bridge the gap between the middle class and the poor by "Americanizing" immigrant newcomers. The ideal of the wholesome, sanitary, private home inspired settlement-house workers and volunteer "friendly visitors." Professional "housers" sponsored and finally achieved municipal legislation to upgrade the quality of tenements that would be built for the urban poor. Their premises derived from exacting statistical studies of ventilation, overcrowding, and morbidity, and from their own concepts of proper family life—already a middle-class preoccupation, even before the efforts to domesticate the poor.

Concern for the health and welfare of their families made many immigrant women in urban tenements receptive to the advice of the reformers. But rooms filled with mementos from their past, with prized ornate furniture, and with pretty gaudy bits of cloth and paper reminded the residents of their own cultural backgrounds, even if this aesthetic simply looked unsanitary and primitive to most social workers. Despite the reformers' efforts, through laws and personal instruction designed to extend their ideal of domesticity, there was no universal standard for the dwelling, the domestic interior, or the family.

In fact, during this part of the nineteenth century, another type of residential architecture was also beginning to characterize American cities. For some time, neither legal definitions nor common usage differentiated tenement buildings from apartment buildings. Both were multiple-unit dwellings. The wealthy families who chose to live in the cities, rather than moving out to the suburbs, found the majestic, stately architecture of the apartment-hotel appropriately distinguished and artistic. They enjoyed the convenience of innumerable services and technological features, unavailable in most private homes of the day. At first, a large segment of the general public was fascinated by the scale and fittings of these apartment houses. Some saw them as utopian settings: auguring a cooperative society, providing technological precision and infinitely available comforts. For a few decades, the apartment house represented a positive alternative to suburban privatism.

The suburbs were, nonetheless, growing at an astounding rate. During these decades they became the preferred living environment for a majority of middle-income families and for many workers as well. The suburbs provided a clear expression of the private home as a haven for the family, a temple of refined culture, and a sound investment in land and property. In theory, each suburban home was unique. Its façade, shape, the size and decoration of rooms, offered recognizable signs of the family's taste, interests, and place in the social order. In theory, too, these bucolic homes were retreats from commercialism and industry. Yet it was new technology—building techniques, transportation systems, and communication lines—that opened up the suburbs to the families of clerks, accountants, and skilled workers, and made the dwellings look the way they did. Despite the inconsistencies, many people came to see the suburbs as the materialization of what America was supposed to offer. They found idyllic natural beauty, personal expression, and security for the nuclear family. The suburban home was the apotheosis of late-Victorian culture.

CHAPTER SIX

VICTORIAN SUBURBS AND THE CULT OF DOMESTICITY

In the furnishing of home, the leading principle should be that it is a place of repose, a refuge from the excitements and distractions of life outside. Hence it should be provided with every attainable means of rest and recreation, and this implies also, with every attainable refinement of form and color.

—Robert W. Shoppell and the Co-Operative Building Plan Association, *How To Build, Furnish, and Decorate* (1883)

WHEN POST–CIVIL WAR SUBURBAN BUILDERS advertised through brochures and newspapers, they promised potential buyers more than comfortable surroundings and well-built houses. Those who moved to the new suburbs were assured of an escape from the problems of poor health, social unrest, and vice associated with urban life. The private dwelling in a safe residential neighborhood would protect the wife and children from the dangers of the wicked city. The theme of redemption for one's own family—less often now for the nation as a whole—occurred again and again. Picturesque site planning and natural building materials evoked a return to nature, to a lost innocence and an earlier stability. Individuality was attainable here, too. The diversity of floor plans and ornament for façades proclaimed unequivocally the unique qualities of each family. And finally, as the note of progress in this idyllic reverie, each house, street, and depot would be equipped with "A. M. I.—All Modern Improvements."

It was an appealing package. Several million American households put their savings and dreams into a new suburban home. The great migration began in the 1870s and gathered momentum as the century wore on. Builders' guides and construction journals, books on political economy and magazines of domestic tips, unleashed a deluge of advice, encouragement, and images about the model home. The authors all reiterated the same themes of suburban salvation and security. This chorus, extolling the personalized, arcadian dwelling, marked the opening up of the American suburbs to Victorian middle-class and working-class families.

Planned suburbs of the ante-bellum years had been rare and exclusive havens for the wealthy, who could afford leisurely trips into town in their own horse-drawn carriages. Roads were still notoriously bad in most outlying areas, and public transportation nonexistent, except for a few expensive commuter railroad lines. The pattern of aristocratic suburbs was an inevitable result of the fact that most people had to walk to work

. . . .

An advertisement for S. E. Gross & Company, Chicago's largest builder and subdivider of the late nineteenth century, plays upon the symbolism of one's own home as a reward for industrious labor. The angel, carrying a sword labeled "Justice," promises the workingman a cottage for his family on the "easy payment plan."

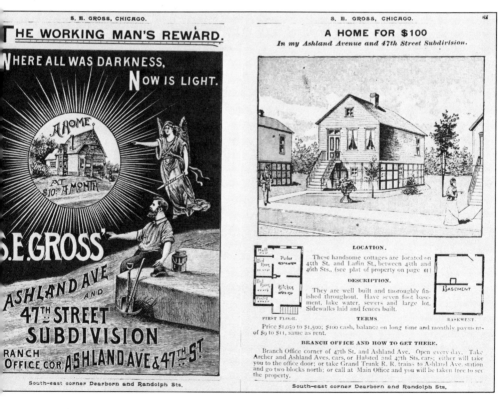

—and remain at their jobs for ten or more hours. True, Brooklyn was growing at a rate exceeding Manhattan's, since commuters could take advantage of regular ferry service over the river; but Brooklyn was itself a bustling city, filled with varied activities and a mix of social classes. It was not a residential suburb.

The inhabitants of these few select places enjoyed expertly controlled and luxuriously romantic settings. When Alexander Jackson Davis laid out Llewelyn Park, near Orange, New Jersey, in 1855, an imitation English gate lodge at the entrance to the 400-acre estate marked a clear social boundary. Within, rambling roads, carefully sited to promote good drainage, led to fifty houses, each set on a spacious property, each with its own private stable. Styles were varied, ranging from Italianate castles to Gothic mansions. Another suburb of that same year, at Lake Forest, north of Chicago, was intended for the well-to-do Presbyterian families who endowed the adjacent college. The site plan featured curving paths, picturesque English garden landscaping, and houses set well back from the road. Such preserves for the wealthy were conspicuously different

. . . .

An illustration from Thomas Hill's *Right and Wrong, Contrasted* (1884) juxtaposes the social life of a tenement neighborhood with the more refined world of private suburban homes.

As we Sow, we Shall Reap.

Poverty, Squalor, Intemperance and Crime.

Pleasant, Beautiful, Happy Homes.

THE neighborhood here shown is a representation and true type of hundreds of localities which exist all over the face of this fair land. The scene tells its own story—a tale of brutal passion, poverty, base desires, wretchedness and crime.

NOW great the difference! Intelligence, re fined taste and prosperity are indicated i these beautiful dwellings. There may b error committed even here, but whatever mora ity, good sense and culture can do to make peopl better and happier is to be sought in such home from the closely packed checkerboard plans of small-town cottages or urban row houses.

In the decades after the Civil War, suburbs took on a new meaning and social organization. Promoters tried to identify their projects with the more exclusive, picturesque retreats for the wealthy, but they were aiming for a different market. Subdivisions of small or moderate-sized lots, near transit lines, were intended to attract the families of salesmen, schoolteachers, clerks, and carpenters. Those who could afford to own a suburban house can be labeled "middle class," comprising, in income, the upper half of the population in an average city. Even among this group there were restrictions, for most of the new communities were implicitly segregated by income and ethnic group. By no means were all suburbanites able to buy their houses. In fact, statistics for Boston, like those for many other cities, show that only a quarter of the suburban households owned their homes in 1890, and half of these homesteads were actually held by mortgage-financing institutions.[1] Yet the move itself was considered crucial, whether the household had a lease or a mortgage, whatever size lot or caliber of suburb could be afforded. The suburban home, how it was furnished, and the family life the housewife oversaw, contributed to the definition of "middle class," at least as much as did the husband's income.

The exodus of middle-class families radically altered the social order and the morphology of the cities they were trying to escape. Within the single decade of the 1880s, Chicago, Omaha, Boston, and Minneapolis surged out beyond their earlier limits. Farther west, Los Angeles experienced a fantastic boom; its population, only six thousand in 1870, had reached nearly a hundred thousand by 1887.[2] Sixty new communities were spawned around the earlier city to absorb the newcomers. Annexation was a favorite topic as municipalities sought to add the tax dollars of suburbanites to their coffers—aware, as they are today, that suburbanites require city services, since they work and shop downtown —but many outlying villages, recently transformed into bedroom suburbs, refused to be incorporated into the larger nearby cities.

Whether annexed or independent, suburban areas were booming with building activity by 1880. Shaker Heights outside Cleveland, Chestnut Hill outside Philadelphia, and the many small towns of Long Island drew urban upper-middle-class professionals. Chicago's Ravenswood and the aptly named Normal Park, Boston's Roxbury and Dorchester, much of Queens, outside Manhattan, Milwaukee's Humboldt and Wauwatosa, offered inexpensive lots. A few of the subdividers financed transit lines, installed sewer lines and streets, and built houses, although most of them sold the lots to smaller builders after they had platted the streets. Chicago's Samuel Eberly Gross completed forty thousand lots, developed sixteen towns and 150 subdivisions, built and sold over seven thousand houses, all between 1880 and 1892.[3] He produced as many simple $800 workers' cottages as he did more elaborate, $3,000–$4,000 houses for middle-class families.

Building and loan associations were responsible for much of this sudden growth. First operative in the United States in 1831, they expanded considerably in the years after the Civil War. Philadelphia, one of the centers of the movement, had over four hundred associations by 1874.[4] These institutions offered working-class families the opportunity, as members of a corporation, to borrow mortgage money safely and at minimum interest rates, provided the association's directors approved the lot or the house, which usually cost between $1,000 and $2,500. Most associations adamantly preferred suburban sites, though they also financed mortgages for urban row houses. Idealistic hope for the suburbs is evident in the official "model American home" painting, commissioned in 1893 by Judge Seymour Dexter of Elmira, New York, founder of the United States League of Building and Loan Associations. In the background, behind the healthy family and their large, handsomely ornamented dwelling, stands a New England schoolhouse, a Protestant church, an American flag, and a village of other picturesque homes.

In many ways, the Victorian dwelling embodied both an ideal and its antithesis. These supposedly individualized and expressive homes depended on industry for their naturalistic effect and their wide availability. New machinery accelerated and systematized the production of construction materials. Using exacting templets, factory workers now cut flat, recessed panels or rough blocks of stone for foundations and façades. Brickworks also shifted to machine production. By the late 1870s, they offered several varieties: inexpensive, durable common bricks; smooth, dry-pressed bricks of superior quality and uniformity; thin Roman bricks; or shiny glazed and enamel bricks. All of these were available in a wide spectrum of colors, in cream, buff, yellow, crimson, even metallic sheens, no matter what color the local clay.

Earlier factory-produced finish work for house façades had been fairly plain and crude; but with the use of steam power in the late 1850s, experimentation began in earnest. After 1871, there was a rush of inventions for faster, cheaper machines. Factory workers produced strips of detailing in a wide assortment of shapes, sizes, and grades. Shingles were cut to resemble fish scales or snowflakes, or left rough-edged and "natural"; moldings were available in elegant beading or floral designs; spindles, in delicate cylindrical shapes; Venetian blinds, in beveled slats; panels adorned with urns or sunbursts. In addition, many styles of window frames could be purchased from architectural supply companies, and entire porches and stairs could be ordered from catalogues. New processes for grinding tints and for mixing mineral paints and stains expanded the colors that could be applied to the finished house.

A façade of different materials, abundant detailing, and many colors

. . . .

"The American Home, Safeguard of American Liberties," a painting commissioned in 1893 by Judge Seymour Dexter, founder of the United States League of Building and Loan Associations, claimed that mortgage lending companies protect all the important institutions of American life.

was not necessarily an expensive undertaking. By the late 1870s, most of the supposedly individualized craftsmanship on a Victorian house consisted of ornament that had been made in a factory, shipped to the site along the railroad routes, and then tacked or glued into place by a carpenter. The new industrialism did encourage extravagant, even garish display, as many architects charged, because it made abundant ornament accessible to American builders and homeowners of all classes.

Industrial processes were also transforming the environment within the home. Builders alternated lengths of factory-made cornices, chair rails and plate rails, latticework screens, wainscotting and dadoes, and then filled in the spaces between with various patterns of wallpaper. After 1875, the domestic production of plate glass became more profitable; and plain, stained, or ornamentally beveled window glass could be ordered in any size. Every space was adorned, first by the builder and then by the occupant.

New mechanical equipment for the middle-class dwelling emphasized comfort, health, and fashion. No matter what the size or shape of a house, it was easier to keep rooms at a reasonably even temperature, either with the costly system of basement furnace and room registers, or with individual room stoves. Styles and standards changed quickly. Hot-air furnaces with names like "Crown Jewel" or "Art Garland," appropriately encrusted with cast-iron rosettes and ribbons, revolutionized home heating. Any household item could be, and usually was, beautified as much as possible.

Manufacturers of plumbing equipment reported soaring sales during the 1880s. Modern flush toilets, porcelain sinks, and permanent zinc-lined bathtubs became more familiar fixtures in middle-class dwellings. Many homes, old and new, still had only a kitchen pump and hot water from a vat on the back of the stove, although one found more precise traps and valves, together with a visible maze of cast-iron pipes. Bedroom washstands, bathtubs that folded out from the wall, and an earth closet (in which fresh soil was scattered to relieve odors) provided the most common forms of personal sanitation. Many housewives or servants still had to carry hot water upstairs, dirty bath suds down, and change the soil in the earth closet. They welcomed any improvements.

Recognizing this interest, new journals on construction and home life multiplied in the 1880s and especially the 1890s. *The American Home, Sanitary News, Careful Builders, Good Housekeeping,* and other magazines offered men and women all over America detailed advice about the latest technology and the brightest fashions for their parlors, porches, and pantries. Clarence Cook, a well-known New York art critic for *Scribner's* and the *Tribune,* declared zealously: "There never was a time when so many books and magazines written for the purpose of bringing the subject of architecture—its history, its theory, its practice—down to the level of popular understanding were produced as in this time of ours."[5] These publications stirred popular interest in decoration and architecture, while they standardized taste and dictated the correct domestic protocol.

The suburban expansion of the period depended directly and indirectly on many different forms of technological innovation. The suburbs of the 1870s had been contained by the public transportation

· ·

A typical late-nineteenth-century Queen Anne–style house built in Ottawa, Illinois, ca. 1880, has numerous nooks, crannies, and bay windows. The façade features various kinds of machine-turned shingles, wooden ornament for the porches, and an elaborate chimney.

networks of slow horsecars and infrequent, expensive railroads. Then a real revolution in public transportation occurred. The introduction of the San Francisco cable car in 1882, followed by the electric trolley—first installed in Richmond, Virginia, in 1888—and Chicago's experiment with an elevated railroad in 1892, launched a drive outward. To compete with the electric streetcars, railway services opened up more lines and reduced fares. Commuting was suddenly easier, faster, and less costly. Speeds on the electric streetcar were twice those of the horse-drawn omnibuses, which had served the early suburbs. By 1890, fifty-one cities had installed electric streetcar lines; five years later, 850 were in operation, with service covering ten thousand miles.[6] "Streetcar suburbs" sprang up along all these routes. On Sundays, free excursion cars, often decked out with banners, flags, and a brass band, would take crowds of potential buyers out to the open fields where they might purchase their suburban home. Subdividers promised the felicitous unity of urban comforts and rustic simplicity, progress and nostalgia that characterized the ideal American community.

Like the fashionable, upper-class suburbs, moderate-cost communities prided themselves on natural amenities. Usually, however, the area chosen for a subdivision was a rather barren and flat site. For the sake of economy and efficiency, most subdividers preferred to lay out gridirons rather than curving streets, and undertook as little improvement work as possible. Many suburban residents had to pave their own streets and lay their own sidewalks. Except for an occasional tree-lined boulevard or a small country club (but only for a prestigious enclave), there were few planned public amenities unless the municipality decided to erect a public library or to set aside land for a park. The "Escrow Indians," as one guidebook to southern California called the subdividers, "came here not to build up the country, but to make money, honestly if they can not make it any other way."[7]

Builders were aware of the spartan natural surroundings in most suburbs, so their chromolithographs of model homes sold the illusion of independence, not that of elegant community. Brochures focused on the private setting, portraying a house set off against its own exuberantly overgrown yard. Often there was a cheerful group playing croquet, badminton, or some other popular outdoor sport. In reality, the sites tended to be small and square, especially for the narrow workers' cottages, yet the publicity encouraged a sense of spacious property.

At a time when summer camps, national parks, and resort hotels had captured the fancy of the middle class, the pleasures of outdoor life, fresh

A Victorian worker's house, built in Paterson, New Jersey, ca. 1880, was a miniature version of popular architectural themes for larger houses, even though it measured only sixteen feet across.

air, and exercise were a major promotional theme for the suburbs. Physicians' textbooks on household sanitation and home upkeep, which appeared in great numbers during the 1870s and 1880s, strongly endorsed suburban living. Nature supposedly offered health and well-being. Most of these books commended large yards, open windows, dry foundations —and diligent housewives. A major worry was that "sewer gas" escaping from poorly installed plumbing fixtures, held inside by inadequate ventilation, would poison the inhabitants of a badly designed house. Consequently, promoters of new subdivisions stressed setback lines, which supposedly prevented contamination from other houses; spacious yards; and carefully laid pipes and drains. But there were few controls other than precautions against fires. Housewives had to take the principal responsibility for judging sanitary facilities and keeping them operative. Public-health debate divided those reformers who advocated more efficient city sewage lines and well-maintained municipal water supplies from the doctors, ministers, and builders who argued that the foundation for public health had to be laid in private homes—outside the cities.

Suburbanites also considered the natural environment as a potent nationalist metaphor. An author in *Cosmopolitan* hoped that each suburban dwelling would have "stateliness enough to comport with the general dignity and breadth of the American landscape."[8] A miniature vision of the bounty and splendor of their country was difficult to attain in the bare, muddy, and often rather cramped lots of most new subdivisions, yet it was part of the allure.

Builders claimed that architecture could assert almost as much natural imagery as the landscape itself. They considered the irregular shape of a house as a sign of organic complexity, and writers of popular literature echoed that sentiment. Rough limestone, wide clapboards, cedar shingles, green patina on slate tiles, all used for a single façade, gave the look of natural materials and venerable aging to a new house. It was common to simulate the hues of nature with mineral paints and stains. Builders of the 1870s and 1880s favored the reds and golds of autumn leaves, the greens of ferns and lichens, the soft browns and grays of weathered woods. Unlike earlier ante-bellum carpenters, they daringly combined four and five colors on one house front. Even the lines of the house—the deeply sloping irregular roof, with overhanging eaves and decorative shingle patterns, together with the horizontal emphasis from different materials being used for each story—were meant to bring it closer to the ground plane.

Porches, too, were being handled in a new way to accentuate the house's relationship to the natural environment. Of varied shapes and sizes, they were always more commodious than those of the ante-bellum Greek or Gothic house. Most suburban dwellings had several porches. There might be an entrance portico, a simple back service porch, an open veranda along the side, a wide rounded piazza, and a porte-cochere for carriages. Above the first floor, balconies or half-moon arches cut into corner towers provided additional places for surveying the out-of-doors. Builders favored such accouterments because they were not considered violations of building lines, even on a street with cramped lots. But the commercial appeal of naturalistic architecture was as deep as such utilitarian issues.

The widespread interest in presenting the house as part of a well-ordered natural system affected the design of the parlor as well. By the late 1870s, windows had become much larger and were often grouped together to create a wall of light and view. Bay-window conservatories of potted plants filled up a corner of many a sitting room or dining room. Popular decorations included pine-cone frames and gray southern moss draped over a molding, leaves pinned up to make a cornice or suspended with thread as if they were falling. Ferneries protected delicate ferns under glass. Displays of shells, seeds, corals, and other objects of natural history instructed the young. Just as the house now opened more to the outdoors, so women were eager to bring nature into the home and cultivate it. By making even the smallest twigs and flowers into decorative motifs, the Victorian builder and the housewife attempted to evoke natural beauty. They clearly tried to contain and preserve it as well.

Victorian ideology perceived women and children as especially close to nature, much more so than men, who could withstand the harsh demands of supposedly unnatural city life—provided they had their retreats in the suburbs. During the last decades of the nineteenth century, the cult of home and motherhood, which had emerged in the 1830s, reached its pinnacle. Novels, poems, lithographs, children's books, and domestic guides extolled the virtues of domesticity so much that the good family and their suburban home became almost interchangeable concepts. George Palliser, a New York builder, could open his pattern book of house designs with the sentimental exclamation: "Home, what tender associations and infinite meanings cluster around that blessed word!"[9] Authors of guides for women likewise insisted that the best domestic architecture, which was not necessarily the most expensive, would evoke the most lofty associations.

The very qualities that made the home so meaningful also made it precarious. Victorian Americans worried about the rising divorce rate and the declining number of births among white women of the educated classes, a trend they called race suicide. They recognized the restlessness of many homebound women, and a child's desire for excitement that could lead that son or daughter astray. The potential influence of the home over family behavior, for good or for evil, therefore loomed dramatically large. "Who knows how much of the incompatability of temper, sorrow, passionate discontent, mutual disgust, may not have grown out of these unhappy surroundings," wondered Mrs. M. E. W. Sherwood, the editor of *Harper's Bazaar.* "Nay," she continued, "Indiana divorce laws may be perhaps directly traced to some frightful inharmoniousness in wall-paper. The soothing influence of an Eastlake bookcase on an irritated husband has never been sufficiently calculated."[10]

Since women and children were considered the most susceptible to the dangerous influences associated with the city, they had to be sheltered from urban life. The search for isolated, purified protection in the suburbs was obviously a middle-class ideal, for many women had labored long hours in factories or stores before their marriages, and then took in boarders or did laundry or piecework in an urban tenement to make ends meet. At the other end of the spectrum, it was fashionable for women to spend afternoons going about town enjoying theaters, museums, shopping, or calling on one's friends, perhaps undertaking philanthropic work among the poor, all pastimes available in the city. Nor was the ideology of the domestic retreat binding on the middle-class woman. The streetcars that took husbands to work also carried their wives and daughters to the downtown corner, where department stores offered the latest items for their homes and wardrobes, and even special restaurants and reading rooms, exclusively for ladies, where they could relax from the demands of shopping. Against this backdrop, the sentiments celebrating the pure suburban home, isolated from contact with market values and factory conditions, took on a heightened intensity. With the expansion of the suburbs, concepts of the home as a private refuge, a place of peace and inspiration, a reward for diligence and thrift, became something more than abstract images.

What did this ideal expect of the middle-class home and the women who saw over it? First, home would be as unlike the world of business and industry as possible. The spheres of men and women, city and suburbs, were cast as fiercely antagonistic to one another in every way.

The widely held expectation that the impersonal market was grueling and cutthroat, harshly competitive and draining, posed the home as compensation. "[T]his stirring career away from home," wrote one contented husband, "renders home to him so necessary as a place of repose, where he may take off his armor, relax his strained attention, and surrender himself to perfect rest."[11] Home was to be a setting of luxury and comfort, softness and frivolity, at once a place of refinement and exotica. It was to be private, contrasting with the frenzied activity of the skyscraper, which now symbolized the business environment.

Home should never be simply a sensuous indulgence, though, for it was the source of spiritual education; a mother's guiding values and the indelible images of home were supposed to carry her son or daughter safely through the difficulties of adult life. In the late nineteenth century, middle-class children spent much of their time at home. Despite compulsory school attendance laws in many states, the average American received four years of formal schooling in 1880, and only five years a decade later.[12] The mother was responsible for education, as well as character training and social skills; and the home was the principal place for every aspect of this training. One text for children's moral education captures the spirit, if not the actual procedure, for domestic influence: "From such homes the children go out into the world only when necessity calls them; they return to its hallowed precincts with delight, and the remembrance of its pleasant associations is ever a silent monitor standing guard over them."[13] The suburban home was part of a strategy to keep children far from the world of the city streets, to ensure their entry into the proper, disciplined class of present and future suburbanites.

In the parlor, the housewife would show off the family's best possessions, striving to impress guests and to teach her children about universal principles of beauty and refinement. One popular symbol of domesticity was the fireplace. By the 1870s, although furnaces or room stoves had taken over the task of heating most suburban homes, fireplaces had become popular as symbols of the family hearth. Elaborately carved mantels, some in marble but most in inexpensive painted and incised wood, provided the suburban home with its ritual center; it did not matter if some hearths were fitted with imitation logs, fired by gas, or hid a furnace register. Here too were the "artistic" pieces the wife had purchased: sculpture, vases, chinoiserie, and all manner of bric-a-brac. These objects she skillfully juxtaposed with her own handmade creations, or "household elegancies," which might include crocheted lambrequins, hand-painted cabinets, rustic furniture, shadow boxes and Easter eggs, screens and easels bedecked with ribbons and flowers. The balance, however, was shifting toward items purchased from a store or catalogue, which captured the refinement and culture that the home was supposed to encourage. Taste, according to most decorating books, was a matter of "art groupings," arrangements of objects that had the stamp of universal beauty. When friends came by for an afternoon tea party, or a daughter's beau was received in the parlor, Japanese scrolls and casts of Greek statues would give the proper impression. Since the mother sought to teach her children values in and through the home, she had spared no expense in acquiring beautiful works of art that were both "interesting and instructive."

Guides insisted that quantity would increase the effect of "home-training" for one's children and spouse. As Harriet Spofford explained:

. . . .

The parlor of the Dr. J. G. Bailey House in Santa Ana, California, photographed ca. 1876, combined many of the fashionable details of the model Victorian interior, including a painting on an easel, a piece of sculpture draped with vines, a tiled fireplace, and abundant artistic bric-a-brac.

"Provided there is space to move about, without knocking over the furniture, there is hardly likely to be too much in the room."[14] Comparing taste in the 1880s to that of the 1840s, an editorial in *Harper's Bazaar* exclaimed: "What a desert was that old parlor to this! This which, if a little overcrowded, and giving scarcely rest enough to eye or mind, is yet crowded only with beauty."[15] Interior designers, hired by department stores in the late 1880s to set up model rooms and advise clients, favored the same approach. In order to make the home an alternative to the commercial world, the housewife had to become a diligent consumer. Ironically, the home as haven from the world was actually filled with worldly goods, industrial products, and fashionable details.

The intricate floor plans of middle-class Victorian houses, especially those in the suburbs, created distinct zones for different activities. The formal social spaces, the kitchen/work area, the private rooms upstairs, each had its particular aesthetic. The Victorian home was, in this way, a splendid setting for family life, providing places for children to hide and for friends to visit, places for disarray and for formality under the same roof.

The kitchen was almost always isolated in the back of the house. This was a commodious work space, often shared by several women. In most urban and suburban areas in 1880, only 20–25 percent of all households employed a servant, and this ratio was noticeably higher than the national average.[16] Even with a daily servant, who was both housemaid and cook, and perhaps a weekly laundress as well, the average housewife and her daughters had a great deal to do in the kitchen. Washing entailed boiling water on the stove, mixing up one's own soap and starch, rubbing the clothes fiercely up and down on a washboard, then hanging them up to dry. Most meals, even breakfasts, consisted of many courses, and each dish underwent an elaborate ritual of presentation. Fanny Farmer's cookbook explained how to make a green aspic for a ham, how to wrap a meatloaf in crackers so that it resembled a box, how to cut radishes and celery into decorative floral shapes. Consequently, given this approach to food preparation, special storage space was required. One usually found a rear pantry, which contained bins for flour and sugar, which had been bought in bulk, next to open shelves for the food put up by the household—preserved fruits and vegetables, jellies and pickles —and for recently available canned foods like tomatoes, corn, milk, corned beef, and sardines. A cooler, either in a window or in the cellar, protected from insects by a screen, kept such perishables as homemade pies and cakes, dairy products, and oleomargarine. The large amount of space allocated to the kitchen and pantry reflected the quantity of work that women still did in the suburban home.

Places for privacy within the home were carefully defined. Guides to home decoration passed over the sleeping areas with a slight blush, but general guidelines emerged. Bedrooms were usually large enough to serve as sitting rooms, where a mother might spend the afternoon with her child, or a young woman with her girlfriend. Mementos and handmade objects would be proudly displayed in an artistic, stylized arrangement. It was primarily in well-to-do families that the husband and wife would keep separate rooms. Most married couples shared a double bed, and their children usually shared rooms with siblings of the same sex. Often the servant woman was allocated a room on the same floor with the family bedrooms, off a common hallway, instead of being assigned to the attic. But it was increasingly likely that she was married and "lived out."

As family size decreased, so did the pressure on domestic space. The average American family had slightly more than five children in 1870 and only four in 1890.[17] Despite the smaller size, separate rooms for each individual were not considered necessary. Privacy for the Victorian family was still associated with short periods of time alone, in a special place in the house: a window seat, a cubbyhole under the stairs, a man's library, or "growlery." Within the home, there was always somewhere to retreat from the intensity of family life.

The irregular outline of Victorian houses revealed the occupants' search for individuality and their interest in functional design. Each bay window, porch, and other protrusion was considered evidence of some particular activity taking place within; it made the space exactly right for playing the piano, sewing, reading, or tending a hot stove. As the number of rooms in a moderate-cost suburban house increased, floor plans burst into extraordinary shapes. Closets and storage rooms provided for a larger number of possessions; a special music room or nursery or library could be found in quite unpretentious houses. The names of these many rooms were a further statement about family life. Debates about sitting rooms, family rooms, parlors, living rooms, and living halls filled builders' guides as well as many novels. The characters in William Dean Howells's *The Rise of Silas Lapham* (1885), H. C. Bunner's *The Suburban Sage* (1896), or Henry Blake Fuller's *With the Procession* (1895) wanted houses that fit their needs and announced their social aspirations.

According to the housing guides, each detail of a dwelling, inside and out, revealed both the personality of a particular family and the virtues of family life as an institution. An article in *Godey's* by decorator Ella Rodman Church likened the parlor to "the *face* of a house—the most noticeable part—and that from which visitors take their impressions of the whole."[18] The architecture as well as the decor was anthropomorphized. Each dwelling was to be singular and personal, a creation specially adapted to the family who resided there, an expression of their taste and their preferences.

The books of Eugene C. Gardner, an amateur architect-author from Springfield, Massachusetts, evangelized about personalized design. His whimsical writings, with their rough but charming sketches of houses and interior vignettes, remained popular for three decades. One book, *Illustrated Homes* (1875), was a series of tales in which various archetypical clients—the poet, the parson, the philanthropist, the professor's wife —conferred with their local architect about their dream house. Each of the resulting designs was unique, Gardner claimed, intended for that particular family. All information about the family was pertinent, for the diligent designer must know everything about a client, "who his grandfather was and where his wife was 'raised'; to what church he belongs, or doesn't belong; how he made his money and whether he believes in a future state of rewards and punishments; the size of his family, present and prospective; the number of his servants, and how he treats them; his own business, and how his daughters spend their time, whether they are domestic, musical, literary, or stylish."[19] This information would then generate the house form and its ornament.

Middle-class Victorians wanted to believe that their houses were impressively unique. At the same time, certain patterns were necessary so that other people could clearly read the symbolism of social status and contented family life in the details. Many suburban Americans connected their highly ornate dwellings with their own individualism, just as they connected the separateness of each suburban household with the self-sufficiency and autonomy of the family. In fact, the majority of moderate-cost suburban houses were built on speculation, not for a particular family; yet the ideal of personalized expression was a principal selling point. Ignoring the evidence of standardization, people identified themselves with their homes. The legacy of that rhetoric of domestic bliss, so closely associated with detached houses and elaborate architectural ornament, still resides, to a great extent, in the suburbs today.

CHAPTER SEVEN

AMERICANIZATION AND ETHNICITY IN URBAN TENEMENTS

By far the largest part—eighty percent at least—of crimes against property and against the person are perpetrated by individuals who have either lost connection with home life, or never had any, or whose *homes had ceased to be sufficiently separate, decent, and desirable to afford what are regarded as ordinary wholesome influences of home and family.*

—Jacob Riis, *How the Other Half Lives* (1890)

AS MIDDLE-CLASS AMERICANS HEADED FOR THE NEW suburbs, they turned back to exclaim in horror about the condition of the cities. Throughout the 1870s and 1880s, and especially during the 1890s, an influx of new and larger populations transformed every major American metropolis. Blacks from the American South, Italians, Eastern Europeans, and Russian Jews arrived in unprecedented numbers. In California, the earlier immigration of Chinese and the more recent arrival of Japanese brought about violent opposition from white native-born groups, even though the minorities were prevented from owning or renting property outside special areas. Mostly unskilled, these immigrants had to live in the center city, where small businesses and factories hired on a daily basis. Poverty, overcrowding, and segregation existed in distinct ghettos, most of which were multi-ethnic.

Housing in these areas was supposed to accommodate both large families and single men and women as cheaply as possible. Some habitations were adapted from existing warehouses, breweries, or residences; others were erected as multiple-unit dwellings on a site that had been razed or where earlier frame structures had been moved to the rear of the lot. A few philanthropists erected "model tenements," yet even these had to be remunerative, for the donors did not seek to be charitable but to set viable examples for private builders.

Books and magazine or newspaper articles describing city life seldom mentioned the landlords' avarice. Instead, they revealed a frightened fascination with what life was like in Manhattan's Lower East Side or Chicago's Near West Side, in "The Swamp," "The Tenderloin," or "Nigger Hill." Titles, too, conveyed public attitudes. Peter Stryler's *The Lower Depths of the Great American Metropolis* (1866), George Ellington's *The Women of New York; or, The Under-World of the Great City* (1869), Henry William Herbert's *The Spider and the Fly; or, Tricks, Traps and Pitfalls of City Life by One Who Knows* (1873), and Anthony Comstock's *Traps for the Young* (1883) presented lurid accounts of depravity and downfall. Charles Loring Brace's *The Dangerous Classes*

. . . .

Lewis Hine's 1908 photograph of frame tenements near DuPont Circle in Washington, D.C., showed the dilapidated dwellings and the active street life of black families who had recently migrated to the northern cities.

of New York (1872) balanced the horror with proposed remedies, one of which was to ship young boys away to farms in the West. By the mid-1890s, his Children's Aid Society had transported some ninety thousand boys out of Baltimore, Boston, Philadelphia, Saint Louis, Cleveland, San Francisco, Washington, and New York.[1] The Reverend Josiah Strong's *Our Country* (1885), which sold half a million copies in the next twenty years, vehemently attacked immigrants for having turned American cities into "tainted spots in the body-politic."[2]

Blaming the poor for the deplorable conditions around them was common. However, in the 1870s, many reform-oriented men and women began to shift the terms of analysis, arguing that the environ-

· ·

The "Street of the Gamblers" in San Francisco's Chinatown, photographed ca. 1905 by Arnold Genthe, presents several aspects of the housing problem. Since the Chinese were not allowed to own property in any other part of the city until 1948, conditions were extremely crowded and unsanitary in the district to which they were segregated.

ment itself could demoralize and even physically destroy its residents; the abysmal poverty, disease, and discontent of the inner city were attributed to overcrowded tenement dwellings. Those who wanted to uplift the victims of poverty now viewed tenement-house reform as a key to changing the residents' lives. Housing conditions were evidence of every failing of character, the cause of every social problem, and the surest path to improvement. "Home improvement" for the urban poor, like "home improvement" for the middle class itself, was considered the direct route to virtue; bad home environments were the inevitable road to despair.

Campaigns for improved tenements took several forms. Ernest Flagg, a prominent New York architect, asserted that the best approach was to show speculative builders that they could still make money on better-quality structures. "Reform can only be brought about through the pockets of the landlords," he wrote in *Scribner's*. "Show them how they can build good houses for less than it now costs them to build bad ones."[3] Other educational crusades addressed the residents through model housekeeping classes for immigrant girls and anti-tuberculosis exhibitions carried into tenement homes. The general public saw an outpouring of journalistic prose, statistical data, poignant photographs, and well-attended exhibitions, complete with scale models of tenements.

Although Americans began to recognize the extent and the pathos of urban poverty during the post–Civil War decades, the housing associated with this phenomenon had come into existence long before. In the early 1830s, landlords in New York, Boston, Philadelphia, and other cities converted warehouses into cheap housing for Irish and black workers. Sometimes several hundred people would live in a single building. The "tenant house" emerged during this decade, as landlords constructed buildings initially intended to house numerous groups of residents. Usually three or four stories high, with two families on each floor —including the damp, subterranean basement—and another building squeezed into the backyard, these residences offered only a minimum of space, light, and air. Despite occasional criticism, the structures proliferated. By 1850, the average tenement in New York or Boston contained sixty-five people.[4] A major responsibility for the crowding lay with the middle man, or "housekeeper," a speculative agent or sublandlord (often a compatriot of the tenants), who chose residents, frequently packing as many people as possible into a building, and gauged their rent payments. The term "tenement house," as we now know it, is an Americanism dating from the mid-nineteenth century, although based on the medieval English etymology of "tenement" as an abode for a person or for the soul, in which someone else owned the property.

By the 1850s, every American city had concentrations of crowded tenement houses and converted buildings. As in England, such neighborhoods were often called rookeries, a word derived from the medieval English slang term for a group of thieves. One of the most notorious of the American rookeries was New York's Five Points, just below Canal Street, inhabited mostly by Irish and blacks. Charles Dickens, familiar with the least seemly sides of London, wrote upon his visit here that Five Points was a "kind of square of leprous houses" filled with "all that is loathesome, drooping, and decayed."[5] Similar neighborhoods existed in Louisville, Charleston, and in the industrial towns of New England. In Milwaukee, landowners moved frame buildings that were no longer desirable in other areas to the Third Ward, where they became substandard, crowded tenements for Irish and then Italian workers.

In the 1850s, a new kind of structure appeared in the cities. Larger, more crowded than earlier types of housing, the "railroad tenement" was a ninety-foot-long solid rectangular block that left only a narrow alley in the back. Of the twelve to sixteen rooms per floor, only those facing the street or the alley received direct light and air. There were no hallways, so people had to walk through every room to cross an apartment, and privacy proved difficult. The open sewers outside, usually clogged and overflowing, a single privy at best in the backyard, garbage that went uncollected, and mud and dust in alleys and streets made these environments unpleasant and unsanitary.

Prompted by draft riots, an alarming death rate, and fear of cholera and typhus epidemics, a group of prominent New Yorkers formed a Citizens' Association in 1864. The subcommittee on hygiene began an investigation of the tenant houses and soon issued the first of numerous reports on housing conditions for the poor, complete with maps, diagrams, and photographs. The report proposed four approaches to the problem: collection of vital statistics; moral uplift through church missions; public-health control and information dispersal throughout the population; and the encouragement of resettlement to working-class cottages outside the city. This four-part program united the principal ways in which Americans of the period would analyze poverty and its effects. Statistical fact-gathering was added to the religious and reform campaigns for moral character-building. A staunch refusal to accept the necessity of urban life for most workers led reformers to believe that the suburbs and countryside offered solutions. At the same time, the growing awareness of public-health dangers, not only for tenement populations but for the entire city, necessitated some more systematic way of grappling with bad urban housing. New York's Metropolitan Board of Health and a local tenement house law (the first in the country) were results of the report. But the legislation provided no basis for enforcement.

Public health became a major issue after the 1880s, when Americans learned that Louis Pasteur and Robert Koch had isolated the specific bacilli and the general "germ culture" conditions for certain dangerous

· ·

The evolution of New York's tenement house types, from the earliest structures of the 1830s to the mid-nineteenth-century railroad tenements and then the notorious dumbbell—which predominated until it was outlawed in 1901—shows the minor changes in the sizes of rooms and the amount of light and air in typical habitations for the poor. Each of these buildings would have had another structure abutting on both sides.

diseases. Now reformers had purportedly "scientific evidence" for connecting a dark, damp environment with physical disease. They pointed out that tuberculosis, pneumonia, and typhoid were "house diseases," three to five times more prevalent in the crowded, dimly lit, unventilated, and perpetually damp houses of the poor. No evidence actually connected the tenements per se to specific diseases. Sanitary conditions, especially contaminated sewage and water, and the overworked, undernourished condition of the tenants proved to be more significant factors. Yet the argument had a powerful effect in exciting opposition to crowded multiple-family dwellings.

Health conditions in the tenements were of particular concern because of hand-manufacturing done by the tenants in their rooms. It was common practice for families to take in "homework" from small businesses and subcontractors. The rolling of cigars and the making of garters, paper flowers, boxes, and other small items were all tasks frequently performed at home, for which a family would receive a small amount per unit completed. A dozen men's pants, for instance, brought a dime in 1890. By the 1890s, it was possible for a Russian Jewish family in New York's Lower East Side to set up their own tiny women's wear "factory" at home, as described in Abraham Cahan's 1917 novel, *The Rise of David Levinsky.* In such apartments, whatever the enterprise, almost every room would be filled with the materials a family worked on and sometimes the special equipment they needed, such as a sewing machine or a German-made wooden mold for packing and rolling cigars.

To most middle-class Americans, the problem with this system was not poor wages or the lack of benefits for the workers, but rather the possibility that the products would be contaminated. Realizing that they would have to play up this danger in order to change tenement conditions, reformers cited case after case of tubercular women, fevered children, and ailing grandparents lying in the same room where an expensive coat or suit was being made. Consequently, efforts to condemn—if not actually to improve—tenement health conditions took on a fervent intensity after each epidemic scare or bacteriological breakthrough.

Harper's, the *Atlantic,* the *Arena, Municipal Affairs, Scribner's,* the *Forum,* building trades journals, professional architectural and social work publications, and almost every local newspaper took up the issue of tenement housing and sanitation in the late 1870s, criticizing tenement family life and lamenting the "promiscuity in human beehives, rendering independence and isolation of the family impossible."[6] The breakdown of social organization and family ties was considered an inevitable result of crowding. The stable, elaborate social networks of ethnic ghettos escaped most of these observers, many of whom still blamed the poor for their misery. *The Chicago Herald* declared that "it is not abject poverty which causes such nasty and cheap living; it is simply an imported habit from Southern Italy."[7]

The ideal solution, for it favored the "deserving poor," continued to be the promotion of inexpensive cottages in the suburbs. Accordingly, New York, Boston, Philadelphia, and other cities instituted programs for reduced rates of 5 cents at rush hours on their elevated railways and trolleys, and workers' building and loan societies flourished. Nonetheless, the reality of urban tenements for those who could not afford a cottage

. . . .

"Finishing Pants," a Jacob Riis photograph of tenement homework, ca. 1898, was intended to document the working conditions of the poor; it also shows a carefully tended room with a canopied bed and valences on every shelf.

or did not want to live in the country remained a visible issue. Architects and planners, including Calvert Vaux, Margaret Hicks, Frederick Law Olmsted, and Ernest Flagg, published critiques of existing tenements, and several magazines sponsored competitions for alternative tenement designs.

In 1879, the New York *Plumber and Sanitary Engineer* announced what would be the most significant of these competitions. The editors specified that the tenement should yield the highest economic return, while providing improved fireproofing, ventilation, and sanitation. The winning entry by James E. Ware, Jr., was immediately labeled the "dumbbell" because its plan had two narrow air shafts within a solid rectangular block. It drew harsh criticism from *The New York Times,* the *American Architect,* and other journals, which branded the solution unsound, unhealthy, and cruel. Yet, because it did fulfill the criterion of economic feasibility, Ware's scheme gained immediate attention from speculative builders. After a state tenement house law later that year took the air shaft dimensions as an approved minimum standard, the dumbbell quickly became the prevailing model for new tenement construction. Legislators, the press, architects, and reformers fought among themselves about what could, in fact, be considered a model tenement: Was it the most healthful housing for the poor, the most dramatic architectural solution, or simply an economical prototype that would be taken as the basis for thousands of real tenement buildings, as the dumbbell, in fact, proved to be?

The typical dumbbell tenement, twenty-five feet wide, stood on a lot of the same width and extended back ninety feet. Indentations twenty-eight inches wide and fifty to sixty feet long broke the solid block. Entirely enclosed on all four sides and rising the full height of the building, these air shafts seldom met their ostensible purpose of providing light and air to the inside rooms. Tenants on the upper floors often threw their garbage down into the shafts, where it was left to rot. This practice could be partially explained by the danger of maneuvering on the stairs, which were usually totally dark. Only the first-floor hallway received light from a small pane of glass in the front door. The first floor contained two small shops, with bedrooms behind them, and another apartment in the rear. On the other floors there were two 4-room apartments in front and two 3-room apartments in the rear. Seven-by-eight-foot bedroom alcoves stood between the kitchen and a parlor bedroom. In the public hallway, opposite the stairs and venting on the air shaft, were one or two toilets and a sink.

In 1893, according to a Board of Health census, over 1 million New Yorkers—70 percent of the population—lived in multiple-family dwellings, four fifths of which were tenements and most of these dumbbells.[8] At least thirty thousand of those buildings remain in use today.[9]

Though other large cities also had an increasing number of crowded multiple-family tenements, converted single-family dwellings were a more prevalent pattern outside New York City. Row houses, frame cottages, and dilapidated shacks were subdivided and shared by more and more people. Cleveland, Buffalo, Washington, Baltimore, Philadelphia, Pittsburgh, San Francisco, and every other American metropolis admitted problems of overcrowding, poor sanitation, jerry-built construction, and health hazards in areas inhabited by the poor.

Despite their concern about these problems, American housing reformers did not even consider the possibility that municipal, state, or federal governments should build or subsidize improved housing. Instead, model tenements were financed by limited-dividend corporations and individual philanthropists who expected that the experiments would raise the construction standards of the average builder and the living standards of the tenants. To show that they were reasonable, the supporters insisted on a profit from these ventures, which came to be known as "philanthropy and 5 percent." But since a speculator could bring in a 20–25 percent return on most tenement property, model tenements were not likely to become widespread prototypes. Although those who promoted them claimed them to be pragmatic and realistic, model tenements had little effect on the private market. The total number was never more than a fraction of the speculatively built housing. In New York, reform organizations erected ten groups of model tenements—the equivalent of two hundred separate buildings—between 1855 and 1905, while speculative builders in that city put up fifty thousand tenement buildings.[10] The model tenements represented neither widespread improvements nor radical alternatives but rather a small though much discussed program which, in fact, did little to relieve the problems of poverty.

The first American model tenements appeared shortly before the Civil War. In 1855 the Working Men's Homes in New York opened to black tenants. The architect, John Ritch, followed the floor plan of one of the city's worst tenements, Gotham Court, even expanding its size two and a half times. His reforms involved subsidized rents and efforts to choose well-behaved tenants; but the building soon became a slum, and the reform campaign was dropped. Ellen Collins's nearby rehabilitation of abandoned row houses also received some publicity. The model tenement then reappeared after the war, first in New York and later in other cities, with great fanfare in the press and a new attention to architectural amenities.

Late-nineteenth-century model tenements differed conspicuously from other housing, not because of architectural embellishment—for many commercially built tenements had ornamental façades—but because of their monumental scale. In Brooklyn, Alfred T. White, influenced by current British practices, sponsored the Home Buildings (1877), the Tower Buildings (1878), and the Riverside (1890). Each block, set around a large quadrangle, incorporated massive corner towers and ornamental stair railings. Vaux and Radford's model tenement for the Improved Dwellings Association of Manhattan, built in 1882, housed 218 families behind a single, smooth brick façade. The companies that backed these projects bought up entire blocks, which would otherwise have contained thirty-two separate buildings, and considered them as single sites, two hundred feet by four hundred feet. While the size of units was usually no larger than that of units in most speculative tenements, each room received more air and sunlight because of the way buildings were arranged on the site.

In addition to large-scale site planning, another major issue that concerned the reformers was sanitary facilities. The average tenement had hall sinks, which drew water pressure from the street. Tenants on the top floors had to use the outdoor hydrants, since water would not rise very high. In model tenements, large tanks on the roofs provided sufficient water pressure for sinks, washtubs, and toilets on every floor. The model buildings also had improved fixtures. In the interest of economy, architects continued to put communal sinks and toilets in the hallways. Some also installed a few partitioned bathtubs in the basement. Occasionally, each apartment had an individual washtub, not really large enough for a bath but nonetheless private, since it was set off in a small alcove behind the kitchen.

The architects' aim was not only modesty for bathing but an emphasis on the kitchen as a room with a specific function. The kitchen in most tenement apartments was the place for bathing, cooking, eating, washing, studying, and socializing. Often a board was folded down over the washtub and a cloth pinned up over its rim to create a second table. If a family was large or took in boarders, the kitchen inevitably doubled as a bedroom at night, as did the parlor. Such mixtures of people and activities seemed disorderly to observers who had larger homes and different notions of domestic propriety.

The practice of taking in boarders, one of the many common and necessary aspects of tenement existence, especially upset reformers. In 1890, forty-four thousand families reported that they shared their apartments with one or more boarders; in 1900, that figure had almost doubled; and by 1910, it had reached 164,000.[11] Most poor and working-class urban families needed the extra money to help make ends meet. In the immigrant novels of Abraham Cahan, Anzia Yezierska, Rose Pesotta, Michael Gold, and others, the boarder appears again and again as a fact of family life. In Yezierska's *The Bread Givers,* for instance, a Russian Jewish family debates whether the father can continue to use a bedroom for his studying of the Torah or whether, in economic desperation, the family must rent it out. Reformers reasoned, rather harshly it would seem, that small rooms in model tenements would discourage boarders. They also sponsored model boardinghouses to relieve the pressure on family apartments. The Liberty Bell and the Friendship in Chicago, the White Rose in Harlem, the Municipal Lodging Houses for men and women in midtown Manhattan, and the 1,554-room Mills Hotel in downtown Manhattan offered cheap, clean accommodations for $2.50 a week.

In other ways, too, reformers used improved tenement design in their attempts to ordain a certain kind of family life. The central courts marked the beginning of a long campaign against street life. They provided places for children to play and adults to socialize, as well as utilitarian areas for drying clothes and lighting apartments. If the residents of the model building, like those of later public housing, were to be successfully rehabilitated, the reformers believed that they had to be isolated from the contaminating influences of their surrounding neighborhood. This meant cutting off the "street habit," as Jacob Riis, Marcus Reynolds, Alfred T. White, and their colleagues labeled the bustling activity on front stoops, sidewalks, and back alleys. Instead, children and adults would take their fresh air and wholesome recreation in the carefully cordoned courtyard of the model structure. By the early twentieth century, the separation became even more distinct, as stairways were placed on the courtyard side and some buildings inaugurated community services—roof playgrounds, kindergartens, communal laundries in the basement—to draw the residents together.

The issue of familial privacy from other tenants proved equally potent for the housing reformers. They saw all sorts of dangers lurking in shared facilities and indistinct boundaries, even within the model tenement. In 1905, Commissioner of Labor Charles P. Neill addressed the New York School of Philanthropy about this issue: "In my own estimation home, above all things, means privacy. It means the possibility of keeping your family off from other families. There must be a separate house, and as far as possible, separate rooms, so that at an early period of life the idea of rights to property, the right to things, to privacy, may be instilled."[12] Most model tenements were embellished with the accouterments of

• •

In 1890, architect William Field built Brooklyn's Riverside Apartments for philanthropist Alfred Tredway White and the Improved Dwellings Association. The creation of a courtyard—which provided a music pavilion, drying yard, and play space for children—was one of the ways in which reformers tried to get residents off the street and into a controlled outdoor environment.

single-family residences. For example, Frank Lloyd Wright's Francisco Terrace in Chicago, built for philanthropist Edward Waller in 1895, maintained a residential scale of only two stories. Wright used elegant brick detailing, together with hoods over each entry (on the courtyard side, of course) to delineate the individual units. The Labor Department touted the use of front doorbells, private entrances, and bay windows on tenement buildings, since they echoed the single-family home.[13]

Reform groups which sponsored suburban cottages could take this ideal much further. In Boston, Robert T. Paine erected 116 tiny dwellings for the "substantial workingman" in the 1890s. The New York City and Suburban Homes Company, the largest American limited-dividend corporation, sponsored a Brooklyn project called Homewood. A typical cottage in this 53-acre tract consisted of a diminutive two-story brick-and-timber structure with a porch and gabled roof to "add quaintness."[14] The company insisted on a firmly authoritarian policy: each resident was required to take out life insurance for the cost of his home. Multiple-family dwellings, saloons, and factories were prohibited in the neighborhood, as were flat-roofed buildings.

To the reformers, a lack of visible privacy for every family suggested numerous temptations. Communal toilets, bathrooms, stairs, and laundries, boarders within an apartment, and the multiple-family dwellings themselves harbored an association with communism for these reformers and, they feared, for the residents as well. As Professor Charles R. Henderson of the University of Chicago sociology department warned in 1902: "A communistic habitation [that is, a tenement house] forces the members of a family to conform insensibly to communistic modes of thought."[15] Of course, in these pre-Bolshevik years, communism had fewer political overtones. It referred to the more idealistic sharing of property in biblical communism and in American communitarian settlements. All the same, communism did imply a lack of proper respect for private property—an ironic commentary on the tendency to link poverty itself with political radicalism.

Even more discussion centered around enticements to sexual immorality. Children would have to pass the rooms on a tenement's first floor that were often rented out, at a higher rate, to professional prostitutes; therefore, from the 1880s on, commissions asked higher penalties for prostitutes who took customers to their tenement house rooms. Equally threatening were the lewd thoughts that would form in impressionable minds when children saw older girls and women washing themselves in hallway sinks. Parents sharing their bedroom with young offspring or doors left open for ventilation were considered invitations to incest. In response to this perceived danger, the Citizens Association of Chicago tried to require dormitories for all boys over the age of fifteen; 150 beds and a communal urinal on the top floor of a tenement building seemed far better than adolescent boys eyeing their sisters.[16] An Indianapolis social worker summed up the sentiment: "If a number of persons of low standards of different sexes and ages all live together in one room, it is almost bound to result in vice. So it is when a number of families have to use the same yard, yard closet, hall and stairs, especially when the latter are dark."[17]

Housing reformers saw themselves as a moral police force, using environmental change to enforce propriety. While professional social workers sought to translate problems into statistics and statistics into laws, other concerned citizens continued to regard the ante-bellum approach of direct contact as the best way to encourage real improvement. Volunteer women focused on instructing individuals, moving between the offices of charity organization societies and the homes in poor neighborhoods. In weekly visits, they offered suggestions on economical meals, good housekeeping routines, educational goals for children, and artistic influence through home surroundings. By the early 1890s, over four thousand "friendly visitors" were paying their calls in Boston, New York, Baltimore, Cleveland, and other cities, under the auspices of local charity organization societies.[18] In addition, visiting nurses instructed residents about health precautions; visiting housekeepers promoted cleaning standards; and visiting statisticians collected information. As the mission became less precise, the tactics took on a more abstract aura. One visitor wrote that she always wore white dresses for their "suggestion value," even though she had to boil them clean after each day's work.[19]

The settlement houses provided personal direction through even closer contact. First the Neighborhood Guild, and then the College Settlement in New York's Lower East Side, Chicago's Hull House, Boston's South End House, and by 1897, seventy other settlements brought idealistic, college-educated women and men to live among the poor and provide an uplifting example. The residents of these settlements chose the architecture and furnishings of their quarters with care. The parlors gave immigrant women a glimpse of middle-class luxury and refinement. Isabel Hyams of Boston's Louisa May Alcott Club claimed that the settlement house offered her Italian and Jewish neighbors "an idealized home" where "all the activities of a natural home are taught."[20] "Social housekeepers" like Hyams did bring much genuine concern, but they brought moralistic middle-class biases to their crusade as well.

By the 1880s and 1890s, trained social workers insisted that such humanitarianism was too personal, too diffuse, and too subjective to change conditions. "Scientific philanthropy" came into vogue as several nationally known professional "housers" led the campaign to make housing reform more objective, centralized, and effective. The names E.R.L. Gould, Carol Aronovici, Bleecker Marquette, Emily Dinwiddie, and especially Lawrence Veiller appeared on municipal commissions and private committees all over the country. They believed that centralized bureaucracies would distribute services more efficiently, technically precise laws would define minimum construction and sanitation standards, and statistical data about conditions in the tenement slums would prove their case unequivocally. In 1893 Congress directed Carroll D. Wright, commissioner of the U.S. Bureau of Labor, to undertake a statistical study of the slums in four cities: Chicago, Baltimore, Philadelphia, and New York. In his research, Wright ruled out questions such as what caused poverty and what led to slums as "too vague for the application of the statistical method."[21] No one in this group advocated any form of public housing, only public enforcement of certain legal standards and public investigation of slum conditions.

The great accomplishment of the housers was the New York Tenement Law of 1901. This landmark legislation, authored by Veiller, set strict standards for ventilation, fireproofing, overcrowding, private sanitary facilities, basement apartments, and courtyard dimensions. The stipulations proved so strict that few speculative builders would divert their money into this kind of construction any more, and the housing shortage for the poor grew worse. Moreover, no provisions existed for enforcing the higher standards in existing buildings. The same situation prevailed in other cities and states as they followed New York's legislative lead. Consequently, while the letter of the law pleased reformers, it did little for the poor.

The first model tenement house planned especially for blacks, the Tuskegee, built in New York in 1901, met the specifications of the recent law. Soon after the Tuskegee was completed, former Surgeon-General George M. Sternberg organized the Sanitary Housing Company to provide housing for black families in Washington, D.C. Although he continued to have difficulties raising capital, Sternberg built a hundred 2-flat dwellings in the next ten years. In 1911, Cincinnati's Jacob G.

Schmidlapp joined in, providing Washington Terrace, a group of eighty-eight small row houses for 326 promising black families.[22]

Despite such efforts, the major forces governing the housing available to urban blacks and most other minority groups continued as before. Segregation did not abate. Even when a black residential area expanded, it quickly became a ghetto. Rents rose as services were cut back, but black families were so anxious to leave the worst slums that they would pay exorbitant rents and undergo extreme crowding in the hope of finding a better neighborhood. Difficulties were intensified by the overwhelming majority of black women over men in cities (for it was easier for them to find work, mostly as domestic servants) and the rental discrimination against women with children.

. . . .

Jacob Schmidlapp's Washington Terrace model tenements for black families, built in Cincinnati in 1911, presents a very different prototype from the monumental Riverside Apartments. Each family had its own two-room or three-room row house to reinforce privacy. The environment, once again, was presented as a force that encouraged children to give up bad habits.

Slum clearance, which destroyed existing, already overcrowded housing, also put great pressure on every poor neighborhood. Clearance had been authorized on health grounds in most American cities since the early nineteenth century and was carried out by the hundreds of units after the 1890s. Tenements with high rates of tuberculosis or other supposedly contagious diseases could be leveled, and the owners would be compensated. Officials saw the problem only in terms of dangerous environments, not as the lack of decent, affordable housing. According to a leading advocate, the New York architect I.N. Phelps Stokes, slum clearance supplied "lungs for the poor" by replacing bad housing with parks. Yet a third of the original residents were left unaccounted for in most new neighborhood plans. When Chicago razed two city blocks to form Eckhart Park in 1905, over 3,500 people were forced to leave two hundred buildings.[23] Large numbers of poor families and individuals had to find new homes wherever they could, at whatever price and condition, while the owners of the razed tenements recouped their losses.

The impetus for slum clearance derived, in part, from pictures of deplorable conditions and human despair in the tenements. Lewis Hine's photographs of families working in their homes, sewing pants or making cigars, equaled his compassionate and proud factory portraits. Robert Hunter filled his survey of *Tenement Conditions in Chicago* (1901) with pictures of that city's tiny frame cottages, back alleys, and young waifs. R.R. Earle contributed family scenes to the 1910 series on *The Housing Problem in Chicago*. By far the best-known, most sentimental, and incensed were the photographs of Jacob Riis, a Danish-American journalist who walked the police beat for the *New York Tribune*. In *How the Other Half Lives* (1890), *The Children of the Poor* (1892), *A Ten Years War* (1900), *The Battle with the Slum* (1902), and *Children of the Tenements* (1903), Riis attacked the tenement as the source of all social pathology in the slum. He provided images rather than social theory to make his point. His most famous pictures focused on children, evoking a lost innocence, a premature toughness in these "street arabs." Like other "muckrakers," Riis took scores of flash-lit photographs of filthy sanitary facilities.

In the eyes of most middle-class Americans, these journalistic photographs showed the squalor and depravity of tenement existence. What was disparaged as debris were often family portraits, religious mementos, and objects the residents had brought with them from their former homes. Though the rooms were furnished on very little money, and the circumstances for housewives were demanding (for instance, many women had to carry water up and down several flights of stairs), tenement interiors often displayed a carefully conceived aesthetic. Fancy paper or gaily printed fabric valances covered mantels, cabinet shelves, furniture arms, tabletops, and even the kitchen table and washbin. Lace curtains hung in the windows, providing a glimpse of personal expression when seen from the outside and a bit of privacy within. Elaborate wallpaper in mismatched pieces, creating a vibrant optical effect, covered the cracks and stains on the walls. Portraits of the Madonna in gilt frames, images torn from magazines, Sunday newspapers, free merchants' calendars, or inexpensive gaudy prints appeared in every room, even in the hallway toilets. Most settlement workers tried to encourage families to do away with the fuss, or at least to substitute reproductions of famous paintings in order to bring the uplifting influence of true art into the home. But some public-health volunteers realized that they could use the immigrants' desire for beauty and tradition by giving them brightly colored pictures of Old World landscapes, with disease warnings printed in their native language.

Furnishings were a mixture of family heirlooms, dowry gifts, and fancy mass-produced pieces purchased on the installment plan. In the 1880s, factories in Grand Rapids and Chicago began producing special lines of inexpensive, highly ornamented furniture, prompting stores in working-class neighborhoods to extend credit. Preferences for heavy, ornate pieces like sideboards, bureaus, and chiffoniers (derived perhaps from a long tradition of dowry chests and wardrobes in European rural homes) made tenement rooms very crowded, but the pride in these objects was undeniable. Beds, piled high with feather comforters, stood in the center of many parlors. While social workers regarded this as a shocking sign of sexual license and overcrowding (worsened by the probability that the frames, bedding, and fancy linens were probably unwashed), most immigrant groups considered the marriage bed an important symbol of family stability, and a reminder of the deeply emotional ceremonies surrounding death and mourning.

Friendly visitors and trained social workers abhorred this aesthetic of proud display and cheap abundance. A New York Tenement Investigation Committee in 1894 demanded the removal of wallpaper from all existing buildings and its prohibition in the future, arguing that germs and bugs lived in the layers of paste and paper. President Roosevelt's Homes Commission struck this same chord, counseling against furnishings and ornamentation that might harbor dust or germs:

Hygiene, therefore, condemns all carpets and interior finishes which serve as dust and germ traps, such as heavy cornices, elaborate moldings or door and window frames, wardrobes, cumbersome draperies, and unnecessary furniture. Hygiene, on the other hand, approves of neatly polished floors with small rugs, which can be easily taken up and cleaned outside of the house, curves instead of cornices and angles, smooth and nonabsorbent walls instead of embossed wall papers, simplicity of furniture, closets instead of bureaus and wardrobes.[24]

· ·

When public-health workers came to tenement apartments, they often tried to use the residents' desire for beauty and tradition to teach them about health dangers. In 1908 this woman in white from New York's Charity Organization Society presented an Italian family with a colorful Venetian landscape; at the bottom of the picture, in their native language, was a description of the symptoms of tuberculosis.

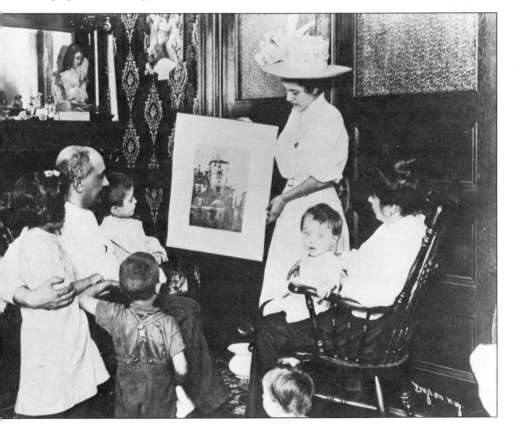

Vanity and wastefulness seemed dangers almost as grave as disease.

Reformers expected that immigrant housewives and their daughters, under the personal tutelage of friendly visitors and settlement-house teachers, would discard the extravagant furnishings and change their living habits. The housers believed that legal codes could end inequalities. Both groups considered their own taste to be a universal standard of beauty, hygiene, and human sentiment. As Edith Abbott wrote in 1913, musing upon the destruction of Chicago's Plymouth Court and the eviction of its Italian residents: "It was strange to find people so attached to homes that were so lacking in all the attributes of comfort and decency."[25]

CHAPTER EIGHT

THE ADVANTAGES OF APARTMENT LIFE

> Many elaborate domestic conveniences are
> practicable in a house of many suites of rooms
> that a cottage could not have, to the great
> welfare of our too-much-worked womankind.
>
> —"Editor's Table," *Appleton's Journal of
> Popular Literature, Science and Art* (1876)

DURING THE LAST QUARTER OF THE NINETEENTH century, when tenements and apartments came to characterize housing in American cities, few legal or semantic distinctions existed between them. Both words referred to dwellings designed to accommodate three or more separate sets of tenants under a single roof; both connoted dense urban living, although tenements and apartments also appeared in suburbs and industrial towns. When municipal governments attempted to regulate the construction of tenement buildings, the legislation specifying room size, fireproofing, ventilation, and plumbing was taken from recent ordinances that protected the upper-middle-class residents of multiple-unit dwellings. The early instances of journalistic debate about urban multifamily living for Americans—already encompassing fears about communism and promiscuity, but also a fascination with the possibilities for efficiency, cooperation, and good financial investments—frequently concerned apartments. There were numerous articles on modern upper-class apartments prior to the outpouring of facts and photos on tenements at the end of the century. All in all, at least for several decades, the middle-class public was highly ambivalent—suspicious but enthusiastic—about the potential of the apartment building as a means for reorganizing certain aspects of American domesticity.

In England and France, since the mid-seventeenth century, the word "apartment" had designated simply a set of rooms, not necessarily in a building shared with other people. When American real-estate developers first hired society architects to construct multiple-unit dwellings, the planning premise was seen as a deviation from the prevailing pattern of owner-occupied detached or row houses for private families. Indeed, the early apartment buildings in New York and Boston were called French flats, evoking a cosmopolitan social life, the glamorous influence of the continent, and the slightly risqué practice of living in close proximity to one's neighbors. Soon after the Civil War, "apartment-hotel" came into general use in the United States, referring to the centralized services and professional staffs at one time attainable only at luxury hotels.

America's earliest apartment buildings, the Hotel Pelham in Boston, constructed for Dr. John H. Dix in 1855, probably by Arthur Gilman, and the Stuyvesant Flats of New York, an 1869 project of the French-trained Richard Morris Hunt for Rutherford Stuyvesant, consisted of one continuous roof over separate suites of rooms for a small number of well-to-do families and bachelors. Both buildings relied on architectural elegance and luxurious décors to attract stylish residents. To the passerby, the fashionable Frenchness was most visible in the mansard roofs, which evoked the glamour of Louis Napoleon's Second Empire. ("Mansard" referred to François Mansard, the seventeenth-century French architect who first popularized this roofline.) Steeply pitched for ten to fifteen feet, then flattened out on top, this roof had rows of windows in the lower slope and rich ornament under the curved eaves. One reason for its widespread use in mid-nineteenth-century French cities was that the top floor of a residential apartment, under the roof, would not be taxed as an additional floor. Though this was no advantage under American law, the cultural associations with French art and elegance made the mansard roof extremely popular, especially since the just-emerging American architectural profession considered the Parisian École des Beaux-Arts the supreme authority on beauty. In addition, the mansard roof had the visual effect of making a structure seem heavier and closer to the ground by weighting the top and disguising the uppermost story. This diminished the dramatic change in scale from single-family row houses and detached dwellings.

Although the Pelham was built before the Civil War, the New York French Flats—as Stuyvesant's building came to be known—marked the beginning of a movement. The tenants of the French Flats were the city's elite. Each of the six-room to ten-room suites on the first four floors rented for $1,200 to $1,800 per year, while the fifth-floor studios commanded $920. A month before Hunt completed construction, Stuyvesant was beseiged with two hundred applications. The building, which had cost $150,000, brought in a profit of $23,000 during its first year.[1] The message to investors and to prospective tenants was quite clear; and in New York alone, nearly two hundred sets of French flats were erected between 1869 and 1876. By 1878, one Boston directory listed 108

. . . .

Boston's Hotel Pelham, America's first apartment building, was probably designed by Arthur Gilman in 1855. It offered permanent residences for families and bachelors, all under one elegant mansard roof.

apartment-hotels for middle-class residents. In Chicago, little more than a decade after the fire of 1871, which initiated an apartment-construction boom, 1,142 apartment buildings went up in a single year, and one reporter observed that flats had appeared "almost as if by magic on every main and cross street of the city."[2]

Returns of 10–30 percent stimulated investors to erect apartment buildings, but the more general urban economic trends of the day also encouraged this kind of structure. The tall apartment building represented a rational way to utilize expensive land. During the years following the Civil War, American cities grew rapidly. In downtown business areas and in the surrounding residential neighborhoods, land speculation inflated prices. Business blocks and apartments quickly rose several floors above existing structures, so that investors could take the fast-rising real-estate values into account in charting their future profits. The demolition and rebuilding of large downtown sections in the major cities stamped this pattern irrevocably onto their terrains. Adventurous capitalists tried to anticipate the direction in which the central business district would grow by erecting tall apartments and offices in areas of probable expansion while land prices were still affordable.

Yet there was more to the apartment phenomenon than purely economic motives. The apartment house captured the nation's fancy with unheard-of technological advances and the efficient organization of domestic chores. While neither the Pelham nor the New York French Flats were equipped with elevators, both featured the latest central hot-water heating, central gas mains for lighting, and fully equipped bathrooms for each unit. (At this time, bathrooms and running water were considered luxuries, even in most well-to-do homes.) Promoters of each new building advertised some technological breakthrough in comfort or convenience over its predecessors. Architects paid almost as much attention to these hidden systems as to the façades. Soon every apartment building was fitted with steam elevators, including an elevator with a uniformed attendant for the residents and their guests, and a service elevator for servants and deliveries. Bathrooms became more elaborate. Hot and cold running water and the immaculate removal of wastes became standard. Fittings included hand-painted china basins, and hand-carved wooden seats and screens in the shower stalls. Beginning in the late 1870s, switchboard operators answered and connected telephone calls at any hour. Architects experimented with electric lights, providing a generator until the 1890s, when power from the street lines became available. Engineers installed central vacuum-cleaning systems, with nozzles in each room connected to a large pump in the basement; individual attachments could be used as hair dryers or reversed as dust collectors. The cavernous basements of these buildings housed the modern equipment that provided heating, ventilation, plumbing, transportation, clean clothes, clean rooms, and sometimes even food for the residents.

The emphasis on efficiency resulted in some unusual rearrangements of domestic activities in the new apartment buildings. Hotels and men's clubs had separated the kitchen from living quarters long ago, removing the heat and discomfort of cooking and laundering from the quiet pleasures of entertaining and privacy. Now the new apartment-hotels offered the same comforts to their permanent residents, both families and individuals. In New York City, Detlef Lienau's Grosvenor Apartments on Tenth Street and Fifth Avenue, completed in 1871, inaugurated the first public kitchens, public dining rooms, and basement steam laundries in an apartment-hotel. The management provided each of the forty units with two servants—a maid and a waiter. Residents had two options for meals: they could descend to the elegant main dining room on the first floor, or they could have their waiter bring up the food on the staff elevator. He would serve piping hot or perfectly chilled dishes in the apartment's private dining room. Then, at the end of the meal, he would whisk away the dirty dishes to the kitchen scullery below. Laundry was also centralized. The maid took the family's clothes to the basement tubs and drying room. For rents ranging between $650 and $2,200 a year (and most apartments at the Grosvenor were leased for two years before the building was even finished), it was possible to do away with many of the smells, sounds, and wasted space of household drudgery.[3]

The centralized kitchens and laundries which characterized the apartment-hotel seemed promising innovations to many observers. An article in Scribner's of 1874 declared: "How far space could be economized, and the general wholesomeness of the entire building increased by the abandonment of private kitchens, and the cooking of all the food in one place, is a matter yet untested among people of moderate means."[4] By 1878, the quality of these public services in apartment-hotels for the well-to-do had reached such a high level that a New York City court ruled that the efficient distribution of cooking and laundering from a central source was the distinguishing mark of an apartment building. The claimant in the case was a Fifth Avenue matron protesting the construction of a large apartment near her property; she argued that there was a prior agreement that no "tenement house" would be erected on the site. The judge declared that whereas a tenement consisted of three or more families living independently under one roof, an apartment house contained collective services for all its residents.[5]

In some structures, the public kitchen was located on the top floor, under the roof; in most instances, it was in the basement. From these gleaming, busy rooms, food could be hurried to private apartments or to the lobby-level dining rooms, banquet rooms, cafés, and restaurants. Delivery systems for carrying the food included special elevators with metal-lined warming boxes and ammonia-cooled refrigerator cabinets, and subterranean railways with delivery wagons or conveyor belts. Some buildings installed warming boxes at the back entrance of each unit so that food could be left unobtrusively by the apartment staff and the family could dine, enjoying a hot meal, whenever they wished.

Residences for artists or bachelors, such as the Everett in Washington,

· ·

In the basement of a large, turn-of-the-century apartment-hotel, a centralized kitchen staff prepared food that could be sent to the lobby-level restaurants and cafés, or to the residents' private dining rooms.

D.C., built in 1883, continued to be constructed without public or private kitchens. These all-male apartment-hotels were designed solely for entertaining, sleeping, and reading; the men were expected to take their meals at their clubs or with family or friends in private homes. In this way, the bachelors had some exposure to "home comforts," though there were fears that young men would become addicted to the independence of living outside a family structure. Apartment-hotels for women were more controversial, since it was considered a grave threat when women abandoned domesticity; nonetheless, several philanthropists funded such buildings. The Working Women's Hotel in New York City, completed in 1878, had five hundred sleeping rooms, an ironing room, laundry room, library, and several dining rooms for the residents. To prevent associations with tenements, since the residents of the Working Women's Hotel were women of "reduced circumstances," no sewing machines or other working apparatus was allowed in the bedrooms.[6] The architect claimed that well-appointed dining rooms and slight variations in each bedroom would encourage the women to aspire toward their own private residences when they married. The Trowmat Inn, another New York working women's apartment-hotel, compensated for the centralized services with a purportedly feminine architectural symbolism: all concave or convex curves, and no right angles.[7]

To people who were enthusiastic about apartment-house technology and services, these advances represented a higher stage in the evolution of American society. Apartments were characteristic of an approaching utopian future in William Stead's popular novel, *If Christ Came to Chicago* (1893), and in William Dean Howells's Altrurian romances. In 1876, the editor of *Appleton's* called attention to the advanced plumbing and ventilation, "constructed with the latest scientific knowledge," that graced the apartment buildings of his day.[8] Scientific progress, he announced confidently, would protect and extend the benefits of American home life. The elevator, for example, was a boon to health, relieving women of the taxing chore of climbing up and down stairs all day. Another writer proclaimed that the apartment elevator was an American technological advance that "democratized" the French flat because it overcame the hierarchical structure of European residences, in which poor families were consigned to the basement and upper floors, while wealthy families climbed only a few flights.[9] In American buildings, elevators made every floor equally accessible.

Despite the technological advances, there were many difficulties in the early experiments in apartment living. The layout of rooms often resulted in dark back hallways and long trips between the kitchen and the dumbwaiter. Many residents retained bedroom chamberpots and water pitchers because of the distance between the bedrooms and the bathroom. The floor plans of the early buildings often resembled those of a dumbbell tenement, with narrow air shafts spliced between double rows of rooms. The bedrooms had, at most, one window venting onto the air shaft. A commentator in the *American Architect* of 1879 claimed that some model tenements provided better health and comfort than majestic apartments on Fifth Avenue, where a desire for grandeur overrode all other concerns.[10] By the 1880s, most apartment architects provided large interior courtyards and grouped the rooms around central halls and reception areas so that bedrooms had ample sunlight and fresh air. In fact, the basic tenets of model-tenement design had more of an impact on luxury apartment buildings than on speculative tenements.

Other problems with apartment buildings proved more difficult to resolve. Many people disliked the thin walls and floors, which allowed sound to carry between the units. Experimentation in accoustical insulation was an offshoot of research in construction technology. Load-bearing walls of solid masonry, hollow-tile fireproofing, heavy interior partitions, massive floors of rolled iron beams, and masonry arches helped reduce the noise level. But the uncomfortable awareness of neighbors—and the possibility of their eavesdropping—remained a common criticism.

Too little space was another complaint, especially in the less expensive buildings. In a four-room or five-room middle-class apartment (as opposed to the customary six to ten rooms a wealthier family enjoyed), dimensions were cramped and inconvenient. The one or two closets were tiny; a typical parlor was only twelve feet by fifteen feet; a bedroom, eight feet square. Sometimes the furnishings a family brought with them from their former house would not fit into the new quarters. A New York newspaper cartoon of 1880 ridiculed the awkward spaces, the steep stairs, and the breakdowns in equipment that plagued the inhabitants of middle-income apartment buildings.

Accommodations were especially close for a family with children. Apartment life continued to be associated with young childless couples, bachelors and working women, widows or widowers, whose space needs were less demanding. "The newly wed and the nearly dead" could contend with the situation more easily. A few apartment managers took children into account, all the same. The moderate-priced Hyde Park Hotel in Chicago incorporated a special enclosed indoor area for small

An 1880 cartoon of middle-class apartments in New York City spoofed the awkward spaces and faulty technology that made apartment life less pleasant than it was promoted to be.

children and their nursemaids. Others, like Boston's Charlesgate, had supervised courtyard play areas and special dining rooms for children and servants, so as to keep them out of the way while their mothers entertained upstairs. The feminist Charlotte Perkins Gilman, an ardent advocate of apartment life, recognized the need to plan for children. In an appeal published in *Cosmopolitan,* she called for all-day nursery programs in every apartment house so that women could take advantage of the potential freedom apartments could bring them. This, she wrote, was the American spirit of progress, always experimenting, "throwing aside good for better, and better for best."[11]

Even if private rooms were small, the public rooms, and especially the main entrance, were always sumptuous. Marble floors and paneling, crystal chandeliers, imported carpets, and walnut or mahogony wainscotting adorned public doorways, lobbies, staircases, and elevator carriages. Lavish detailing in the manner of a Gothic lord, an Elizabethan ruler, a Renaissance prince, or a Byzantine potentate created a distinctive aura for the most costly buildings, where the foyer often measured one hundred feet by fifty feet. In each individual apartment, a high percentage of floor space was given over to rooms for entertaining, much more than was so allocated in most single-family dwellings. In large suites there might be a parlor, a reception hall, a library, a dining room, a smoking room for men off the dining room, and an informal living room. After all, one of the reasons a family preferred to rent an apartment in the city, rather than move out to the suburbs, was to be able to entertain in a regular and lavish manner. Apartments were conspicuously different from most suburban homes, which tended to emphasize family privacy and practical housekeeping matters in their organization of space.

At the end of the 1880s, the instant ballyhoo over Edward Bellamy's *Looking Backward* (first published in 1888) brought another strong endorsement of apartment life. Bellamy's enormously popular utopian novel described a future in which apartment buildings, centralized services, and trained staffs of specialists had become the norm for all Americans. The cooperative services, technical advances, and attention to public spaces in the contemporary apartment-hotel made it seem one of the most advanced institutions in American society. Apartments were praised as a way of accelerating the movement toward a better future for everyone.

In 1890, the prominent Boston architect John Pickering Putnam, sponsored by an organization of Bellamyites, published *Architecture Under Nationalism.* Putnam, who had specialized in apartment-house design since the 1870s, claimed numerous benefits for apartment complexes: economic savings, architectural interest, social cooperation, increased health and efficiency, decreased crime through group surveillance, and freedom for women to work outside the home. In time, Putnam wrote, the discomfort about living so close to other people one did not know would give way to a sense of shared community. He optimistically predicted that "under nationalism, the only valid objection to the apartment-house, namely, the uncongeniality of the people, will disappear, and with it half the expenses of living."[12] Once again, architecture would play a major role in effecting social change.

Despite the associations with Bellamy's cooperative, technological utopia, there were still reservations, even in the heyday of enthusiasm for apartments. To many Americans, any kind of shared dwelling seemed an aberration of the model home. Given their idealization of the personal benefits and moral influences of the private residence, a belief that prompted the flight to the suburbs, this is not entirely surprising. As publicity about deplorable tenement conditions became a regular feature in the American press, associations with tenements for the poor tainted even luxurious multiple-unit dwellings. Charges that close proximity and shared facilities encouraged promiscuity fired opposition to both types of habitations. Critics also insisted that wifely negligence of duties toward home and children would inevitably result from the reduction of housekeeping chores in the apartment-hotel or even a more conventional but small and efficient apartment. Finally, imitation of decadent European living patterns did not seem fitting for good American families.

As a consequence of these criticisms, even though they were still a minority opinion during the first three decades of apartment building in America, some architects began trying to re-create the symbolic details of more conventional home life, aiming, as they were, for a conservative upper-middle-class market. Fireplaces were one sign of domesticity, so architects installed them, even though central heating in most buildings was quite advanced. Carl Pfeiffer's Berkshire Apartments, a cooperative built in 1883 on Fifty-second Street and Madison Avenue in New York, featured fireplaces with ornate mantelpieces in the main lobby and in every private room except the kitchens. Philip Hubert, a Frenchman who established a successful apartment practice in New York, described his buildings as "small private dwelling houses" stacked on top of one another.[13] He emphasized the separateness of each unit, which provided good insulation for sound and separate entrances to each building, rather than grand public lobbies. Even collective services could be seen as a heightening of domesticity, because they allowed the family to focus entirely on the social and familial aspects of home life, thereby placing production tasks outside the home. The servants often lived in rooms at the top of the building, isolated from the family group. Some residents pooled their domestic staffs rather than maintaining the more personal mistress-maid relationship. Call buttons with levers for meals, linens, tea, cleaning, and other needs sent silent messages to the staff's headquarters in another part of the building.

To many observers, the strangeness of apartment life lay not so much in the lavish display or even the collective services but in the close proximity of public spaces and private bedrooms within a given unit. Although a few architects experimented with duplexes as early as the mid–1870s, the expense of installing so many interior staircases made it more practical to keep all the rooms on a single floor. In *The Age of Innocence* (1920), Edith Wharton described an elderly woman of the late nineteenth century who appreciated the convenience of a single-floor apartment. "Her visitors were startled and fascinated," Wharton wrote, "by the foreignness of this arrangement, which recalled scenes in French fiction, and architectural incentives to immorality such as the simple American had never dreamed of. That was how women with lovers lived in the wicked old societies, in apartments with all the rooms on one floor, and all the indecent propinquities that their novels described."[14] A view of an apartment in Chicago's plush Mentone, taken in 1891, reveals such a daring vista. From the parlor, with its mantelpiece, its vine-draped works of art, and other signs of domesticity, one glances into the dining room and catches a glimpse of the bedroom bureau beyond.

At the end of the century, the apartment house again underwent major changes. Especially in New York but also in Boston and San Francisco, majestic, opulent towers appeared, making no concessions to the appearance of conventional residences. Between twelve and fifteen stories high, and spreading out over entire city blocks, these structures asserted a palatial grandeur. The Dorilton, the Ansonia, and Graham Court in New York, and the Ponce de Leon in Los Angeles, were encrusted with ornament, inside and out: associations with aristocratic wealth rather than democratic cooperation were unmistakable. In other cities where new apartments were not so monumental, they now evoke an air of fantasy rather than of technological progress. There was no longer a discourse that contended that apartment-hotels promoted egalitarian communities. Restraint was no longer so fashionable, although the tradition of architectural reserve and technological prowess did persist in Chicago, where Pond & Pond and Dwight Perkins built eminently sensible structures. All in all, most Americans now thought of apartment buildings as grandiose, exclusive, and decidedly undomestic structures.

At the same time, there was a shift toward more conventional domesticity in that each unit was treated as a separate entity. The emphasis on public kitchens and efficient, centralized services sharply declined. Gas companies and electric companies installed stoves and refrigerators in each household's tiny private kitchen. There were still massive refrigeration plants, water lines and heaters, gas mains, and electrical wiring circuits in the basements; but these services were not visible to any guest or resident, and they connected to hundreds of private appliances.

A photograph of the Wheeler apartment in Chicago's elegant Mentone, taken in 1890, shows the view from the proper Victorian parlor into the dining room and bedroom bureau beyond.

Even as these changes were taking place, the apartment-hotel suddenly came under vehement attack in the popular press. *The Child Welfare Manual,* a guidebook for families issued by a group of New York ministers and university faculty, warned of the dangers: "It is hard to think of a real home stored in diminutive pigeon-holes. . . . The quarters are so crowded that not only is it necessary to use folding Christmas-

· ·

The Dorilton, built in New York in 1902 by architects Janes and Leo, was criticized in the *Architectural Record* as an "architectural aberration" because of its grandiose scale and overly lavish ornament.

trees, but the natural, free intercourse of the family is crowded out; there is no room to play, no place for reading-room and music and hearth-side; and so families fold up their affections too."[15] One architect castigated women who chose this life. "A woman who lives in an apartment-hotel," he charged, "has nothing to do. She resigns in favor of the manager. Her personal preferences and standards are completely swallowed up in the

The 1901 Lucas Apartments in Galveston, Texas, a seaside resort city, show fanciful imagery embellishing the more reserved outlines of late-nineteenth-century American apartment buildings.

general public standards of the institution. . . . She cannot create that atmosphere of manner and things around her own personality, which is the chief source of her effectiveness and power."[16] An architectural journal of 1903 united the two separate themes of immorality and undemocratic extravagance, declaring that the "promiscuous exclusivity" of the apartment-hotel made it "the most dangerous enemy American domesticity has had to encounter."[17] Another zealous critic announced at a national housing conference that "sex morality often is by subtle ways weakened through long-established apartment house living." Marital discord, he continued, would easily breed in close quarters where every word could be overheard by nosy nieghbors. Then "it is a shortcut from the apartment house to the divorce court."[18]

This onslaught of criticism should by no means lead one to think that fewer apartment buildings were erected in the early twentieth century. Apartments were practical, and they were good investments; the arguments against them, though highly charged, were ineffective in and around the cities, where the price of real estate was high. In fact, while some professional architects publicly condemned apartments, others made their living principally by designing them. By the 1920s, in many cities, more apartments than single-family houses were being built. In fact, three quarters of Chicago's building permits for the decade were for apartments. In Los Angeles, the proportion rose from 8 percent of new construction in 1920 to 53 percent by 1928.[19] Experimental garden apartments, which left a major part of the site open, won favor on both coasts. Apartment houses had become the characteristic dwelling type for the metropolis, although most of the new construction was still aimed at a wealthy market.

Middle-class attacks on apartments as inadequate homes did not abate. The *Ladies' Home Journal* issued dire warnings of Bolshevik influence over American women exerted through the increasing number of apartments; and James Ford, executive director of an organization called Better Homes in America, captured the sense of alarm when he reported to the 1921 National Conference on Housing that a child's sense of individuality, moral character, and intellectual efficiency could only develop in a private, detached dwelling. In 1928, a branch of the Chicago Public School Association and the Cook County Federation of Women's Organizations passed a resolution that all "parents living in kitchenette apartments, presumably for economic reasons, but in reality because of the inconvenience of home-making in a cottage home or bungalow, thus lessening the free hours that the woman who is an apartment dweller devotes to club life, *be urged to become home owners for the sake of the younger generation.*"[20]

Charges that apartment houses could encourage promiscuous sexuality, female rebelliousness, communistic sentiments, or warped children reiterated the American myth that the domestic environment could, indeed, influence behavior, for good or for evil. Curiously, the thousands who lived in apartments and liked them did not develop a moralistic defense of their environment, as had the earlier generation. The persistence of the charges, when the economics of urban land dictated such a large number of apartment buildings, intensified the dichotomy between urban and suburban dwellers: they by no means saw apartments in the same light. Urbanites who enjoyed the comforts of apartments dismissed the moralism of suburbanites as provincial; while suburban groups, and even some city people, criticized the apartment dweller as irresponsible and flighty. In their discourse on the dangers of apartment life, critics voiced their alarm about the large numbers of women taking on work outside the home. They blamed the apartment for the rising divorce rate, the declining birth rate, premarital sex, and the social and economic disparities between rich and poor. The apartment became a scapegoat for these larger social problems, just as the suburban bungalow now seemed a solution.

PART FOUR

DOMESTICATION OF MODERN LIVING

DURING THE FIRST DECADES OF THE TWENTIETH century, the inequalities and sentimentality of the Victorians came under sharp attack. Feminists demanded radical changes in society's treatment of women; progressive reformers called for a more rational approach to government, education, and homemaking; sociologists and engineers inaugurated an appeal for "scientific management" in all aspects of modern life; and architects and popular journalists decried the excesses of nineteenth-century home decoration, endorsing simpler lines and uncluttered spaces. While trained experts led the various movements, ordinary middle-class men and women also espoused a modern approach to American life. Professionals and nonprofessionals alike considered the modernized home as a key to the larger political, social, and aesthetic reforms they espoused.

The pervasive use of the word "standards" in every field testifies to the high status of science. Direct parallels with industrial production or big-business efficiency created new models for the home, the school, and the government. Saving time, saving steps, increasing output, standardizing the final product: the vocabulary of Taylorism was applied to dusting a mantelpiece, raising children, or running a factory. Modernization had become a goal for its own sake.

The social sciences came into their own and took an active part in modernizing homes. Fledgling professional organizations of sociologists, economists, and political scientists suddenly found their members in demand, not only as teachers, but in other capacities as well. In the early 1900s, industrialists hired "social secretaries" to help develop social welfare programs for their workers and the workers' families. Home economics departments, women's magazines, and women's organizations turned to sociologists and anthropologists for expert counsel about the nature of family life and the changing role of women. By the 1920s, the jargon of the psychologist was familiar to educated Americans who were concerned about marital satisfaction and proper child-rearing.

The progressive movement at the turn of the century announced that all classes of Americans needed better homes and asked how science could improve domesticity. Amateurs and professionals analyzed the needs of rich and poor, working women and housewives, rural and urban households. They asked what should be discarded, what collectivized, what preserved, in the modern home. By 1910, the formula for a progressive home resembled the proposal for an efficient factory. According to Orison Swett Marden, advocate of a new self-motivation psychology and editor of *Success* magazine, "The ideal of modern efficiency demands a reorganized and standardized home."[1]

Changes in the middle-class dwelling were most conspicuous. The bric-à-brac of the Victorian parlor was put out of sight; the elaborate combinations of wooden detailing were peeled off the façade. Though new houses declined in square footage, prices remained high, largely because of technological improvements, which were now considered "standard." Modern bungalows were simpler to make housekeeping easier, which in turn was supposed to facilitate women in their pursuit of jobs and other non-domestic interests. However, the re-educated housewife, now a "household efficiency expert," still had much to do.

In industrial towns, professional planners, working in tandem with sociologists, devised housing schemes in which every aspect of the occupants' lives would be supervised. Many improvements resulted: better sanitation and ventilation in the houses; more outdoor space; less crowding; and in some cases, possibilities for homeownership. The industrial managers who funded these programs were also calculating their own self-interest. Workers' homes in corporate industrial towns were conceived as part of a multi-industry effort to increase management control over the work force, and signaled an update of the early-nineteenth-century concept of forming the worker's character through his or her environment.

The period following World War I seemingly represented a resurgence of individualism and an indulgence in residential architecture, a reaction to the standardization of the previous two decades. Fanciful cottages in fairy-tale styles were part of that image. Yet the developers who planned the housing of this generation actually extended the aesthetic and social controls of the progressive period. The middle-class suburb of the 1920s had covenants with regulations governing their style of architecture, the size of houses, policy toward cars, proximity of business and commerce, and restriction of entry to ethnic and religious minorities. The limited-dividend "model suburbs" of the decade, such as Radburn and Sunnyside, used similar but less discriminatory planning techniques to achieve a carefully worked-out balance of public amenities and private comforts. Experimental cooperative apartment projects in the cities, such as the Amalgamated Clothing Workers' complex in the Bronx, showed even more attention to public spaces and cooperatively run services as a substitute for each family's isolated self-sufficiency. Each of these planned living environments would influence the range of housing models in the decades to come. Here were the images of collective domestic stability for the twentieth century.

CHAPTER NINE

THE PROGRESSIVE HOUSEWIFE AND THE BUNGALOW

The house will become the first lesson in the use of mechanical appliances, in control of the harnessed forces of nature, and of that spirit of cooperation which alone can bring the benefits of modern science to the doors of all.

Ellen H. Richards, *The Cost of Shelter* (1915)

AS THE TIDE OF PROGRESSIVE REFORM BEGAN TO rise in the 1890s, middle-class American women insisted on the need for changes. Many of them believed that the home had to be revamped in order for women to be able to spend their time as they wished, in clubs and philanthropic activities, in offices and department stores. "A busy woman," Mary Gay Humphries wrote in *The House and Home,* edited by the Social Gospel minister Lyman Abbott, "is accustomed to say that her idea of the house of the future is one that can be cleaned with a hose."[1] While this particular suggestion never found its way into builders' specifications, housing of the early 1900s certainly reflected a concern for simplicity and efficiency.

The revitalized home economics movement—whose leaders now preferred the appellation "domestic science" or "household administration" to indicate their professional standards—helped stimulate such demands for housing reform. In the 1880s, under the leadership of Ellen H. Richards, a small group of Boston women had initiated the campaign for a more scientific, professionalized approach to the house, its upkeep, and its daily life. At the 1893 World's Columbian Exposition in Chicago, these women founded the National Household Economics Association to promote their cause. Under the impetus of the NHEA, homemaking departments were soon established in major universities and colleges, including Northwestern, Cornell, Vassar, and Stanford. In 1890, only four land-grant colleges had home-economics departments; by 1899, there were twenty-one; and by 1916, 17,778 students in 195 institutions were studying various aspects of the household.[2] High schools and grade schools tried to instill in young girls a scientific approach toward their future career of homemaking. Many schools had "practice houses" where students could compare laundering techniques and rearrange the latest styles of furniture, which had been donated by local merchants. U. S. government bulletins and the Cornell Farmers' Wives bulletins brought information to farm wives; and by 1911, over ten thousand women had enrolled in correspondence courses on family sociology, domestic architecture, and scientific cooking offered by the American School of Home Economics.[3]

Initially, the home-economics courses at schools like Simmons College in Boston, Carnegie School in Pittsburgh, and New York's Pratt Institute, were designed to train future servants. Settlement-house programs concentrated on helping immigrant women by preparing them for jobs as waitresses and servants while teaching them to keep spotless apartments. Middle-class housewives were also interested in recasting their own relationship with the domestic environment, and the proliferation of courses after 1900 primarily addressed this group. Feminists wanted to help women become more efficient so that they could pursue interests outside the home. Conservatives proposed that the only way to preserve the family and the private home was to treat housewives as professionals, to transform their role into that of the exacting, highly skilled "household administrator."

In the first years of the twentieth century, a new, highly motivated generation of home economists modernized the Victorian ideal of the woman who uplifts society; this was accomplished by giving women a new weapon: science. By treating the home as a laboratory, domestic scientists believed that they could promote better health, better families, and more satisfied women.

In some cases, the new scientific techniques resulted in a parody of laboratory conditions. Ellen Richards suggested that her readers leave out petri dishes, as did scientists who grew germ cultures, to see if they had successfully eliminated the bacteria in their living rooms. Mary Pattison, attempting to apply the principles of Frederick Winslow Taylor's scientific management to housework, called for a desk, a dictaphone, files, even a card index with the location and uses of the several rooms and closets in the house. More often, domestic scientists encouraged real improvements in the home and in women's attitudes toward their work. The leaders of the movement endorsed a radical simplification of the dwelling, condemning styles of decoration and architecture that might be fashionable but that were neither practical nor comfortable. They cited William Morris on the benefits of simplicity and adaptability: "Have nothing in your homes that you do not know to be useful, or believe to be beautiful."[4] They criticized the Victorian ornament, still popular in the 1890s, charging that it was unhealthy because dust collected in the crevices; hard to keep clean because it was heavy and plush and easily chipped; uncomfortable; and ugly.

In the interest of eliminating unnecessary housework, an almost austere simplicity became the basis for domestic design. Uncluttered space and smooth surfaces were easier to clean. Instead of crevices or cornices, which had to be dusted, painted stencils began to adorn living rooms. New coverings in dyed cotton, jute, burlap, or the recently improved rolls of wallpapers replaced carved or machine-made plaster ornament, and walls often simply received a coat of smooth, white plaster. On the floor one found straw mats, small rag throw rugs, or the novel product called linoleum. Materials for walls and floors were supposed to be easy to wash and restful to gaze upon.

Every detail was simpler and looked more functional. Plain rectilinear screens replaced the elegant curves and minute carvings of the Victorian stairway balustrade. Built-in conveniences abounded: bookshelves and cabinets in the living room; fold-down tables, benches, and ironing boards in the kitchen; medicine cabinets in the bathroom; and more closets throughout the house. Venetian blinds replaced curtains in many houses. Rows of simple casement windows with small leaded panes eliminated the need for curtains, as the leadwork obscured the view of the interior. Where draperies persisted, they were of almost transparent materials and barely covered the window sills, since anything sweeping the floor seemed dirty.

While modern home economists continued the tradition of moralistic rhetoric about the home, they dropped the celebration of softness and abundance; their ideal was purity and simplicity. The Chicago home economist and decorator Mabel Tuke Priestman wrote: "All superfluous ornament and drapery are done away with, and homes such as these in their appointments are conducive to plain living and high thinking."[5] Unlike the Victorian domestic moralists, this generation invoked an industrial association for the model home. Modern order, wrote Helen Campbell in 1897, derived its organization from "an office, . . . the kitchen of a buffet car or a steamship, the arrangement of a laboratory or a store."[6]

The goal of simplicity led to unpretentious amateur house designs and a suspicion of professional expertise. The early domestic scientists sought the active involvement of as many women as possible. Women were encouraged to learn to draw floor plans and to judge the quality of plumbing systems so that they would be able to choose well for their own families and influence the course of residential architecture. The idea was not that women should become architects, contractors, or building inspectors, but that they should demand good housing for their own families and play an important role in civic improvement associations. At the University of Chicago, professors Marion Talbot and Sophonisba P. Breckinridge concentrated on the responsibilities of "the citizen as householder."[7] In a world that had to reckon with inadequate municipal services, graft in construction inspection, and the lack of decent urban housing for the poor, the private house was no longer the main issue, they argued. Women had to become politically active in order to improve the quality of all housing.

In the early twentieth century, many different groups were campaigning for what they called a progressive approach to house design and upkeep. While their social goals often were based on conflicting values, public-health nurses, arts and crafts advocates, feminists, domestic scientists, and settlement-house workers favored the same simplified, standardized home to represent those values. Though a number of architects were experimenting with simplified forms, sometimes discarding historical styles in favor of pure geometric shapes, a broadly based popular interest in domestic architecture was, in large part, responsible for the sudden transformation in residential environments for middle-class Americans.

The public-health movement, for instance, was concerned with all classes of housing, not only the tenements of the poor. The educational campaigns geared to teaching personal and domestic hygiene to immigrant women also reached middle-class housewives through women's club meetings, books, and pamphlets. General acceptance of the germ theory of disease provided ammunition for their attacks on dust, dark corners, and inadequate sanitation.

Architectural specifications for the sanitary house were numerous. Sleeping porches and screened-in "sun parlors," which could be glazed in wintertime, provided fresh air and sunshine. Physicians and domestic scientists who considered dust a primary carrier of germs located dangerous "abiding-places for germs" in draperies, upholstered furniture, wall-to-wall carpets, and bric-à-brac. They urged that doorways and window casings be simpler; moldings and statuary niches disappear; cornices and other features where dust could collect be eliminated. White was revered as a sign of sanitary awareness. At first, concrete basements were whitewashed; then living rooms and dining rooms were whitewashed as well. Specifications for kitchen walls called for washable tiles or less expensive enameled sheet metal, lightweight oilcloth, or enamel paint—always white. Even appliances had touches of shiny white porcelain. Combining recent awareness of public-health criteria with emerging studies of mental health, architect Una Nixson Hopkins told readers of *The House Beautiful* that physicians who studied the effects of color on the mind considered bare white walls as effective as a rest cure.

In the arts and crafts movement of the early 1900s, architects and designers mixed with poets and writers, housewives and reformers, combining a sentimental reverence for hand-crafted goods with a more up-to-date endorsement of simplified, wholesome environments. Some designers acclaimed a self-consciously rustic aesthetic for the home, using massive tree trunks and uncut stone for structural elements, which they left exposed. While the fashionable family might display Indian handicrafts or folk art in the living room, most American arts and crafts enthusiasts simply called for "good taste" through quiet lines and minimal ornament. In contrast to their English counterparts who had initiated the arts and crafts movement as a reaction against the abuses of industrialization, most members of the numerous American organizations claimed that it was possible to produce pleasing forms in a factory as well as in a crafts workshop. They focused predominantly on the final product rather than on the actual conditions of making that product.

One of the most prominent popularizers of the arts and crafts movement in the United States was Gustav Stickley of Syracuse, New York. A furniture maker, Stickley had first redesigned the practices in his shop so that all work was done with hand tools. Simple, rectilinear lines and unvarnished oak became characteristic of his "Craftsman" furniture. In 1901 Stickley began publication of a magazine, *The Craftsman*, hoping to lead a social and artistic revolution in America. The journal featured articles on tenements in New York City, Kropotkin's utopian anarchism, factory working conditions, flower arranging, and glass blowing. The following year, Stickley began to offer his readers model house designs, and continued to feature both interior and exterior plans until the magazine's demise in 1916. In 1903 he established the Craftsman Home Builder's Club, which gave free advice on "well-built, democratic, well-planned homes."[8]

According to Stickley, "The Craftsman type of building is largely the result not of elaboration, but of elimination."[9] The houses in his magazine had simple, rectilinear, built-in furniture, plain surfaces of native stone or wood, unpretentious plans and elevations. Stickley did not insist that every dwelling be a highly personalized design, even though he clearly enjoyed experimenting with the texture and variety of materials. To him, "democratic architecture" meant good homes available to all Americans through economy of construction and materials, together with necessary standardization. Though Craftsman designs suggested time-consuming construction techniques, the exposed beams were often simply tacked on under the eaves and the rough "clinker brick," produced in a factory to look like hand-molded brick.

. . . .

The typical Craftsman cottage, such as this one in Virginia, Minnesota, ca. 1908, used rustic materials and self-consciously simple lines.

Stickley claimed that his approach to design could remedy almost every problem facing the middle-class family, from lack of servants to the increased divorce rate. He also saw the well-crafted home as a key to solving larger social problems, such as crime and civil disorder. Small, inexpensive versions of the Craftsman house would make working-class families homeowners. Apprentice training programs in house construction and furniture making, run by the state and by private business, would provide uplifting employment for young men. The pages of *The Craftsman* carried the message that housing and social issues were related in their need for good design. Though Stickley's expectations of immediate, lasting social harmony through aesthetic reform were obviously unrealistic, he found a sizable audience that regarded residential architecture as the preferred American approach to reform.

Other magazines also offered detailed specifications for modern model houses, as well as more general advice on decoration and domesticity. By the time Edward Bok retired in 1919 as editor of *Ladies' Home Journal*, this magazine had a circulation of 2 million largely because of Bok's crusade for "model *Journal* houses." Bok wanted to encourage middle-class women to become more involved with the home, thereby relinquishing their recent tendencies to abandon domestic duties for jobs or women's club activities. He was emphatic about architectural standards for the modern home. The house should be free from "senseless ornamentation"; it should be equipped with the latest sanitary fixtures; it should be decorated with unpretentious furnishings and a few handmade niceties. These dicta did not, by any means, imply a spartan setting. The *Journal*'s 1901 series of room designs by the St. Louis artist Will Bradley were opulent Art Nouveau décors. Yet Bok's taste was not all-embracing. He laid down exacting specifications for every detail, from pillows to room dimensions, often showing comparisons of "Good Taste vs. Bad Taste" in furnishings.

At first, no architects would deign to accept Bok's offer to design "model *Journal* houses," but with the depression of the 1890s, they became more willing. Beginning in 1895, suburban dwellings in Colonial Revival, Elizabethan, and Queen Anne styles, costing between $3,500 and $7,000, regularly appeared. In 1901, Bok launched the first of a series of modern model dwellings by Frank Lloyd Wright and his associates in Chicago. Thousands of readers sent in $5 for a complete set of plans and specifications, which would enable them to build duplicates of these model houses. As Theodore Roosevelt supposedly said of the *Journal*'s editor: "Bok is the only man I ever heard of who changed, for

Frank Lloyd Wright's third model house for the *Ladies' Home Journal*—"A Fireproof House for $5000," published in April 1907—made the prairie-style design of a master architect available to anyone for the minimal fee of $5.00.

· ·

This San Francisco house of 1915 was one of hundreds around the country that were based on Wright's 1907 model house that appeared in the *Ladies' Home Journal*. (In much the same way, complete plans of Wright houses, and of many other major architects' work, are available today from the Library of Congress at a minimal fee.)

the better, the architecture of an entire nation, and he did it so quickly and yet so effectively that we didn't know it was begun before it was finished."[10]

While there were many words for the new house of the early twentieth century, "bungalow" was certainly the most widely used. It usually referred to a relatively unpretentious small house, although more exotic, expansive, hand-crafted dwellings created by architects like Charles and Henry Greene in southern California were also called bungalows. In general, though, the term implied a one-story or story-and-a-half dwelling of between six hundred and eight hundred square feet. Bedrooms were only bunk spaces. The kitchen, fitted like a ship's galley, accommodated a single person, and she (it was assumed) had a squeeze. The family ate their meals in the large central area, a combination living/dining space. This room usually featured exposed ceiling beams and sometimes exposed stud walls, a rough brick or stone fireplace, and bands of windows, which let the sunlight in. Stickley's Craftsman look, also known as New Art, made its mark in houses of every class.

Styles for the façades of these bungalows varied. The most prevalent, usually identified with Stickley, combined heavy porch supports, overhanging eaves, and either stucco or shingled walls. Often a porch or a pergola extended across the front of the house. The Bungalow Building Company of Seattle and Bungalowcraft of Los Angeles turned out thousands of similar designs in a single year. Several *Bungalow* magazines and specialized pattern books gave builders precise specifications for cobblestone chimneys and wooden roof brackets. The large mail-order houses of Sears, Roebuck & Company and Montgomery Ward's offered do-it-yourself owner-builders all the material and fixtures needed for entire bungalows in this style. The lumber, doors, windows, and porches were sent precut and ready to assemble. A Craftsman bungalow from a mail-order company combined mass-production techniques with the allure of personal craftsmanship in the final assembly.

Despite the common aesthetic of simplicity, regionalism had a strong effect. Builders and architects sought to use local materials and to evoke particular memories or associations. In southern California and throughout the Southwest, Mediterranean influences flourished. The early missions, Spanish and Italian villas, and even North African habitations served as bungalow models. Smooth planes of white stucco, large windows and doors, interior courtyards, and carefully landscaped gardens made the most of the warm climate. Regional publications, such as *Outwest, Sunset,* and the more professionally oriented *Architect and*

Engineer, extolled California hybrid styles to such an extent that the bungalow was often portrayed as a West Coast innovation.

In the San Francisco Bay Area, the "hillside cottage" appeared, representing a moral crusade for "the simple life" through another regional aesthetic. A group of Berkeley professors, artists, and architects worked out the tenets of the style in their meetings at the Hillside Club. They became enamored of uncluttered façades of dark-brown redwood shingles, interlocking woodwork, and open-air sleeping porches. Informality and a studied casualness pervaded the large, open living spaces. Charles Keeler, spokesman for the group, described the connection between the architecture and their values, explaining that "the thought of the simple

· ·

The living room in a bungalow in Tacoma, Washington, ca. 1910, shows a "progressive" interior: easy to clean, simple, and fashionable. The furniture combined straight-backed Mission oak and curved wicker porch chairs. Some remaining bric-a-brac has been put behind the leaded-glass doors in the built-in bookshelves flanking the plain brick fireplace.

life is being worked out in the home [with] harmony, craft, dignity, restraint. Blessed is he who lives in such a home and who makes life conform to his surroundings."[11]

From the Midwest came another prototype, as the English Tudor, favored by arts and crafts advocates, merged with the sharp horizontal lines employed by Frank Lloyd Wright and his associates. The resulting "prairie style" was almost devoid of historical references. The white stucco cube with simple bands of dark wood and casement windows did not look back to any period of the past. Builders across the country, but especially in the Midwest, quickly adopted this idiom. Writing in the *National Builder,* James Casey praised the prairie-style bungalow, declaring: "The new type of home, now so popular, has utility for its fundamental principle. It aims to eliminate all that is superfluous, and to embody all modern improvements."[12]

The Colonial Revival also found advocates across the nation. Its simple foursquare plan and white clapboard façade evoked the moral tone of restraint and sound judgment in yet another way. *Carpentry and Building* magazine proclaimed the New England colonial cottage to be an architectural expression of the entire country's common heritage of good sense and egalitarian principles. "The people really want a combination of wholesome, strong, simple effects, and especially good, livable things, with fair and moderate cost," wrote the editors. "And that is what the present generation is getting at last."[13]

These new and simpler bungalows did not necessarily cost less than the elaborate Victorian dwellings of a generation before. Interest in regulating health and increasing domestic efficiency meant that a larger proportion of construction expenses—often 25 percent—now went into household technology. Modern systems supplied the home with power, heat, and numerous services. The first House Furnishing Exhibition, held at New York's Madison Square Garden in 1906, was a multi-industry effort to educate the public on the immense quantity of labor-saving devices and economical mechanisms available to homemakers. Magazine advertisements became more numerous, and they began to suggest the more elusive aspects of products: their scientific exactness, modern allure, and relationship to family comfort and pride.

Once residential construction picked up after 1905, the bathroom was considered an essential part of the middle-class house. The production of porcelain fixtures—toilets, bathtubs, sinks, and trendy features such as toothbrush faucets and sitz baths—increased markedly during the first decade of the new century. Factory-produced lead pipes replaced wooden pipes made on the site. At first, pipes were left exposed, partly from pride in the shining sanitary aesthetic, partly from lingering doubts about the danger of trapped gases. By 1913, built-in bathtubs and sinks were on the market, making claw feet and visible pipes seem like old-fashioned clutter. The compact bathroom, its walls and fixtures gleaming white, became the mark of modernization.

The sudden prominence of the kitchen also confirms that the cult of household technology drew from a generalized popular interest in science as well as particular technical innovations. The kitchen replaced the parlor as the focus of attention in many builders' pattern books, and certainly in domestic science textbooks and women's magazines. Isabell McDougall, describing "An Ideal Kitchen" for readers of *The House Beautiful* in 1902, evoked the by-now familiar metaphors of impeccable laboratory order to be enforced by the housewife, or household administrator. "Everything in her temple is clean," she explained, "with the

· ·

Christine Frederick's *Household Engineering,* published by the American School of Correspondence in 1915 as a home-economics text, praised the housewife who looked to scientific-management techniques.

scientific cleanliness of a surgery, which we all know to be far ahead of any mere housewifely neatness."[14]

The average kitchen in the turn-of-the-century bungalow or larger house was compact and carefully planned. It measured approximately 120 square feet, and everything had its place. The commodious Hoosier cabinet, with numerous wooden drawers and bins, stood against one wall. Wooden worktables were positioned to cut down on unnecessary steps —a principle that domestic scientists borrowed from Taylorism. By 1910, the built-in breakfast nook had become popular; and in many houses, the kitchen had been reduced to a Pullman kitchen, or "kitchenette."

New appliances held center stage. The sink and drainboard were of shiny white porcelain or enameled iron. An automatic pump supplied hot and cold running water. If there was no brine-cooled or ammonia-cooled icebox on the back porch, where the iceman had easy access, a metal basin in one corner sufficed. A hood hung over the gas range to cut smells, and porcelain-enameled cookware hung on wall hooks. Unfortunately, the new appliances were not necessarily reliable. As one textbook on domestic architecture admitted, most laundry machines "are not economical on account of the severity of the process on the clothes being washed."[15] Most households still used a washboard and hung the clothes in the yard to dry.

To many Americans, mechanical devices for the home were the essence of progressive improvements and a bright future. Writing in the *Congregationalist*, Henry Demarest Lloyd, the Chicago muckraking journalist, extolled the benefits he envisioned:

> Equal industrial power will be as invariable a function of citizenship as the equal franchise. Power will flow in every house and shop as freely as water. All men will become capitalists and all capitalists co-operators. . . . Women, released from the economic pressure which has forced them to deny their best nature and compete in unnatural industry with men, will be re-sexed. . . . Every house will be a center of sunshine and scenery.[16]

According to Lloyd, technology promised individual freedom and social equality. Men and women of all classes would share the infinite power of electricity, the "modern servant." Lloyd envisioned women returning to their homes, leaving their jobs because of increased economic abundance brought about by electrical power. But other reformers, especially feminists, foresaw a future wherein more women would be able to take on jobs outside the home because electricity had freed them from household drudgery.

A few domestic scientists were skeptical about the tendency to rely on technology to solve all domestic problems. "It is a paradox," wrote the English home economist Mrs. W. N. Shaw in an American edition of a textbook, "that one of the difficulties with which the modern mistress has to contend is the fact that her house is 'replete with every modern convenience.' Every labour-saving contrivance, every mechanical convenience, calls for vigilance to ensure its proper use, and for knowledge as to the ways in which it may fail, and of the method of readjustment should it happen to do so."[17] But such opinions were in a minority.

In most new houses of the early twentieth century, square footage was dramatically reduced to compensate for the increased expenses of plumbing, heating, and other technological improvements. Magazines like the *Journal* had regular features on "The Little House Home," with tips on practical ways to create a sense of "coziness" rather than asceticism. By 1910 it was rare to have single-purpose rooms such as libraries, pantries, sewing rooms, and spare bedrooms, which had comprised the Victorians' sense of family uniqueness and complex domestic life. In a moderately priced two-story house there were usually only three downstairs rooms: living room, dining room, and kitchen. On the second floor, bedrooms were only alcoves for sleep and privacy, no longer receiving rooms for one's friends and children.

Changes in the middle-class house signaled new patterns in family life. The average number of children decreased to three and a half by 1900, and many middle-class families had only one or two.[18] Housing studies also related the reduced square footage to the decline in domestic production of goods. There was no longer a need for places to store away quilts, home-canned vegetables, and dowry linens for future use. Even the home economists declared that the modern housewife's principal role was that of consumer, not producer. Better distribution of food meant that the kitchen need not be stocked for long periods of time.

Formality in the home was declining. As dining habits became more relaxed, doors between dining room and living room could be left out or the wall itself removed so that the two rooms became one. Meals were much simpler and shorter. Often a housewife simply served prepared foods or cereals in the breakfast nook, and had a sandwich or salad by herself for lunch. Family dinners had fewer courses than they had in the previous generation, as youthfully slim figures became the vogue. Entrance halls no longer seemed necessary for receiving guests. Rather than bring suitors home, the daughter was likely to be going out on the town with her boyfriend. *Ladies' Home Journal, The House Beautiful,* and *Carpentry and Building* all condemned the parlor as outdated, pretentious, and a waste of space.

The home was no longer the main locus for training children. The school year was longer, and compulsory attendance laws were enforced. More mothers sent their children to kindergarten for expert early education. There were twice as many high schools in 1914 as there had been in 1898, offering training in manual skills such as woodworking for boys and cooking for girls, training which once had been an integral part of home life.[19] After school, a child might attend Boy Scout or Campfire Girl meetings. As a result, many mothers saw less of their children in the home.

In more and more cases, the housewife worked alone in her kitchen. Between 1900 and 1920, the number of domestic servants in the United States declined by half—from eighty per thousand families to thirty-nine.[20] (Most of these were day workers, usually black married women rather than live-in servants.) Yet no builders considered opening up the kitchen and ending the housewife's isolation there. Rather, they praised the smaller, better-equipped kitchen, planned for the domestic scientist who had no need of a servant, since she had learned the most efficient techniques for housework. The kitchen was not to be a place for playing with children or visiting with neighbors but a modern "home laboratory."

One of the principal justifications for the smaller kitchen and the minimum-upkeep materials of the progressive house was the middle-class woman's demand for more time of her own outside the house. By 1900, women held jobs in almost every occupation listed in the census. Although most of these women were unmarried, and a quarter of them domestics or factory workers, college-educated women did enter the professions. Other young women donned the starched shirtwaist and ankle-length skirt of the Gibson girl and entered offices as receptionists, clerical workers, and typewriters (the same word was used for the machine and the person working at it).

Middle-class women who did not hold regular jobs often worked as volunteers in charity or civic organizations, promoting the numerous improvement campaigns of the National Consumers' League or their local women's club, lobbying for reform legislation or neighborhood parks. These women still considered domestic issues their primary concern, but now the entire city was their home. In 1910, the president of the General Federation of Women's Clubs declared that their platform was based on protecting "women and children, and the home, the latter meaning the four walls of the city as well as the four walls of brick and mortar."[21]

Private homes were often the focus of debate, all the same. In order for women to have time for their non-domestic activities, they wanted both simpler houses that were easier to keep clean and more labor-saving appliances. The single-family dwelling was condemned in the pages of *Harper's Bazaar* as "a prison and a burden and a tyrant."[22] The Philadelphia economist Robert E. Thompson and Charlotte Perkins Gilman and other radical feminists demanded kitchenless houses and public child-care facilities to ease the domestic demands on women.

There was some reservation about architectural changes that were tied to new sex roles. The restlessness that characterized "the modern woman" caused a stir among many conservatives. Journalists, physicians, and politicians raised the issues of "race suicide" and "desexualization," which they connected to the declining birth rate among white women. In *The Foes of Our Own Household* (1917) and in articles for *Ladies' Home Journal,* Theodore Roosevelt spoke about the dangers of women abandoning the traditional roles of wife and mother for more exciting challenges outside the home. Higher education for women came under attack, since college-educated women often did not marry, and when they did, they had one or two children at most. The modern home and, even worse, the apartment, requiring as little time as they did, seemed to encourage these tendencies.

Despite their misgivings, architects, builders, and the editors of women's magazines recognized the growing market of working women. Even the married woman who worked was not necessarily considered a pariah. *Ladies' Home Journal* carried several articles on ways to earn one's living both inside and outside the home; and a full-page color spread in February 1911 considered the best house plan for a woman with a family and a career at home. Her bungalow had two separate entrances, a living room that doubled as a reception room for clients, and many built-in conveniences to accelerate housekeeping chores. Bungalows designed for single "business-girls" or "girl-bachelors" were featured in magazines and home-economics texts in the 1910s. Space allotted for cooking and laundering was minimal, for it was assumed that such tasks were done commercially, outside the private home. For defenders and critics of the trend, the large proportion of unmarried independent women was connected to this kind of housing.

An elaboration of this model was the bungalow court—a group of ten or twenty almost identical dwellings, first designed as winter housing in southern California—which appeared in all parts of the country in the 1910s. Since the bungalows were quite small, there was usually a community "playhouse," where residents entertained guests and organized evening entertainments. Those who promoted the bungalow court as a modern living environment suggested that it could domesticate single working women, demonstrating to them the progressive side of home life. According to many advocates, this setting also represented "The Community Problem Solved."[23] The harmonious uniform aesthetic and the shared outdoor spaces, playhouse, and garages were evidence that the residents had established strong social ties among themselves.

. . . .

The Alexandria Bungalow Court in Pasadena, California, built in 1915 by Arthur S. Heineman, combined stately architecture and aesthetic controls with appeals to efficiency and community.

Visual appeals to community in the bungalow court implied that neighborly contact was infrequent in the modern city or suburb. After 1900, fears of isolation and a romantic nostalgia for the homogeneous fellowship associated with small towns infused much of the discussion about housing. Most middle-class Americans wanted to know that they lived with other people who were like them, who shared the same values and might become friends. Civic-improvement societies and suburban neighborhood associations multiplied as residents lobbied for sanitation and temperance laws, for clean streets and well-mown lawns. In the neighborhood club or the block organization, the incorporated suburb or the bungalow court, people hoped to find companionship. Middle-class women, both single and married, formerly isolated in their private homes, were in the forefront of movements to promote community and ensure better living environments.

The plight of the farm wife, who had the most extreme isolation as well as the most primitive facilities for housework and cooking, received special attention. When sociological studies described the high incidence of depression among farm wives, home economists and architects considered what kind of house might raise these women's spirits and encourage their daughters to become farmers' wives rather than moving to the city. In 1913 the Minnesota State Art Association sponsored a competition for "progressive farm houses," with the published plans available to farmers at a nominal fee. These twelve-room dwellings were designed to make work easier for the woman, to separate the family from the farm hands, and to improve the appearance of the rural landscape. New appliances and telephones for the model homes were strongly recommended by architects, who argued that these would buoy the farm wife's state of mind.

While more than half the nation's farmers owned their homes in 1910, only one third of non-farm households did, and that number dropped to one quarter in Philadelphia and one fifth in Cincinnati.[24] It was increasingly difficult for Americans to afford to become homeowners. In particular, the growing number of unmarried women and men usually rented rather than owned. The smaller, plainer dwelling, especially one set on a common court rather than on a large private yard, was an attempt to find a solution to the economic problem and to the seemingly related problem of a growing population of unmarried persons. Participants at the annual National Conference on City Planning, whose meetings began in 1909, and the National Conference on Housing, which commenced in 1911, hoped to find innovative ways to increase homeownership without moving toward any sort of federal subsidies. They endorsed architectural solutions to economic and social dilemmas. The Model Street display at the St. Louis Exposition of 1904, the Model Bungalow installed at the Indiana State House for the 1913 National Conservation Congress, and the flurry of competitions for model suburban developments were all expressions of a nationwide enthusiasm for the "progressive house," which began to look much the same, wherever it appeared.

The uniform image appealed to a range of people who hoped that domestic architecture would encourage social cooperation. The Victorian suburb was branded as a "labyrinth of unreason," reflecting a time of "rabid democracy," of social and aesthetic license.[25] Settlement workers Jane Addams and Graham R. Taylor, Jr., the domestic scientist Marion Talbot, the statistician Adna Weber, and the political journalist Herbert Croly concurred: houses conceived as individualistic display encouraged class differences and competition among neighbors. They argued for common architectural standards that would visually reinforce their ideal of a balanced, egalitarian social life for women and men. Both feminists and conservatives asserted that it was possible to solve "the woman question" through a more rational approach toward living environments. In 1912, Grosvenor Atterbury, who designed the model suburb of Forest Hills Gardens in Queens and championed planned industrial towns, wrote an appeal for progressive residential planning in *Scribner's*. He too argued that domestic architecture could reinforce the higher social values of residents, subordinating individual desires to the general good. "[T]he truth is that with any kind of control anarchy ceases," Atterbury claimed. "With the elimination of lawless eccentricity and disregard of architectural decency, the good elements begin to count."[26]

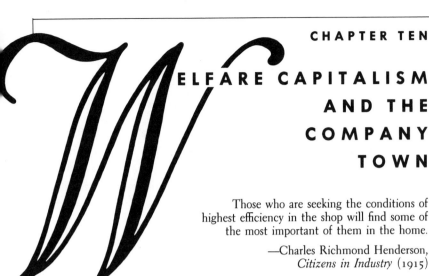

CHAPTER TEN

WELFARE CAPITALISM AND THE COMPANY TOWN

> Those who are seeking the conditions of
> highest efficiency in the shop will find some of
> the most important of them in the home.
>
> —Charles Richmond Henderson,
> *Citizens in Industry* (1915)

IN 1894, UNDER THE LEADERSHIP OF SOCIOLOGIST William Howe Tolman, a number of New York–based social scientists organized the Get-Together Club to discuss current civic and social problems. A few years later the club added several business leaders to its ranks in an effort to promote a more scientific approach to social welfare programs in American industry; the members also recognized the potential employment and research opportunities for professional social scientists. In 1898, Tolman and Josiah Strong formed the League for Social Service and the New York Social Museum to publicize nationally the message of "Industrial Betterment" through a more systematic approach to "welfare work," especially in planned industrial towns.[1] Their modern approach to industrial management would extend to every level of the worker's life, from the factory to the school to the home.

The National Civic Federation (NCF) provided another impetus for systematic welfare work in industry and in the homes of industrial workers. The organization was founded in 1900 by Elbert H. Gary, George W. Perkins, Andrew Carnegie, Marcus A. Hanna, other business leaders, and a few labor leaders who shared their goals, notably Samuel Gompers of the A.F. of L. and John Mitchell of the United Mine Workers. The NCF sought to promote social reforms that would defuse the demands of radical political groups by providing benefits to working-class families. Participating corporate leaders pledged to promote "peace between capital and labor" through "good work" in all spheres of the laborer's life.[2] By providing services, employers could tie their workers more closely to the corporation. Although NCF officials could act as arbitrators in labor disputes, they sought to prevent strikes altogether by encouraging employers to win their workers' confidence and dependency. Apprenticeship training and factory safety measures alone were thought to be insufficient incentives. Improved working conditions had to be linked to other reforms that reached workers' families in their homes.

In 1904, the NCF set up a welfare department to publicize its reform goals. Interested employers received descriptions of social service programs and drawings of company-built dwellings, clubhouses, and other facilities. The NCF Welfare Department also functioned as an employment service. "Welfare secretaries," or "social secretaries," received job offers through this office. The men and women who took these positions had backgrounds in social work, philanthropy, public health, education, and religion. In the industrial towns, they functioned as moral police, statisticians, teachers, recreational planners, and counselors. Membership in the NCF Welfare Department grew from one hundred in 1904 to 250 two years later and five hundred in 1911.[3] The sociological department became a familiar feature in large factories, lumber and mining towns, and even in department stores.

The principal responsibility of social secretaries was to ensure that employees conformed to employers' regulations governing cleanliness, living habits, boarders, and other such domestic matters. They did so through classes, educational programs, competitions, and prizes. They also undertook investigations of the workers' homes to observe how families actually lived. Leaders of the industrial welfare movement claimed that the findings would prove useful for the larger society as well as the private company. Strong described the mission of the League for Social Service as the "study of the science of life by the putting on file of all manner of human experience."[4] Yet, to the workers and their families, always subject to the scrutiny of the professional social secre-

• •

(Opposite) An advertisement for the Connecticut Mills in Danielson, Connecticut, was featured in *Homes for Workmen* (1919) as a good example of how industrialists could use improved housing to attract skilled workers.

TAKE YOUR CHOICE

If you and your wife and your babies lived in this unhealthful hovel do you think you would work as cheerfully and well as you could if —

You all lived in this handsome modern home where you could hold up your head and your children would not be ashamed?

The Connecticut Mills Company in Danielson, Conn., offers you a beautiful, modern home at the same rental you often have to pay for tumble-down shacks in many mill-housing colonies. It offers better incomes.

It Is Called "The Village Beautiful"

It offers an opportunity for its operatives not only to work FOR the company, but WITH it!

tary, such visits were invasions of privacy. The home as well as the workplace had become the scene of conflict between classes.

The industrial town of the early twentieth century offered the professional urban planner unparalleled opportunities to carry out projects based on modern theories of urban organization. Principles of land use, zoning, sanitation, and transportation planning could be put into practice, analyzed, and compared. Under the auspices of the industrial managers, the planner had extraordinary centralized authority. He could direct the arrangement of facilities, roads, and people, combining an elegant, axial Beaux-Arts aesthetic with more scientific considerations derived from sociology, statistics, and public-health and management studies. The industrial town (or the section dominated by a single industry) provided a laboratory for the emerging profession of urban planning.

One example of the planned industrial town was Kaulton, Alabama, a lumber town on the outskirts of Tuscaloosa, founded in 1912. Boston planner George H. Miller designed a fan-shaped site plan, with broad avenues and narrow, curving paths repeating the overall shape. The fact that the minor axes were actually dirt roads did not dissuade him from imposing an elegant pattern. The complex of machine shops, mills, and railway lines; a large playing field; and space set aside for a civic center were grouped together as the focal point of the town. While planners endorsed zoning for other kinds of suburbs, they did not try to separate industrial, recreational, and residential areas in company towns. Protecting individual real-estate investments was not an issue here, whereas efforts to protect the workers' physical well-being was a primary consideration. Miller emphasized a strictly rational, business-oriented approach to planning, noting that "heretofore scientific management has not given sufficient attention to the preservation or creation of fitness of a workman for work in those non-working hours when there is being determined the potential ability of whether he is to give a high or low percentage in work."[5]

Heads of large corporations, owners of mining camps, and manufacturers with only a few hundred employees sought expert advice from social secretaries and town planners. Many industrialists recognized the potential value of residential as well as factory planning, although the degree of implementing social welfare programs varied considerably. One report declared that two thousand American firms were engaged in "welfare work" in 1917, while the U. S. Bureau of Labor Statistics estimated that same year that at least one thousand industrial firms provided housing for employees.[6] Still, Graham R. Taylor, Jr., of the

Chicago Commons Social Settlement, criticized the "do-as-little-as-you-like" approach that characterized most company towns, and chastised the short-sighted executives of U. S. Steel, who refused to allocate money for a professional city planner when they built Gary, Indiana, in 1905.[7] A monotonous grid extended eleven miles along the lakefront, and tens of thousands of workers were housed in poorly built frame tenements and spartan concrete bungalows. Taylor predicted that the family relations, political views, and work efficiency of all the residents would suffer as a consequence of the environmental problems.

Planned industrial towns had existed long before the fanfare of the early twentieth century. Lowell had been famous since the 1820s. Other small New England mill villages had provided housing and some social

· ·

Kaulton, Alabama, laid out in 1912 by Boston planner George H. Miller, applied formal Beaux-Arts planning principles to the dirt roads and plain wooden bungalows of a company town.

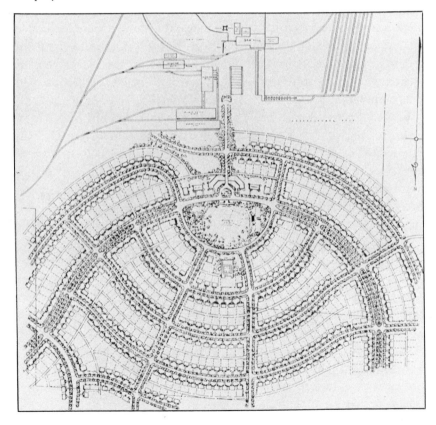

services since the mid-1800s. Several European ventures offered prototypes for Americans: Essen in Germany; Saltaire, Port Sunlight, and
Bourneville in England. There were, however, major differences between nineteenth-century and twentieth-century industrial towns. The
scale of the later enterprises was generally much larger. In 1836 the eight
firms in Lowell employed six thousand workers. The Colorado Fuel and
Iron Company had seventy-five thousand people in thirty-eight camps
in 1901; Grosvenor Atterbury laid out the Carolina, Clinchford, and
Ohio railway town of Erwin, Tennessee, to accommodate forty thousand
people.[8] Even if a company provided housing for only one third or one
half of its workers, the enterprise was enormous compared to nineteenth-
century standards.

American industrialists insisted that the new industrial planning did
not represent philanthropic schemes but rather sound business investments. In *Homes for Workmen*, a compendium of recent American
industrial towns published in 1919, planners claimed that workmen in
model towns would be between 25 and 33 percent more efficient on the
job.[9] Professional town planners and sociologists were meant to comple-
ment scientific management experts inside the factory to help increase
production. As Miller wrote of Kaulton: "Every feature in such a town
is designed to have some constructive influence for specifically benefit-
ting the workman for his work, and he gets nothing he does not pay for,
thus eliminating the element of paternalism."[10]

Books such as *Homes for Workmen*, Georges Benoit-Lévy's *Cités-
Jardins d'Amérique* (1905), E. Wake Cook's *Betterment* (1906), William Tolman's *Social Engineering* (1909), and numerous reports sponsored by the federal government confirm that in the early part of the
twentieth century, American management depended on sociological and
architectural expertise to develop more refined techniques for controlling their work force. Major industrialists were worried about labor
uprisings; strikes and violence had become frequent occurrences in the
late nineteenth century. They also wanted to forestall certain progressive
reform movements. Government and consumer group demands for
changes in factories—inspections, occupational safety regulations, laws
limiting the hours and risks in the work of women and children—forced
management to put forth their own reforms. Furthermore, a shortage
of properly trained workers and the increasing complexity of production
techniques in many industries prompted forward-looking managers to
find new ways to lure and keep skilled workers. And welfare work—
especially housing programs—was one solution.

Pullman, Illinois, set the most important precedent for the welfare-oriented industrialists of the early twentieth century. With Nathan F. Barrett as landscape designer and Solon S. Beman as architect-planner, George Pullman completed his model town on the outskirts of Chicago in 1884. It cost $8 million and covered four thousand acres. Pullman wanted to protect the skilled mechanics who built his railway cars from the "baneful influences" of the city, especially its radical political activity and strong unions.[11] He sought complete control over his workers. He constructed over fourteen hundred dwelling units—brick row houses of uniform size for the skilled mechanics and a few detached houses for the managers' families. Pullman owned every one of these houses, as well as the town's church, library, stores, and other buildings. All were rented at a profit. He also owned the eighteen hundred ramschackle tenement apartments where the unskilled manual laborers, most of them Slavic immigrants, lived. Only a few critics commented on Pullman's "feudalistic" control, branding the model town a "slave pen" and portraying the special plight of the laborers.[12]

Then, in 1894, in the wake of a nationwide depression, the vision of paternalistic control and profitable philanthropy fell apart. Under the auspices of Eugene V. Debs and the American Railway Union, the Pullman workers called a strike to retaliate against Pullman's cutbacks in wages, the exorbitant rents he charged (which he did not lower), and his dictatorial control. President Grover Cleveland sent in federal troops to break the strike, thereby intensifying the violence and bitter condemnations on both sides. Many American industrialists were already skeptical of the possibility of encouraging social order through physical planning. In the light of the events at Pullman, the continuation of systematic welfare work and home-building campaigns in American industry is, in fact, rather surprising. However, critics contended that it had been Pullman's authoritarian control that had precipitated the violent reaction. His desires to convert every aspect of the model town into monetary returns and to wield absolute authority represented an outdated, reactionary approach to industrial welfare.

There were a few concurrent examples of successful planning to offset Pullman's notorious failure. Vandergrift, Pennsylvania, site of the Apollo Iron and Steel Company, perpetuated the belief that men and women in a "clean, healthy, beautiful town" would become model citizens and contented workers.[13] Visitors admired the suburban quality of the town, with its curvilinear streets, small parks, and pleasant, detached cottages. The N. O. Nelson Company, a producer of plumbing equipment in

Leclaire, Illinois, provided housing, social, recreational, and educational facilities, as well as a short-lived profit-sharing plan, to counter unrest among employees. Leclaire had neither written laws nor a police force, for Nelson claimed that the residents' mutual interests precluded any serious conflict. The new housing and the generous homeownership opportunities won the workers' guarded approval. The NCF and the League for Social Service publicized the success of these model towns.

The best-known example of the model town was the large section of Dayton, Ohio, dominated by the National Cash Register Company. The company had been founded in 1882; eight years later, the president, John H. Patterson, hired Frederick Law Olmsted, Jr., to supervise the construction of a clubhouse, called the House of Usefulness. In this rustic Craftsman building of stone and exposed timber, employees and their families attended classes in hygiene and physical fitness, or classes in homemaking, manual arts, and traditional crafts, designed to counterbalance the exacting demands of their jobs. Like Nelson, Patterson encouraged employees to decorate their houses with fancy shingles, brackets, and railings, which had been turned out in the manual arts classes, and to plant flowers and shrubs in their gardens. These benefits proved to be inadequate curbs against union activity. Patterson was incensed when his workers organized a strike. He persuaded the strike leaders to come to the NCF headquarters in New York for arbitration, where they agreed to establish a labor bureau, with Patterson as director, to mediate disputes. The workers' principal gain was the promise of company-built housing, available for sale or rent to approximately half the work force.

By 1910, the publicity campaigns of the NCF and the League for Social Service had excited a new interest in modern industrial town planning. Reformers, journalists, and federal investigators for the Bureau of Labor Statistics toured American industrial towns. Their reports often included summaries of discussions with individual managers and owners, who explained the intentions behind their welfare programs. Desire for control over workers was a primary reason for sponsoring housing. One text presented responses from a study of 350 manufacturers and yielded the collective opinion that "A Housed Labor Supply Is a Controlled Labor Supply."[14] Managers reasoned that a stable work force would be more loyal and less likely to go out on strike, and would save the firm the expense of training new employees. Good housing would increase the proportions of married men, who were considered more stable and less volatile than roving single males. Advertisements for skilled workers stressed the benefits for a man's wife and children in a model town with company-built housing. In exchange, the family would be dependent on the company for their improved way of life.

Dependency was considered stronger if the company retained ownership of the houses, renting them below the going private market rates. (The rents were usually a week's salary.) Programs of hiring and firing —or threatening to discharge an employee—worked most efficaciously in conjunction with company control of the housing stock. Nonetheless, the memory of Pullman dissuaded many industrialists from total ownership of the town. The Stetson Hat Company of Philadelphia and the Procter & Gamble Company of Ivorydale, near Cincinnati, encouraged homeownership. Industrial suburbs like Firestone Park and Goodyear Heights, outside Akron, Ohio, were responses not only to employee pressure but to the fact that Akron could not meet housing and recreational needs during the rapid expansion of the two companies. The presidents of Firestone and Goodyear set up banks to make houses available to their employees at 5 percent down and $20–$30 per month.[15] Both believed that the worker who was able to invest in private property had a stake in social and political stability; he would become provident, in his savings and his actions, and would be less likely to participate in union activity.

Improving workers' health was another goal of model-town planning. Sanitary houses meant fewer days lost due to illness. Improved plumbing figured prominently in all descriptions of the towns, even if the facilities were only outhouses, a pattern that continued in the South, especially for black and Appalachian workers. Planners paid special attention to water supplies, sewage treatment, drainage, and such details as window screens. Classes in home medical care, nursing, and nutrition were offered to housewives in the town, and temperance campaigns became a routine aspect of "constructive welfare work." Saloons were outlawed, and clubhouses and social halls were "dry."

Employers recognized the publicity potential of planned communities and special services. Firms that hired many women and children were especially aware of their image as responsible employers. The managers claimed to protect these fragile beings from the onorous, unpleasant, and slightly immoral aspects of industrial life. Kindergartens and company-built schools provided a few hours of reading, writing, and manual training. The matron hired by the Wagner Electric Company of St. Louis had all the machines where women worked painted white in order to "cater to the neatness and innate delicacy of women."[16] Different schedules for women and men, modest uniforms or dress codes for female employees, and women's clubhouses, lunchrooms, and boarding-houses were common features.

Leifur Magnusson's 1917 survey of 350 industrialists noted their consensus that model towns "advertise the company and keep it favorable before the public."[17] Judge Gary and George Perkins, the main forces behind the welfare programs initiated at U. S. Steel, sought to promote a good trust image while retaining skilled employees and forestalling unionization. The Rockefeller Foundation's Bureau for Social Hygiene undertook extensive research all over the country on the benefits—to worker and management alike—of decent housing. *Camp and Plant,* a weekly magazine of local gossip and company propaganda published between 1901 and 1904 by the Sociological Department of the Rockefellers' Colorado Fuel and Iron Company, showed both model homes and workplaces on its cover.

Even in the best model towns, not all employees received the attentions of both an architect and a social secretary. Generally, only skilled workers lived in company-built houses and attended company-financed social programs. Welfare work was designed to reinforce hierarchy and upward mobility among employees. (The wives of lower-paid workmen were sometimes required to attend domestic-science classes in a large model home which encouraged them to aspire to a higher level of domesticity and homeownership.) In industries with many immigrant or black employees, the white native-born Americans received significantly more benefits. In 1920, the average model industrial town provided company-built housing for only a third of the workers.[18] Higher proportions of company-built houses in southern textile villages and western mining camps reflected out-of-the-way locations.

The less-skilled workers in any industrial town usually had to live in very crowded quarters. Although planners and managers disapproved of boarding—asserting that it broke down the "home influence" of the nuclear family—many families had to take in additional persons to augment the man's paycheck. Single men preferred to live with a family, since conditions in lodging houses were notoriously poor. The boarder usually looked forward to bringing over his family from Europe or saving money in order to start a household of his own. Working-class families also considered this a temporary situation, hoping to improve their financial circumstances. Yet economic pressures meant that between one quarter and one half of all working-class households, in cities and in company towns, included boarders or lodgers.[19]

The cover of a weekly publication issued by the Colorado Fuel and Iron Company emphasized that the company officials were equally concerned with the employees' working conditions and their homes.

Settlements of Slavic laborers, known as "Hunkeyvilles" in most company towns, often had the most severe overcrowding problems. The average unskilled steelworker in Homestead, Pennsylvania, earned $1.65 a day, making it almost imperative that his wife earn additional money by seeing after boarders.[20] Sociologists reported many households where every room served as a bedroom for several people. Sometimes a folding bed did double service: first during the twelve-hour day shift, and then during the night shift. Yet, the system was not as fragmented as it seemed to company social workers. Many boarders were relatives: an unmarried uncle, a widower grandfather, a young second cousin. Others had come from the same village in Europe. (Italians were even more likely to maintain strong village ties, naming old friends *compari*, or godfathers, to strengthen the bonds.) The families who shared a court behind their tenement dwellings generally tended to be of the same ethnic group and often intermarried. In the earliest stages of industrialization, men had been able to select the relatives and friends who would work alongside them in the factories; but by the turn of the century, domestic ties and fraternal organizations played the major role in maintaining extended family and ethnic relations.

All sorts of social activities took place outside the houses. At weddings or christenings, the courtyard or street was given over to music and dancing. On fortnightly Pay Fridays, the streets were filled with roving bands and merrymakers, and stores stayed open all evening. Churches and lodges or ethnic organizations sponsored many events. The nickelodeon, skating rink, dance hall, and saloon also functioned as extensions of the cramped houses. Men spent many of their non-working hours socializing in saloons and lodge halls, or meeting with fellow workers in union headquarters. Often these public activities were scenes of conflict and tensions. Saloons that brought together people from different ethnic backgrounds were likely to be the scene of fights. Gambling halls and brothels—which provided a few of the limited jobs open to blacks in many company towns—erupted with brawls and police raids from time to time.

Most immigrant groups, especially the Italians and the Irish, protected their womenfolk almost to the point of confinement. Few Italian women, and almost none who were married, were permitted to work in the factories; and fathers and brothers often prohibited their unmarried daughters or sisters from visiting dance halls. Young women might attend the company-sponsored classes in homemaking and nutrition, where they learned domestic habits that were quite different from those of their families; yet most of them held to their mothers' traditions, in part because it was so expensive to implement the "scientific" standards of classes. While immigrant women participated in church-related events, charity organizations, kindergartens, and female service clubs in their towns, home and family were the focus of their lives.

For most working-class people, the enlightened employer's emphasis on the home was not necessarily considered inappropriate, especially if he promoted homeownership. Property as well as occupation conferred status. Families often sacrificed their children's education so that the offspring could contribute wages as soon as possible; women did extra work inside the home; and men labored at several jobs—rather than advancing careers at one—in order to buy a house. Few of these households foreclosed on mortgages, except during depressions, when mass layoffs occurred.

In towns where the company retained ownership of all housing, or in cases where the family could not afford a down payment, the upkeep of the dwelling was a central concern. The smallest home testified to the occupants' attention to appearance and detail. Margaret Byington's account of the discomforts in a typical two-room tenement in Homestead, shared by a Slavic family and their boarders, conveys a sense of continual frustrations, but also of important domestic pleasures:

> The kitchen, perhaps 15 by 12 feet, was steaming with vapor from a big washtub set on a chair in the middle of the room. The mother was trying to wash and at the same time to keep the older of her two babies from tumbling into the tub full of scalding water that was standing on the floor. On one side of the room was a huge puffy bed, with one feather tick to sleep on and another for covering; near the window stood a sewing machine; in the corner, an organ—all these besides the inevitable cook stove upon which in the place of honor was simmering the evening's soup. Upstairs in the second room were one boarder and the man of the house asleep. Two more boarders were at work, but at night would be home to sleep in the bed from which the others would get up.[21]

These descriptions, and the photographs by Lewis Hine that accompanied Byington's study, reveal some of the ways in which immigrant families tried to maximize the pleasant atmosphere of their homes. Even poor families purchased an organ or a piano. There were pictures on the wall, plush chairs and bric-à-brac in the parlor. Newly married couples bought heavy ornamental furniture on the installment plan. Lace curtains, religious icons, family mementos, and shawls and doilies draped over tables and chairs graced the best room, even though it usually served as a bedroom at night. Some families pasted up scraps of printed wallpapers; like the newspapers on the walls in very poor households, these bits and pieces laid over one another served as additional insulation. The home was an important place for family life and entertaining. In the evening, relatives and friends gathered either in the kitchen or the front room to sing, dance, play cards, court, and socialize.

To most observers, who never saw the interiors of these homes, it was the uniform façades that were characteristic of every industrial town, whether or not it had been planned by experts. Speculative builders used

· ·

Frances Johnson photographed the parlor of a miner's cottage in Shenandoah City, Pennsylvania, in 1892, capturing the occupants' desire to maintain traditions in their home with photographs, handed-down furniture, and domestic pride.

only one prototype for economic reasons; planners imposed limits on architectural variations for ideological reasons, contending that a limited number of styles yielded order and economy. Many company towns required that residents use the same materials for their façades and even the same colors of paint or varnish. Houses for employees of the J. B. Cornell Company in Cold Spring, New York, designed by the president himself, were all built according to the same rectilinear plan, with white paint on the first story and stained shingles on the second. All the houses built by the N. O. Nelson Company sported yellow and white paint. Architects imposed one style over an entire town, whether it was Colonial Revival in Eclipse Park, Wisconsin, or pastel-tinted Mission Revival adobe in Tyrone, New Mexico. To the industrialists, the uniformity of the residential environment was a symbol of modern industrial order: a balance between comfort for the residents and control for the employer.

. . . .

The company town of Jenners, Pennsylvania, photographed by the Consolidated Coal Welfare Department around 1915, was a model of industrial welfare. The uniform houses were separated from one another by new fences. In the private gardens, families grew flowers and vegetables. Despite the emphasis on privacy, each family usually took in boarders, especially since these houses were quite large.

Sociologists who described model industrial towns also praised regularity, criticizing the hodgepodge effect of different shapes and styles, and the random placement of buildings when there was no central planning. G. W. W. Hanger, a federal statistician analyzing the model-town phenomenon in 1904, pointed out how the minimal houses built by the Colorado Fuel and Iron Company contrasted with the earlier habitations the miners had built for themselves. "Arranged in regular order upon streets," he wrote, "they appear to decided advantage by the side of the older and more poorly disposed dwellings of the place."[22] The pages of *Camp and Plant* were filled with photographs of new, company-built cottages, juxtaposed with crude huts built of scrap wood, rammed earth, and abandoned debris. Each was labeled as the kind of dwelling an Italian, Navaho, Mexican, or Welsh miner would build on his own.

Control over workers and the visible expression of efficiency were two principal goals of company housing in industrial towns. But employees sometimes demanded more than architectural benefits when working conditions were especially poor. The extent of management control in a group of model towns precipitated one of the more infamous incidents of American industrial repression. The Colorado Fuel and Iron Company had spent money on arms and guards, as well as on workers' housing. In 1913, at Ludlow, guards killed several miners in a dispute over wages and mine safety. The Ludlow Massacre won sympathy for those miners and their strike from people across the nation. Mother Jones came to Colorado to help organize the many different nationalities of men employed in the camps. The New York *Tenants Weekly* called for the nationalization of the mines, declaring that company housing meant very little when the company had such authoritarian control over its workers' lives.[23] The Rockefellers, who owned the company, although obviously opposed to nationalization, testified before Congress that more reforms were in order. As with the strikes at Pullman and Homestead, national debate about this form of industrial control over work and home was widespread and passionate. Details of the specific industrial town were contested; but neither reformers, industrialists, nor union leaders questioned the right for workers to have decent housing and decent working conditions—within the context of company "welfare work."

CHAPTER ELEVEN

LANNED RESIDENTIAL COMMUNITIES

Maintaining a high percentage of individual
home-owners is one of the searching tests that now
challenge the people of the United States. The present
large proportion of families that own their homes is both
the foundation of a sound economic and social system
and a guarantee that our society will continue to develop
rationally as changing conditions demand.

—Herbert Hoover, forward to the U. S. Department of
Commerce publication *How To Own Your Home* (1923)

DESPITE HIS PERSISTENTLY-OPTIMISTIC
tone, Herbert Hoover saw the housing situation in the 1920s as a
critical problem. Although residential construction had increased
dramatically since the First World War, it lay on a precarious
foundation. Booms and collapses plagued the real-estate market;
the residential mortgage debt had tripled in one decade; and the
number of foreclosures mounted precipitously at the decade's end.
In addition, the percentage of homeowners had been steadily declining; and there were reports by such housing reformers as Edith
Elmer Wood that up to one third of the nation was poorly housed.[1]
Hoover was concerned. To him, stable homes were the bulwark of
good citizenship. Private homes encouraged individuality; and residential construction, together with real-estate investments, played
key roles in the national economy.

The new kinds of housing in the 1920s represented attempts to
redress problems in the American housing system without introducing overly radical alternatives. In the process, two conflicting
characteristics—personalized design and uniform planning—were
hastily welded together. Thus, while fanciful cottages with imitation thatch roofs or Mediterranean courtyards evoked the mood of

the decade, the appearance of individuality was often illusory. Most new dwelling units were set in large planned communities, which were almost entirely residential and homogeneous.

A broad coalition of developers and realtors, architects and builders, government officials and sociologists, interior decorators and housewives, union leaders and urban reformers, engineered the residential patterns of the 1920s. Each sought ways to preserve the nuclear family, bolster the economy, provide more affordable houses, or encourage community participation. And they all believed in more tightly organized planning for residential areas. Accordingly, federal agencies, municipal zoning

· ·

A street in St. Paul, Minnesota, with houses of the mid–1920s, shows the decade's fascination with diminutive scale and quaint architecture. The developer balanced this picturesque quality with the obvious repetition of the same overall plan for every house on the block.

boards, incorporated homeowners' associations, and local art juries set building controls to regulate the production, appearance, and social composition of residential environments. Even the celebration of the individual home presumed that neighborhood homogeneity was necessary.

The 1920 census showed that only 46 percent of all American families were homeowners. That figure was even lower in most metropolitan areas: 27 percent in New Orleans, 25 percent in Atlanta, 18 percent in Boston, and 12 percent in New York City.[2] An economic depression in 1921 aggravated the postwar housing shortage, limiting the number of new permits and increasing the price of housing that was being built. (The average cost for a new dwelling rose $1,000, from $3,972 in 1921 to $4,937 in 1928.) *Building Age* estimated early in the decade that 500,000 new dwellings, at a minimum, were needed, yet the construction industry was stagnant.[3] Senator James Wadsworth, promoting a bill to finance housing cooperatives and to research cooperative efforts in the American past, proclaimed that the country had a housing shortage of dangerous proportions. Edith Elmer Wood insisted that the figure was almost always underestimated, given the poor quality of housing available to the poor and working classes.

The census also noted that for the first time in the nation's history, the majority of Americans were classified as urban or suburban. The outlying or suburban areas of metropolitan regions were adding to their populations at a faster rate than the central cores. In the decade of the 1920s, the suburbs grew twice as rapidly as the center cities, reaching a population of 17 million by 1930. The most prestigious developments increased at spectacular rates: Beverly Hills by 2,500 percent; Shaker Heights by 1,000 percent.[4] The entire state of Florida suddenly boomed with instant metropolitan areas. These wildly successful real-estate promotions advertised natural resources, pleasant social life, and sound economic value—all standard suburban claims.

Families who invested in the suburban way of life hoped to find both individual freedom and social stability. Many sociologists and planners considered the suburban trend the saving grace of America, embodying a combination of small-town virtues and urban amenities in a carefully planned environment.

But not everyone was so enthusiastic. Lewis Mumford criticized suburban selfishness and aimlessness. "Household administrator" Christine Frederick told readers of *Outlook* why she wanted to move back to a city apartment and leave behind the "delusion of the suburbs." Looking for rest and community, she had found only "neat little toy houses on their neat little patches of lawn and their neat little colonial lives, to say nothing of the neat little housewives and their neat little children—all set in neat rows, for all the world like children's blocks."[5] Other critics discussed the self-conscious wholesomeness of the suburbs, the social and economic homogeneity, the expense, and the loneliness generated by so much privacy and so artificial a social life. Nonetheless, most popular middle-class literature, housing guides, and even architects' manuals and government documents praised the suburbs as the haven of "normalcy" —the word that had helped Harding and Coolidge, before Hoover's own election, win their way into the White House.

As Secretary of Commerce under these two earlier administrations, Herbert Hoover led the campaign to involve the federal government in promoting normalcy through better housing. His goal was a cooperative, voluntary association between government, business, and civic groups. Hoover believed that the expansion of government programs during the war years, including the construction of housing units for war workers and standardization of many critical materials, would not threaten private enterprise, provided it, too, grew stronger. Hoover's plan was for government to sponsor agencies and committees tied to private groups or local associations. The state would function as a clearing house for information, while business and community organizations developed new markets for continuing national prosperity.

Hoover first advocated a coordinated program to relieve the housing shortage and stimulate the flagging construction industry in 1920. The next year, after taking office, he made such cooperation one of his department's policies. Hoover supported the "Own Your Home" campaign, launched by the Department of Labor to encourage homeownership; this included the sale of federally financed housing for war workers through local realtors. He also backed California's Veterans' Farm and Home Purchase Act of 1921, designed to bolster construction by providing 250 farms and five thousand homes.[6]

Hoover's policies made their mark on Washington's bureaucracies. The Bureau of Standards (created during World War I and greatly expanded in the 1920s) tested fire-retardant materials, waterproofing techniques, accoustics, and such household products as silver polish. It encouraged manufacturers to standardize and reduce the varieties of mattresses, bricks, and carpet tacks. The Bureau of Home Economics, created in 1923, published studies on household efficiency and home appliances. An Advisory Committee on Building Codes was set up to evaluate the 850 separate local codes and to promote uniform practices across the country. The Division of Building and Housing, established in 1921, oversaw a network of committees composed of professional advisers in real estate, construction, and building-materials production, who sought to modernize American building practices. Their goals were mass-production and year-round, rather than seasonal, construction. Results included the first standard grading scales for building materials and a set of uniform construction details. The division also issued a model zoning enabling act for states in 1924 and one for municipalities in 1927. Books, pamphlets, and numerous conferences publicized the new guidelines.

Under Hoover's direction, fourteen Homemaking Information Centers and seven New England Urban Home Bureaus, most of which had been organized as part of war conservation efforts, continued to provide classes and publications on such topics as household budgets, child care, and house planning. Agricultural Extension Services, funded partly through the Department of Agriculture, the Smith-Hughes Act (1917), and the George-Reed Act (1927), sponsored classes for rural women. The Women's National Farm and Garden Association and the National Grange promoted homeownership, convenient and healthy farm homes, and rural beautification programs.

Better Homes in America, Inc., fulfilled Hoover's goal of voluntary cooperation between government and private enterprise in the public interest. The movement began in 1922, under the auspices of Mrs. William Brown Meloney, editor of *The Delineator,* a women's magazine. She asked Hoover to serve as president of the organization; Vice-President Calvin Coolidge served as chairman of the advisory council. Within a year, the organization had branches in over five hundred communities and headquarters in Washington, establishing close ties to the government. Though the national headquarters sponsored conferences, classes, and publications, the primary focus was on local committees. By 1930 there were 7,279 Better Homes committees across the country.[7] During national Better Homes Week (usually the last week in April), each local committee sponsored home-improvement contests, prizes for the most convenient kitchen, demonstrations of construction and remodeling techniques, and lectures on how good homes build character.

The highlight of Better Homes Week was the demonstration house. During the preceding year, local architects, builders, and home economists in each participating community joined forces either to build or choose an exemplary moderate-cost dwelling and then to furnish it. The house was open to the public for tours and special events. In some communities, local builders donated the models as practice houses for home-economics classes. In rural areas, particularly those in the South, committees sponsored home-remodeling campaigns aimed at black families and white industrial workers. During Better Homes Week, they encouraged whitewashing, painting, and home repairs.

Most cities had one model home, but Santa Barbara, an exception, had thirty-two homes on display one year.[8] In 1926, over two hundred communities built model houses at an average cost of $3,500. In 1930, after the stock market crash, 682 brand-new single-family dwellings at an average cost of $1,885 (exclusive of land) were on display across the country, and a total of four thousand houses were open for tours.[9]

Better Homes enthusiasts were not idle during the rest of the year. In towns, suburbs, and rural areas, they came together to discuss zoning, construction standards, decoration, and citizenship. Boys learned to erect "boy-built" houses; girls learned to make them attractive. Topics of Better Homes forums included mortgage financing, sanitation, racial strife, and Communist threats to private enterprise. It was believed that these problems could be attacked through the home.

The Better Homes movement focused on housing in rural areas and suburbs. Urban workers and their families, however, also needed inexpensive, convenient apartments; and a few individuals and companies tried to bring attention to that need. The Metropolitan Life Insurance Company and the estate of Marshall Field erected housing for middle-income workers in New York and Chicago. The philanthropic Paul Lawrence Dunbar Apartments in Harlem and the Michigan Boulevard Garden Apartments in Chicago were subsidized housing that the tenants—lower-income black families in both cases—managed themselves through cooperative boards. New York Governor Alfred E. Smith prodded the legislature to pass the State Housing Act in 1926, which provided tax abatements for limited-dividend companies that sponsored moderate-cost housing projects.

Unions as well as philanthropists took advantage of the New York law. While both groups favored the tenants' cooperative ownership of a project, this approach required residents with moderate rather than low incomes. In 1928, the Amalgamated Clothing Workers completed five brick buildings in the Bronx, and 304 families moved in. There was a long waiting list for rooms renting at $11 per month, plus an initial $500 per room to join the cooperative.[10] These new "co-operators" quickly began organizing. Within five years, the Bronx Coop had its own nursery school, supervised playground, school bus, library, clinic, laundry, electric current generator, and numerous social and political clubs. A grocery cooperative purchased ice, milk, eggs, and other items, and sold them at discount to members.

While the Bronx Coop had supporters and loyal tenants—many of whom still reside there—the cooperative movement as a means of providing moderate-cost housing gained little ground outside New York City. The owner-occupied single-family detached house in the suburbs remained the prevailing ideal, endorsed by government and business, civic groups and labor unions. In fact, several labor organizations raised capital to underwrite mortgages for their members' suburban houses. The Central Labor Union of Minneapolis, the Railroad Trainmen's American Home Builders Association, and six other groups made low-interest loans available to members. The Brotherhood of Locomotive Engineers developed an entire town of detached bungalows in Florida. The black Brotherhood of Sleeping Car Porters, based in Oakland, California, fought for legislation and company policies to help members buy homes and spend more time with their families.

Both cooperatives and union-sponsored mortgage programs existed because of the acknowledged risks of investing in real estate. Prices were rising rapidly, and conventional financing institutions offered difficult terms. A first mortgage, covering only 50–60 percent of the total cost, had to be paid back in five to seven years. A typical second mortgage, necessary for many families, was 18 percent for three years.[11] The contract-for-deed plan, which involved monthly payments of twice the rent until the house was paid off, generally contained a clause by which the house reverted to the title holder if the occupant missed two payments.

Despite the risks, more and more groups expressed an interest in the single-family suburban housing market. Soon after the government launched its drive to increase the number of moderate-cost dwellings, the architectural profession began a campaign to "recapture" that market (though it had never controlled it). In 1921, the Architects' Small House Service Bureau was founded in Minneapolis with the intention of cornering a part of the suburban market, which had nearly tripled between 1920 and 1922, and reached a high of 572,000 units per year at mid-decade.[12] Robert T. Jones, the bureau's technical director, claimed that the architectural profession was demonstrating its sense of civic responsibility by providing a service, making a reasonable profit, and offering a rational approach to the housing business. Hoover and the Commerce Department enthusiastically endorsed the program.

In the bureau's main office, architects and draftsmen produced stock plans for three-room to six-room houses and made them available at the minimal price of $6 per room. For houses larger than six rooms, the staff unequivocally recommended the personalized services of a professional architect. Recognizing the potential profitability to the profession, the American Institute of Architects officially sponsored the bureau, even though some members disavowed this endorsement of standardized designs.

Although its plans were anonymous, produced cooperatively, and intentionally understated, the bureau did not promote a campaign for modern standardization, such as the avante-garde Europeans were espousing. The service offered over 250 rather conservative designs for varying conditions, budgets, and tastes. Subsidiary regional offices, in addition to the Minneapolis headquarters, developed houses that took into account the historic traditions of a particular area, as well as its climate and native building materials. This was not grand architecture and almost never incorporated the flat roofs and severe lines of "modern architecture." Tiny front porches with built-in benches, carefully executed colonial-style doorways, window boxes, and shutters were among the details aimed at pleasing the public. The plans circulated nationwide through home magazines, special plan books, and the monthly bureau magazine, *The Small Home*. Better Homes committees backed the program, and courses on owner-built construction, such as the YMCA's "Own Your Home" curricula, used the bureau service.

Planning by suburban developers of the 1920s extended to every aspect of the residential environment. The new label of "developer" implied large-scale operations. Before developers put up lots for sale, they set standards for all future construction. Decisions determining the width of streets, the choice of a grid or a curved layout, the size of sewer systems and water reservoirs, the bulldozing or preservation of existing land and trees, and provision for transportation facilities all had implications for the size and class base of a subdivision. Regulations might also specify minimum dimensions for lots and houses; placement of outbuildings, such as garages; optimal distance from house to street; even the style of architecture and height of fences. Planner John Nolen praised such "Safe Guards Against Incongruity"; and the National Association of Real Estate Boards, the National Housing Association, and Better Homes in America, Inc., strongly endorsed each of these forms of architectural controls.[13]

Architectural regulations became common in urban and suburban communities throughout the country. Statutes against billboards and motley buildings were upheld in the courts so long as some potential danger, such as fire or loss of property value, was regulated. Southern California had numerous communities with aesthetic "police power" controls.[14] Older established towns like Santa Barbara and Ojai passed ordinances requiring that new downtown buildings conform to the Spanish Colonial Revival style in order to build a tourist trade based on the aristocratic grandee aspects of their Hispanic heritage. Entire new communities—Rancho Santa Fe, San Clemente, Palos Verdes Estates—

. . . .

The Architects' Small House Service Bureau produced hundreds of anonymous plans for detached suburban houses like this one: traditional in sentiment, economical in construction, and modern in its appliances.

were executed in this mode. In Palos Verdes, a 3,000-acre site south of Los Angeles, an art jury had to approve all plans for houses and strongly advocated "California architecture," with light colors in stucco or concrete and low-pitched roofs.

Upper-middle-class communities were especially likely to have a battery of aesthetic and legal regulations. The Country Club District, outside Kansas City, won international renown because of its extensive and effective controls. Jesse Clyde Nichols, developer of the district, began assembling land in 1908 and started building in 1922. By the end of the decade, he had accumulated six thousand acres, supervised construction of six thousand homes in thirty-three separate subdivisions, built four golf clubs, and spent $250,000 on imported art objects to adorn street corners and parks.[15] He had begun with minimum standards of $3,000 houses and six lots to the acre, and then continued increasing the minimum cost and size of the houses.

Nichols's major innovation was the self-perpetuating deed restriction, which provided that stipulations laid down by the developer would continue indefinitely unless a majority of owners in the subdivision voted to change them at least five years before the expiration of the 25-year term. Elected volunteer boards of residents, called Homes Associations, enforced the regulations and saw to it that property owners paid dues, which were used to maintain streets, parks, and unsold lots. The associations also added new ordinances to regulate sub-leases and sales. This aspect of centralized control, which will be discussed in greater detail at the end of the chapter, seemed entirely normal at the time. It was primarily the aesthetic regulations that brought planners from across the nation, from England, South America, and Australia, to the Country Club District, where they admired its harmonious architecture; its subtle controls over form, color, and roof lines; its land-use regulations; and the community spirit of the Homes Associations.

Seeking to create a vision of harmony and community spirit, many other developers and builders of the 1920s used uniform themes for subdivisions and blocks of new houses. Most of the styles were period revivals, the most popular being the "English" style, with a steeply pitched roof and half-timbering. Local architectural traditions were also incorporated. In the Southwest, stucco houses with heavy timber beams, built around patios and arcades that led to living rooms and dining rooms, simulated older adobe houses and Indian pueblos. In the Philadelphia suburbs, architects renovated old German farmhouses, while developers created new communities of picturesque brick-and-stone houses, resembling those quaint farms. The Monterey ranch house, opening onto a patio, with a second-story balcony across its entire width, formed the basis for a vernacular revival in northern California. And in fast-growing Florida, architect Addison Mizner led a Mediterranean renaissance, which resulted in mansions and small houses adorned with terraces, fountains, and tiles—everywhere the allure of resort architecture.

Later in the decade, historical interest led to the establishment of preservation and restoration programs in Santa Fe, New Mexico; Cohasset, Massachusetts; and many other towns. Restoration of colonial Williamsburg, funded by the Rockefellers, began in 1927. Jesse Clyde Nichols preserved a Shawnee mission and a pre–Civil War "colonial homestead" by persuading the state to share the expenses. The architecture of the past, preserving both real and imagined traditions, evoked idealized village life and made people proud of their modern improvements.

However, not all the new suburbs of the decade catered to the wealthy. Mariemont, outside Cincinnati, was established by Mrs. Mary M. Emery and the executor of her estate, Charles J. Livingood, as a residential community "for all classes," but predominantly for industrial workers. There was some ambiguity about whether this was a model suburb, since the purpose of the Mariemont Corporation was to produce "a real-estate development pure and simple, on normal American lines," and not to fund a philanthropy.[16] Architectural controls raised no such controversy. Mariemont's planner, John Nolen, called his scheme "A New Town Built to Produce Local Happiness."[17] All utility lines were hidden underground, and a central steam plant supplied heating for each cottage or group dwelling. Nolen had sixteen architects design the residences in order to create a balance between aesthetic diversity and a definite Tudor-style harmony for the entire community. His efforts to create a planned suburb were costly, but the result did appeal to middle-class families. Although Emery and Livingood had wanted to create a model suburb for a mix of classes, they believed more strongly in allowing the market to function freely. Since they had insisted from the start that industrial workers should have homes separated from industry, just like white-collar workers, it was easy for Mariemont to become a middle-class bedroom suburb of Cincinnati.

Because most moderate-cost suburbs had neither planners nor architects, their "look" was either monotonous or amusingly diversified. Speculative builders bought narrow lots from developers and put up rows of identical bungalows facing bare front yards and a gridiron of wide, paved streets. The construction was often fast and flimsy, and the uniformity, oppressive. In suburbs where middle-class families hired their own builders, there was extraordinary diversity among the tiny cottages. Home magazines provided models for the dream house: an Inca temple of decorated concrete blocks; a Cotswolds cottage, with a steeply pitched "thatch" roof and round tower; a stately Italian villa, with grills on the windows and tiles on the roof. Versions of these incongruous fantasies, each on its own well-tended patch of lawn, stood alongside one another.

By the late 1920s, the more alluring historical styles had become prevalent and were often taken as themes for medium-scale speculative developments. Entire blocks were laid out with quaint Mission bunga-

. . . .

An advertisement, ca. 1928, for the Los Angeles subdivision of Westwood Hills evokes the serenity of a planned residential community. The Spanish colonial revival was one of the favored styles for southern California architects and developers of the 1920s.

lows or enticing English cottages. An advertisement for Westwood Hills, a 1928 single-family residential development in Los Angeles, emphasized the reassuring sense of cohesive, stable community through the view of other similar Spanish Colonial Revival dwellings. There was clearly a relationship between these designs and the alarming state of the real-estate market. After 1925, foreclosures began to increase. As investors turned toward more lucrative fields, especially the stock market, developers sought to attract the attention of prospective buyers with ever more fanciful residential architecture.

A few far-sighted individuals promoted a combination of regional planning, land-use sanctions, and architectural controls. They hoped to stabilize residential development, to modernize the suburbs, and to open them to more moderate-income families. The best-known ventures were sponsored by New York's limited-dividend City Housing Corporation. Their first project, Sunnyside Gardens, was constructed between 1924 and 1928, in Queens. Unable to convince borough authorities to modify the grid pattern of the streets, architects Clarence Stein and Henry Wright built brick row houses enlosing large interior courts, which were cooperatively owned and maintained. Each group of residents decided how to use their court: for common playgrounds or gardens or, in later years, dividing it into conventional backyards. Wright gave each residence some architectural distinction, balancing the standardized layouts with a variety of roof lines, porches, and brick details. The carefully chosen community consisted mostly of teachers and skilled craftsmen, and many of the families remained in Sunnyside for generations.[18]

The City Housing Corporation's next project was a more adventurous and more influential scheme. The suburban location and rather conventional colonial architecture made Radburn, New Jersey, easily acceptable. The town was designed for white-collar families with children, a car, and a decent, but not high, income. It was divided into three "neighborhoods," each with a shopping center and a school. A municipal association of experts appointed by the City Housing Corporation and advised by a local citizens' association administered Radburn, though power eventually shifted to the community group. The designers believed that their plan would result in the best management for the town and would strengthen social bonds among residents. As Stein later wrote: "The wide-spread parks, the safe footpaths for pedestrians, giving easy access to the homes of neighbors, all led the way to friendliness and neighborliness."[19]

Radburn, advertised as "A Town for the Motor Age," had carefully

Sunnyside Gardens, a model suburb of row houses and detached dwellings in Queens, was built in 1928 for New York's City Housing Corporation by architects Clarence Stein and Henry Wright. Seeking to balance the public and the private, they provided communal yards and small private gardens, uniform architecture and personalized brick detailing on each house.

planned road systems for separating pedestrian and vehicular traffic. The roadways formed "superblocks" of thirty to fifty acres. Within each superblock, narrow cul-de-sac streets led to the houses, which faced large interior parks and an elaborate footpath system. Children could walk almost anywhere without crossing traffic, and adults could reach their automobiles quickly. The most highly praised suburban development of the decade planned for its residents, in part, by planning for their cars.

Increasing reliance on the car had many effects on residential planning, as motor vehicle registration jumped from 9 million in 1920 to 20 million in 1930.[20] Across the country, engineers perfected refinements in transportation systems: divided highways, traffic circles, timed traffic lights, great bridges, and the Holland Tunnel. Suburban developers paved roads and installed cement curbs and gutters. Garages became standard in almost every class of development, as even working-class families took out loans in order to buy cars. To make driving easier and

· ·

Radburn, New Jersey, the major project of the City Housing Corporation begun in 1929, suburbanized the planning scheme of Sunnyside. Here were larger colonial revival detached houses and an extensive common green. Its publication in *The Home and the Child,* issued by the 1931 White House Conference on Child Health, shows how quickly this plan was taken up as a positive national prototype for residential developments.

more pleasurable, some developers abandoned the familiar rectilinear grid street and laid out wide, curving streets and cul-de-sacs. Suburban shopping centers, with off-street parking lots, provided new sources of profit for developers. Local officials passed bonds to buy school buses and to improve the quality of roadways leading into the residential neighborhoods.

Electricity was another major technological improvement that affected the home of the 1920s. "A house twenty years old is antiquated," said one historian of housing. "It is likely to be of a type not easily adapted to present-day conditions of living, nor to the installment and economical use of modern equipment."[21] The value of electrical household appliances produced in the United States increased from $23 million in 1915 to $83 million in 1920 and $180 million in 1929. The Commerce Department announced that whereas only 16 percent of the population had lived in dwellings with electric lights in 1912, that figure had risen to 63 percent in 1927.[22] In addition to electric lighting, households acquired vacuum sweepers, irons, refrigerators, stoves, fans, and floor waxers. Sockets were installed at convenient places so that the housewife no longer needed to plug her electric toaster into the ceiling light fixture.

Advertisements proliferated as producers began to promote their products more boldly. Images of progress beamed from General Electric ads linking "The Suffrage and the Switch." Advertisers exploited people's fears of being out of date: four-color spreads told of teenage children meeting friends at a speak-easy because home had the wrong kind of furniture; or of business deals falling through when word got around that the Joneses' house needed a new paint job. Some ads chastised husbands for making their wives suffer needlessly in hot kitchens with unwieldy appliances. Others suggested that social acceptance depended on modern bathroom fixtures and fashionable décor. But most scolding fingers pointed toward the mother and housewife, challenging her choice of products for kitchen, nursery, bathroom, and living room.

The services of interior decorators suddenly seemed necessary to achieve a "cozy," "personalized" home. The color craze of the 1920s assumed that only a trained designer could balance the lively mixtures of bright colors through which families expressed themselves. Decorators also attended to the housewife's peace of mind, often using psychological jargon about "fulfillment," "anxiety," and "status."

Emily Post and other decorators parlayed Sigmund Freud and Havelock Ellis into a formula of "sex psychology" for decorating and architecture. "The kind of room a man likes" had dark colors, substantial furniture, and bold, rugged materials. A study or a corner of the living room might conform to this description. "The lady's touch" was more pervasive, exemplified in chintzes and floral patterns, delicate furniture, and lacy curtains, though the adventurous woman could also express her femininity in colonial antiques or in modern Art Deco "skyscraper furniture."

With the new freedom to discuss women's sexual needs and methods of contraception, the bedroom became a prime topic in women's magazines. The influence of movies was such that twin beds—required for

. . . .

An advertisement in *The House Beautiful* (1928) depicted the spacious suburban house as an ideal setting for child-rearing, since it provided special places for children's play.

The right atmosphere for the children's playroom

bedroom scenes by film decency codes—became a fad. The woman's dressing table, with its large, round mirror and its array of cosmetics and perfume bottles, emphasized sensuality. While some journalists continued to present the parents' bedroom as an extension of the nursery, others suggested that it was a room for adults.

A renewed focus was placed on the close-knit family, and this had its effect throughout the house. Heating manufacturers promoted the conversion of the basement into a family "recreation room." With smaller furnaces, there was room for a pool table or a family pageant, as endorsed by *Better Homes in America Guides.* Advertisements for radios showed contented families gathered together in the living room, listening to a program on their new set. Electrical manufacturers promised that laborsaving devices would give mothers more time to spend with their children. This was, in fact, a period in which many children were choosing *not* to spend free time at home. [Robert and Helen Merrell Lynd's classic study of *Middletown* (1929) describes fights between parents and offspring over sex, alcohol, curfews, movies, and friends.] Advertisements claimed that certain products would bring the family closer together.

The appeal of the suburbs had a great deal to do with anxiety about child-rearing, about giving one's children the space they needed yet controlling the people they met and what they did outside the home. Unlike apartments, suburban dwellings were large enough for children to have their own rooms, and magazines admonished parents to create a darkroom, gymnasium, or hobby workshop as well if they wanted to keep their children at home. The calibre of neighborhood provided social status and limited children's associates to certain desirable groups. One heard talk of the sexual revolution, flappers, bootleg gin, and dangerous foreigners during the 1920s. Many parents hoped that the suburbs would provide a refuge from these influences.

The period styles of architecture that became so popular in the suburbs also suggest deep racial and ethnic sentiments. Diminutive replicas of French châteaux, Spanish haciendas, Norman farmhouses, Georgian manors, Old English cottages, and various Early American homesteads provided acceptable cultural references as well as aesthetic charm. Families were trying to establish their heritage and their place in the world. The Architects' Small House Service Bureau presented an "architectural melting pot" of designs that was predominantly English.[23] The Allied Architects Association of Los Angeles declared that Mediterranean styles were best for their region because "our environment is definitely racial."[24]

What do the neighbors think of *her* children?

To every mother her own are the ideal children. But what do the neighbors think? Do *they* smile at happy, grimy faces acquired in wholesome play? For people have a way of associating unclean clothes and faces with other questionable characteristics.

Fortunately, however, there's soap and water. "Bright, shining faces" and freshly laundered clothes seem to make children welcome anywhere . . . and, in addition, to speak volumes concerning their *parents'* personal habits as well.

There's CHARACTER — in SOAP *&* WATER

PUBLISHED BY THE ASSOCIATION OF AMERICAN SOAP AND GLYCERINE PRODUCERS, INC., TO AID THE WORK OF *CLEANLINESS INSTITUTE*

The New York Cleanliness Institute published this advertisement in *Ladies' Home Journal* (1928), emphasizing the need for suburban parents to pay constant attention to appearances.

The quaint stylistic diversity of American suburban architecture belied hostilities against ethnic minorities. In 1921 and 1924, laws were passed placing quotas on immigration. The rates were based on the census of 1890, after which the tide had turned from English, German, and Scandinavian stock toward Eastern and Southern Europeans. Japanese immigration was barred, as Chinese had been earlier. The Ku Klux Klan advocated "native, white, Protestant" supremacy through violence and propaganda; and race riots erupted in Chicago, Detroit, New York, and other northern cities as over a million blacks moved northward, out of the South.

During the 1920s, the restrictive covenant, preventing the sale of property to such groups as Asians, Mexicans, blacks, and Jews, came into widespread use. Deed restrictions covering a parcel or a new subdivision had been common for a century, but the new covenant applied to entire established neighborhoods and extended into perpetuity. When the Supreme Court struck down municipal residential segregation ordinances in 1917, real-estate boards and property owners' associations turned to contractual agreements between individuals, which were not outlawed by the Supreme Court until 1948. In many cities, realtors openly promoted the covenant as a way to ensure that each neighborhood contained only one ethnic group. The Palos Verdes Homes Association declared: "The type of protective restrictions and high-class scheme of layout which we have provided tends to guide and automatically regulate the class of citizens who are settling here."[25] Better Homes in America, Inc., also supported restrictive covenants in the hope that property owners would thereby be assured of the kinds of people who would become their neighbors in the future.

Stylistic regulations, such as minimum lot sizes and house prices, reinforced economic segregation in the suburbs. The Van Sweringen brothers, who engineered Shaker Heights, outside Cleveland, set up an elaborate code preventing the construction of two-family houses and apartments, outlawing saloons, and restricting the suburb to the class they wanted. At the other end of the scale, the lack of planning in communities like Cicero, Illinois, led to concentrations of foreign-born, working-class families. Thousands of small, detached bungalows went up. Boarding was permitted, and most of the predominantly Eastern European families did take in additional persons. Large factories, such as the Hawthorne Plant of Western Electric, were allowed in the community alongside small houses (many for two families), saloons, and lodge buildings.

Municipal zoning restrictions that separated industrial and residential areas tended to reinforce class segregation. Zoning, like restrictive covenants, had its origins in nineteenth-century laws preventing nuisances such as noise and pollution, and barring certain groups, such as Chinese laundrymen or Japanese fishermen. Yet these laws did not come into widespread use until the early twentieth century, when local governments initiated zoning measures prohibiting any builder to construct houses next to noxious factories or to erect miles of crowded houses on gridiron streets in the open countryside. Hoover's Commerce Department and the Better Homes in America movement endorsed zoning as a means of rationalizing development and thereby stabilizing homes. The principal focus of zoning measures was the insulation of single-family homes in residential neighborhoods. As a 1971 report to the Presidential Council on Environmental Quality made clear, zoning advocates of the 1920s "only sought to prevent land from being used in a manner that would depreciate the value of neighboring land."[26]

Los Angeles passed the first zoning ordinance in 1909, creating three types of districts: residential, light industrial, and heavy industrial. New York's plan of 1916, conceived under pressure from Fifth Avenue retail merchants who were angered over the immigrant garment-trade employees working in nearby lofts, regulated building height and bulk as well as land use. However, it was during the 1920s, in smaller cities and suburbs, that zoning measures had the strongest impact. At the suggestion of local manufacturers, Berkeley, California, banned all new residential construction in industrial areas, thereby reducing the stock of convenient housing for workers. New Jersey voters backed the town of Nutley's ordinance prohibiting immigrant food stands in residential neighborhoods. The suburb of Euclid, Ohio, became famous when it won its 1926 Supreme Court case, which set single-family residential areas as the highest land use and banned other kinds of housing or buildings in those areas. Planners wrote eloquently of the "natural" separation of residential, commercial, and industrial areas. Reports described apartment buildings "polluting" a single-family residential area or stores "tainting" a neighborhood. By 1930, zoning ordinances, affecting more than 46 million people, were in operation in 981 cities, towns, and villages throughout the United States.[27]

In the suburbs, the banning of light industry and commerce reinforced a strictly residential flavor. Zoning boards relegated luncheonettes, clothing stores, garages, and movie houses to commercial strips on the outskirts of the subdivision, although "neighborhood" grocery stores and a few shops were permitted within the residential enclave. The practice was designed to remove the class of people who would have worked in larger stores and to ensure that most suburban women were protected in their homes, affording them little opportunity for employment. Reliance on the private automobile became even greater as planners laid out arterial roads that connected the strictly residential neighborhoods with large shopping centers and more distant workplaces.

Concern about housing during the 1920s focused on the single-family suburban dwelling. As Americans sought to protect their investments in suburban real estate, family life, and social status, they introduced new forms of control over their residential neighborhoods. However, these were not the only values, nor was this the only kind of housing being proposed—and built. The 1920s were a time of choices, not only of period styles but of various kinds of residential communities and modes of home ownership. In addition, there was an interest in experimenting with a range of housing prototypes. From our present perspective, it is that diversity of possible housing types—rather than one neglected solution or the dominant image of quaint suburbia—that makes this period important. Among many other issues, alternative approaches to housing were on the national political agenda. In 1928, when Herbert Hoover ran against New York Governor Alfred E. Smith for the White House, this was a point that exemplified their differences. Smith, who had set up coops and low-cost housing, represented the cities. Yet it was private builders and middle-class suburbanites who won the election for Hoover.

PART FIVE

GOVERNMENT STANDARDS FOR AMERICAN FAMILIES

THE GOVERNMENTAL FACT GATHERING OF THE PROGRESSIVE
period and the bureaucratic apparatus of Hoover's time laid the basis for
more comprehensive federal housing programs later in the century. By
the 1930s, and even more extensively after World War II, Washington
agencies were overseeing the financing and construction of a sizable
segment of American housing. In the process, the government buttressed a chronically weak construction industry, underwrote home-
financing institutions, and indirectly supported numerous related fields,
ranging from the automobile industry to suburban shopping centers. It
also carried out implicit but quite consistent policies designed to stabilize
the nuclear family and to perpetuate an "orderly"—*i.e.*, segregated and
zoned—pattern of development.

By the second half of the twentieth century, the federal government
was administering public-housing programs in urban and rural areas, and
an even broader network of aid was being channeled into the suburbs.
This sometimes bungling, often moralistic involvement in housing
scarcely seemed warranted, or even necessarily democratic, at least to
those who opposed federal subsidies for the poor. Indeed, the outcry
against public housing—"Especially in *my* neighborhood!"—became
more vociferous as the problems of the poor became more visible. On

the other hand, government programs designed to support middle-class families by helping the home-building industry seemed relatively unproblematic, even to those who claimed to look with disfavor on any interference in the marketplace.

This is not to say that there was a single, unified policy on family life officially endorsed by the government, no more than there was only one prototype in government's architectural blueprints. In fact, the very lack of a national policy, to this day, invites the fragmentation that pervades American housing. Each of the programs has had a strange history, characterized by divergent policies and dissimilar architectural results, emanating over time from the same agency. Nonetheless, it is clear that housing in the United States has been circumscribed by federal guidelines since the depression of the 1930s. The government has set standards for construction, for financing, for land-use planning, and, to a certain extent, for family and community life.

The origins of this intervention during the 1930s suggest that, from the outset, it was a politics of desperation and of idealism. The American desire to uplift families through their home environments once again allied with business interests. For either rationale, the need to consider the larger residential community, as well as the individual habitation, had become incontestable.

Certain general attitudes characterized each of the federal housing programs. Most conspicuous was a basic anti-urban sentiment, a conviction that the suburbs were, in fact, the right place to raise a family, that city streets and older, inexpensive housing were dangerous to body and spirit. This belief helped create the kinds of public-housing towers that cause many Americans today to associate cities with violence, anonymity, and poverty.

Explicit endorsement of segregation—by class and by race—was not only an outcome of federal housing policies; it was a stated principle in every government housing program. Public-housing selection and location were based on race. Slum clearance and highway programs affected minority groups more deeply than they did white families. Even the Federal Housing Administration (FHA) guidelines for suburban development supported segregation, despite the fact that this conflicted with their hope that public-housing tenants would move into the homeowning classes.

Finally, there was a peculiar attitude toward time. Public housing, as architecture, was visibly permanent—a solid investment of the taxpayers' money—while the individual units were usually small and spartan, since they were not supposed to encourage the idea that this was a place to settle into for long. In contrast, a timeless quality lay over the suburbs. Everyone assumed that things would continue as they were here, with larger cars and more roads, newer houses and better schools, forever and ever. Real events have hit hard on both of these scenarios.

CHAPTER TWELVE

PUBLIC HOUSING FOR THE WORTHY POOR

> An Act To provide financial assistance to the States and political subdivisions thereof for the elimination of unsafe and insanitary housing conditions, for the eradication of slums, for the provision of decent, safe, and sanitary dwellings for families of low income, and for the reduction of unemployment and the stimulation of business activity.
>
> —Wagner-Steagall Housing Act (1937)

IT WAS DESPERATION THAT BROUGHT ABOUT THE first American programs of federally financed, publicly owned housing for the poor. In the spring of 1933, 15 million people were out of work. Four million families were on relief; in some states, almost half the population received federal payments. The fact that one third of the jobless were in the building trades spurred President Franklin Roosevelt to give cautious support to federal programs to clear slums and build housing in the cities and the countryside. Reformers who backed these programs—notably Edith Elmer Wood, Catherine Bauer, Helen Alfred, and Mary Simkovitch (women were in the forefront of the movement)—argued that it was the government's responsibility to provide decent, affordable homes for the poor. Yet helping the poor was only a minor aspect of early public-housing philosophy.

From the start, a powerful real-estate lobby, underwritten by the National Association of Real Estate Boards, the National Association of Home Builders, the American Savings and Loan League, the Mortgage Bankers Association, and the American Bankers Association, opposed public housing as socialistic and improvident. Representatives of the lobby, based in Washington and Chicago, insisted that public housing would erode such noble virtues as individual dignity and self-sufficiency; their public-education kits appealed to other sentiments such as racial prejudice. "CAN YOU AFFORD TO PAY SOMEBODY ELSE'S RENT?" "PUBLIC HOUSING MEANS THE END OF RACIAL SEGREGATION IN SAVANNAH!" threatened local billboards.[2] For at least two decades, claimed Edith Elmer Wood and Catherine Bauer, the private market had provided housing almost entirely for the upper third of the popula-

. . . .

The U.S. Savings and Loan League sent out information kits and anti-public-housing billboard prototypes. One of their principal themes was that government liberals would waste the hard-earned money of the middle class by giving the poor something for nothing.

tion.[3] Despite this, the lobbyists expressed concern that public housing might take away potential revenue from private builders, realtors, and banks. They also feared increased governmental intervention beyond public housing, envisioning catastrophes along the "road to socialism," a direction that, to them, meant taxpayer support of a dependent poor and government control of rather than aid to the banks and the builders.

The New Deal initiated several home-building programs, although none were officially called public housing. Federal agencies bought land, built dwelling units, and set up programs designed to improve the lives of the resident families. The sense of crisis gave the early New Deal planners a certain amount of autonomy. They were, in general, an idealistic group, interested in creating organic communities among the poor, not just in providing them with shelter. The communities, with their carefully chosen residents, their integration of work and home life, their public squares and cooperative stores, were expressions of the planners' idealized vision. Critics considered them radical and protested against the "Make-America-Over Corps."[4]

Much New Deal public housing was constructed outside the cities. One agency brought electricity to rural areas. A rehabilitation program provided loans to farm families who otherwise would have to foreclose, and helped farmers build houses and outbuildings. These programs were not designed to change the rural way of life, only to sustain it through a time of hardship. The main thrust of other rural housing agencies was to bring people together, to resettle them in planned communities. Of a total of ninety-nine communities built under the New Deal, forty were rural or suburban.[5] The Subsistence Homesteads Division helped finance experimental farm colonies for agricultural workers in depressed areas. It also moved industrial workers to new government-run rural communities. The colonies of Arthurdale, West Virginia, and the Jersey Homesteads, near Hightstown, New Jersey, provided housing and community buildings for former miners in West Virginia and for Jewish garment workers in New Jersey. These families were supposed to combine farming with part-time wage labor in cooperative light industries.

Two other New Deal rural programs emphasized even more emphatically strong governmental control, modern design, and rational planning. In 1935, Rexford Tugwell was appointed head of the Resettlement Administration, responsible only to President Roosevelt. The three suburban greenbelt towns of Greenbelt, Maryland, near Washington, D. C.; Greendale, Wisconsin, near Milwaukee; and Greenhills, Ohio, near Cincinnati, were the principal undertakings of the Resettlement Administration, and the most important communities constructed under the New Deal. The agency selected residents on the basis of economic stability and community activism. They were, for the most part, families of middle-class white-collar workers who commuted to nearby cities. (Tugwell had intended for each town to include both industry and a commercial center.) The fact that these were people who could have been given outright subsidies to buy their own houses on the private market outraged realtors and builders alike. Shortly after World War II, the U. S. Housing and Home Finance Administration issued Public Regulation No. 1, which declared that in order to encourage homeownership by small investors, the greenbelt towns would be subdivided into lots and sold for cash, with preference given to residents who were veterans.

The Farm Security Administration (FSA) was established in 1937 to take over Tugwell's agency and to aid tenant farmers buy their own land. Then the 1937 Dust Bowl added some 350,000 displaced American farm families to the migrant Mexican-American and Oriental workers who followed the crops on the West Coast and in the Southwest. Migrants became another focus of FSA social housing, and the agency laid the groundwork for migrant projects of the 1960s administered by the Office of Economic Opportunity (OEO). The FSA wanted to create self-sufficient production cooperatives modeled on early Zionist *kibbutzim*. FSA architects designed and built dwellings, community centers, cooperative stores, day-care centers, and clinics in over thirty migrant camps for some fifteen thousand families.[6] With an extremely low budget, they used mostly wood-frame construction and eliminated every unnecessary gable and every foot of little-used floor space. They experimented with prefabricated units, hoping also to provide stable industrial work in a few permanent communities. The structures were arranged in parallel lines, based on the avant-garde German *Zeilenbau* system, which combined precise solar orientation analyses with a visual expression of egalitarianism. The severe modern architecture offended many tastes, especially as it came to be associated with the program's radical social ideals and government ownership of the land. In 1946, the FSA was superseded by the Farmers Home Administration (FmHA). This agency, unlike its predecessor, helped individual farmers buy their own traditional farmhouses in much the same way that the FHA helped suburban families invest in private property.

The Public Works Administration (PWA), which undertook slum

clearance and low-rent housing in the cities, was the most widely known of the government's early public-housing efforts. In its first stage, the PWA Housing Division was restricted to 30 percent federal grants for limited-dividend or nonprofit corporations, including labor unions, which sponsored housing. In Philadelphia, for example, the American Federation of Hosiery Workers launched the Carl Mackley Houses under this program. John Edelman, head of the union, together with architect Oscar Stonorov and Catherine Bauer, a principal adviser and executive secretary of the Labor Housing Conference, wanted to do more than provide economical housing; they hoped to promote widespread demand for decent housing among all American workers. Bauer's *Modern Housing* (1934) posited that workers had to organize politically

. . . .

During the depression, the Farm Security Administration (FSA) built housing and other facilities for migrant farmworkers from Texas to California. This camp at Robstown, Texas, was photographed in 1938.

if government-sponsored housing was to become a reality in America. The design of the Mackley Houses expressed this group's beliefs. The common recreational and service facilities—which included rooftop playgrounds, tennis courts, swimming pool, library, laundry buildings, and numerous meeting rooms—received more attention than the 284 tiny living units. Residents were encouraged to organize forums on socialized medicine and political issues. To them, as Bauer had hoped, subsidies for housing represented one of many basic rights the government should guarantee for all citizens.

Within a year, the PWA itself began to buy land, raze slums, and build housing. Over the next four years, it was responsible for destroying more than ten thousand substandard housing units and erecting almost twenty-two thousand new units in fifty-nine different projects.[7] One of the major problems facing the agency was land purchase. Officials rejected suburban applications on the grounds that the available sites were too small to have any meaning, and that the average low-income family would find neither community nor employment in such areas. In cities, it was possible to combine new buildings with slum clearance and to work with larger sites. However, assembling a sufficient number of small parcels from dozens or perhaps hundreds of slum landlords was often extremely expensive and difficult. The task became almost impossible when in 1935, the courts ruled that the federal government had no right to condemn private land for low-cost housing because it was not considered a "public purpose."

Since states and municipalities *did* have the right to purchase and raze property, PWA officials set up local housing authorities, which were then responsible for deciding where to situate public housing and whom to put into that housing. This localization restricted the federal government's ability to promote integration of blacks and whites, of poor and non-poor. Nonetheless, local decision making did have its benefits. As governmental guidelines became more rigid and austere, local housing authorities and the architects they hired often fought to relax or reinterpret strict federal regulations. And so the issue of federal control versus local control came to the fore at the start.

The PWA allocated half its housing for blacks, stipulating that this would not change existing relations between the races. If a neighborhood was white, no blacks would be admitted into the public housing; if it was mixed, new housing would follow the existing proportions. The agency required that housing for blacks have the same amenities as that for whites. Projects for black families provided playgrounds, social services, and pleasant, small-scale buildings of one and two stories.

Black or white, residents of PWA housing were never destitute but "deserving poor," people with steady, moderate incomes. PWA project staffs favored lower-middle-class families who had been hurt by the depression, those who social workers believed would most benefit from the experience. There were no stipulations that a project had to accept people who had been evicted from their homes by slum clearance; and, in fact, the overwhelming majority of those people could not afford the rents set by the PWA. In the Jane Addams Houses in Chicago, only 21 of the 533 families moved off the site could afford to live in the new housing.[8] The others crowded into tenements in different parts of the city. With many more applications than apartments—usually twelve to one—the PWA project staff could and did screen carefully.[9] They considered the housing a way station for the temporarily impoverished, a home these families could take pride in, a social environment that would help them get back on their feet again.

Tenant organizations created with the help of social workers played an important part in community building. Some organizations, dominated by labor unionists, advocated participatory socialism. However, given public-housing selection policies, which favored a mild-mannered workers' consciousness and conspicuous upward mobility, even these groups tended to be liberal and cooperative rather than radical. Most tenants towed the line. The *Techwood News,* a newspaper put out by the tenants in an Atlanta, Georgia, project, reflected the social workers' principles. Even critics of public housing would have been pleased to read that "housing projects serve a wonderful purpose in providing a breathing spell for families in a low-rent bracket."[10] Socialized cooptation became the focus for public-housing tenants' groups. The administrators wanted to bring individuals together so that they would help one another, not to be accused of fomenting socialism.

Criticism plagued the PWA projects from the outset. The National Lumber Dealers Association told Congress that the government's interference in house building was crippling private construction. Merchants charged unfair competition from the storefronts and cooperative groceries that were part of many PWA projects. Father Charles E. Coughlin's demagogic radio program condemned the entire scheme as state socialism. Even the design standards evoked anger. Because the agency was in business to provide jobs, there were few restrictions on cost. Design was of high quality inasmuch as architects wanted to build "demonstration housing" that exemplified the differences between good housing and slum housing. The Williamsburg Houses in New York City had elegant modern façades with horizontal bands of dark concrete and wide corner windows. Even the smallest projects featured copper roofs, elaborate brickwork, and canopies over every door. WPA sculptors carved friezes of muscular 1930s-style workers for doorways and entrance courts. Inside, thickly plastered walls, ceramic tile hallways, large windows, and the latest appliances were common. Administrators insisted that they saved money by buying in bulk; but electric refrigerators and architectural ornament seemed opulent nonetheless. In fact, PWA housing was often of better quality and design than most private housing, and this especially angered builders and realtors, who claimed that public housing would discourage homeownership by making "tenement occupancy so attractive that the urge to buy one's home will be diminished."[11]

With the Wagner-Steagall Housing Act of 1937, power shifted even more to the local communities; instead of owning and operating public housing, the U. S. Housing Authority (USHA) provided guidelines and loaned money to local authorities. Congress allocated $800 million for this purpose. If a new project was approved, a municipality had to raise 10 percent of its cost; government would provide the rest on a low-interest sixty-year loan, which it later helped the municipality repay. In order to keep rents low, the USHA also granted annual contributions to the housing authority that made up the difference between the tenant's rent (based on one fifth of income) and actual operating costs. By the end of 1940, there were 350 USHA projects completed or under construction all over the country.

Advocates of public housing believed that a combination of well-designed new housing and the elimination of tenements would alleviate social problems. They tied slum clearance to new housing construction, requiring the "equivalent elimination" of one substandard dwelling for each new dwelling unit. This pleased private builders, since it meant that the housing stock would not be increased. The provision was intended to curtail moving the poor into the suburban fringe or other parts of the cities. The USHA would, in fact, entrench inner-city ghettos because it moved poor people from substandard housing into better housing but did not alter the existing social order or segregation pattern of the city.

Unlike PWA housing, which met the needs of temporarily impoverished people, the new programs were designed for the very poor. This was as much a victory for builders and realtors as it was for reformers.

Every public-housing tenant had to come from an income level that was at least 20 percent below the bracket that could afford the least expensive private housing. There were serious drawbacks to this approach. Because a family would be forced to vacate the premises if their income rose

· ·

A 1939 editorial cartoon from *The New Orleans Times-Picayune* captures the belief that slum clearance and better housing would rid the cities of many social problems.

above the limit, there was a strong disincentive to increase one's income. In a Chicago court case, a tenant who protested his eviction on income grounds showed that rental housing was extremely hard to find for the "forgotten 20 percent" between public-housing cutoffs and the private market's least expensive options. The court ruled that with the help of government-insured mortgage programs, the tenant nonetheless had enough money to buy a house in the suburbs. This decision supported the view that public housing was still a temporary "slum of hope" for the submerged middle class, who should be encouraged to join the propertied class in the suburbs—even if they did not wish to.[12]

Public housing in the 1940s was sturdy and functional, designed to last through the government's sixty-year mortgage. It was also purposefully cheap and austere. Congressional regulations prevented government support of projects with "elaborate or expensive design or materials," or projects that cost more than the average dwelling unit constructed by private builders in the area. Senator Harry Byrd of Virginia sponsored a cost-limitation provision that prohibited construction of any kind of "extravagance" on government-built housing.[13] No housing authority could spend more than $4,000 per family unit, or $1,000 per room, although slightly higher limits were set for large cities. Few legislators who debated these restrictions considered the idea that good urban architecture benefitted the entire city, while providing decent housing at the same time.

Despite these constraints, some public-housing authorities sanctioned the construction of quality housing. The best work looked to regional traditions rather than universal ideas of modern architecture, so that public housing in a neighborhood would be relatively unobtrusive. Several examples of this approach were the Saudia Mesa Houses in Albuquerque, New Mexico, where the rows of stucco dwellings resembled traditional abode houses; the Magnolia Street and St. Thomas Houses in New Orleans, which incorporated the tall windows and cast-iron balconies of nineteenth-century Louisiana row houses; and those eastern cities that modeled their modern public housing on earlier, brick row houses.

Site planning in projects prior to the Second World War emphasized ample outdoor play areas and walkways for adults rather than the solar orientations of the mid-1930s avant-garde. Los Angeles built twelve federal projects between 1938 and 1941 that all used cheap materials but were low-rise, well-planted, rambling places. Chicago projects had ball fields and city-run playgrounds.

Much early public housing testified to both economy and innovation. In San Francisco, architect William Wurster's Valencia Gardens had continuous balconies overlooking large interior courts. Glass-brick and smooth, concrete façades gave the building such an elegant look that the Museum of Modern Art singled it out as an outstanding example of modern housing. Edison Courts in Miami, Florida, used solar heating units on the roofs; and Savannah's housing authority decided that all its future public housing would use solar heating. There was often a high level of design, technology, and "livability," as public housing gave planners and architects the opportunity to experiment.

Despite the regulations requiring that public-housing authorities accept only the very poor, these agencies continued to exercise a great deal of control over tenant selection. Most staffs accepted only "complete

. . . .

The St. Thomas Housing Project was built in New Orleans by the U.S. Housing Authority in 1940. It combined modern ideas of government-sponsored housing with regional traditions of architecture.

families," two parents with several children. Such families were preferred, since the authorities believed that the experience of living in public housing would make the children better future citizens. Applicants had interviews with social workers, employment verifications, police-record checks, and home visits, which rated both the inadequacy of a family's existing living conditions and their readiness to change in new surroundings. Once a family settled in public housing, their life was strictly regulated. While Corpus Christie, Texas, installed barbeque pits in an effort to promote family togetherness, other practical expressions of public-housing ideology were not so pleasant. Apartments con-

The living room of Mr. and Mrs. Frank Merchant's apartment in the Ida Wells Homes (built in 1940 by the Chicago Housing Authority) seemed a good advertisement of the hope that public housing would help the poor become the middle class. Mr. Merchant was a worker at the Carnegie steel plant.

tained no storage space for such large objects as bicycles or suitcases, as these purchases represented a more comfortable life than the tenant was supposed to enjoy. Closet doors were left off in an effort to reduce costs and encourage neatness. The parents' bedroom was purposefully small so as to eliminate the practice of infants sharing the same room as the adults. The principal considerations in the individual units were those of the turn-of-the-century reformers: sanitation, ventilation, privacy, and order. The architects, social workers, and housing-authority staffs earnestly wanted to improve the domestic life of the tenants by reinforcing certain habits, but they had little real sympathy or respect for those families whose economic situation brought them into these architectural experiments.

Business interests, fearing the socialist implications of greater federal interference in the marketplace, insisted on having a role in housing programs. That role was not to provide low-income housing, however, but to rebuild deteriorated urban sectors, converting slums into tax bases. Within a few years after the Housing Act of 1949, businessmen had become avid supporters of federally funded urban redevelopment. Under Title I of the act, a municipality could redevelop any run-down or even partially deteriorated neighborhood, and the federal government would pay two thirds of the cost. This package and the 1954 Urban Renewal Act offered an excellent opportunity to clear land for new luxury apartments, convention centers, and office buildings without any financial risk. The city won back wealthy tax bases, and investors made large profits.

The people who had no voice were those who lost their homes. Because only 20 percent of the housing in a renewal area had to be classified as "blighted," real-estate promoters and city-hall politicians destroyed many low-income ethnic neighborhoods. Few families who had lived in these neighborhoods could afford to move into the new apartments. Sociologist Herbert J. Gans documented one such neighborhood, Boston's West End, shortly before the bulldozers were sent in to raze this "blighted area." What he found was a community of Italian-American families, not a decaying slum. According to Gans, the exteriors of the buildings had been neglected because the tenants did not see housing as a status symbol; the apartments themselves, on the other hand, were spotlessly clean. The crowded streets and apartments did not bother the West Enders. As one resident put it: "Everyone can hear everyone else, but nobody cares what anybody is saying; they leave their neighbors alone."[14] Here were the freedom and the close ties of an established urban neighborhood, but the area was condemned, people were forced to leave their homes and friends. Boston lost not only 2,300 units of low-rent non-public housing but a real neighborhood as well. Because few West Enders were willing to live in public housing, they had to pay much more for private housing in other parts of the city.

By the 1950s, conditions in public housing had begun to deteriorate seriously. The high cost of the Korean War and the growing antagonism against special services for the poor reduced the number of public-housing units built, and made them even more spartan. Rooms were smaller, site densities were higher, and playgrounds or social areas inside the buildings were fewer. Housing authorities tried to discourage tenants with large families by providing only small units in new projects, and the old minimum standards became the new maximum allowances. Local

· ·

In 1951 Washington officials and local administrators watched the destruction of former slum housing in downtown Chicago. They had slated the area for a 1,404-unit apartment complex, developed by the New York Life Insurance Company.

communities could now vote on public-housing projects, and rejected many proposals, thereby intensifying the demand for what subsidized housing there was.

Segregation and racial tensions also became critical issues. The housing authorities still had to conform to the pattern of segregation in each locality. (It was not until 1962 that an executive order prohibited the use of race as a criterion in public-housing tenant selection.) But they suddenly had long waiting lists of blacks. One explanation was black urban migration during World War II. But urban renewal, which came to be known as "Negro removal," was the major reason so many blacks now needed public housing. Between 1949 and 1968, 425,000 units of low-income housing, mostly the homes of poor minorities, had been razed for redevelopment; and only 125,000 new units had been constructed, over half of which were luxury apartments.[15] At the same time, highway-construction projects eliminated minority neighborhoods, subsequently increasing the proportions of blacks applying for public housing. And housing authorities were required to give first priority to persons displaced by federal programs. More important than numbers was the mood of these people, who had been evicted from their homes and who had few places where they were allowed to live. (Blacks at that time were prohibited from renting in most white residential areas.) Public housing was no longer seen as a temporary community for families who would improve their condition and move back into conventional homes. Rather, it had become the last refuge for people who were disheartened and hostile.

Most housing officials still believed that they could reform poor families by situating them in model environments; but the image of that environment, and the tenants' participation in shaping it, changed dramatically. Champions of public housing declared that it would cut mortality rates and stamp out prostitution, reduce crime and eliminate juvenile delinquency—if housing authorities had enough control. There was less rhetoric about building communities and more talk about enforcing order. Housing authorities in large cities now preferred massive projects of a unified yet distinctive appearance to the small projects that blended into the surrounding neighborhoods. They assumed that a change in scale would help the residents break with their past surroundings and acquaintances. In *Slums and Housing* (1936), Harvard "houser" James Ford had advocated this position, declaring that a large project would have an "increased chance of maintaining its distinctive character because its very size helps it to dominate the neighborhood and discourage regression" to slum life.[16] Elizabeth Wood, for years the head of the Chicago Housing Authority, took up this position in 1945. Planning, she announced, "must be bold and comprehensive—or it is useless and wasted. If it is not bold, the result will be a series of small projects, islands in a wilderness of slums, beaten down by smoke, noise, and fumes."[17] Her scheme included provisions for eighty-acre super-blocks of public-housing towers, with neither cross traffic nor public transit lines to disrupt the community.

Partly in response to this argument and partly in an effort to trim costs and provide more housing, public-housing commissioners across the country planned larger, more monumental projects in the 1950s. Whereas the PWA had maintained a four-story height limit (except for New York City), the USHA approved taller buildings and huge com-

• •

The massive scale and severity of Cedar Apartments, a fourteen-story public-housing tower in Cleveland, Ohio, typified the shift in both architecture and policy for urban public housing after 1950.

plexes. Even before 1950, New York's Queensbridge Houses had contained eleven thousand people in Y-shaped blocks of six-story elevator buildings. When New York's limit was increased to ten and twelve stories, other large cities followed suit. Chicago's Dearborn Homes consisted of sixteen elevator buildings. San Francisco's Yerba Buena Plaza, set in a neighborhood of Victorian row houses, was a massive eleven-story pink concrete slab, with balconies running the length of the street façade.

Housing officials claimed that this approach was economical and provided more play area for children. Yet the per-unit cost at Dearborn was more than twice that of the Ida B. Wells Homes, a project with larger apartments and more social services, built only a decade earlier on a site a few blocks away. Though high-rise structures seemed economical, when calculations were based on the costs of inner-city land, construction, and maintenance, they were actually much more expensive than row houses. In terms of children's needs, these projects also failed. The huge courtyards became empty wastelands where no one felt safe. The few "indestructible" metal climbing structures did not attract children; and without any benches, there were no spectators for games. Rather than leave young children unattended, mothers often kept them inside all day. Yet to housing-authority officials of the early 1950s, the high-rise tower was a visible expression of economic efficiency and social order; and to architects, it was a breakthrough in modern design. While smaller cities and towns continued to erect low-rise, spartan housing, the tower became the new prototype of the central cities.

Interviews showed that twice as many residents, especially those with large families, preferred small-scale, low-rise public housing. The people who undertook the studies, concerned about rising crime and vandalism, often insisted that inhumane high-rise architecture caused the problems. Yet the criticisms sometimes missed the point. When tenants complained about problems of security, maintenance, and apathy, they were talking about more than their immediate environment. Sociologist Lee Rainwater conducted a study of St. Louis's infamous Pruitt-Igoe and found that the majority of residents considered their apartments superior to their previous homes; what they did not like was the larger project, in social more than environmental terms. As one resident explained, the bureaucrats had been "trying to get rid of the slum, but they didn't accomplish too much. Inside the apartment they did, but not outside."[18] "Outside" was as much a matter of management policies as of architecture. Alternate-floor elevators did not work with young children. Long, dark hallways became dangerous places. The rooms were small, in part because residents were expected to use the huge, barren expanses of outdoor space. Another tenant told an interviewer: "You feel like you can't breathe. People are everywhere. Children are in the bathroom when you are using the toilet, somebody is sitting in every chair in the house, you've got to eat in shifts."[19]

Management controlled every aspect of the residents' lives—the keeping of pets, the policy about overnight guests, the color of paint on the walls, the schedules for using the washing machines—but it adopted the attitude that spending too much money on safety or maintenance or public facilities was wasteful, since the fundamental problems were too extreme. The tenants recognized the combination of disdain and high-minded belief that public housing could elevate residents, make them more orderly. The buildings themselves, and the residents' derogatory names for them—the "Pink Palace" for San Francisco's Yerba Buena Plaza, or the "Congo Hilton" for Chicago's Taylor Homes—revealed the contradictory values of the planners and tenants.

Planner Catherine Bauer caused quite a stir with a definitive attack against public-housing policies in her 1957 article, "The Dreary Deadlock of Public Housing." She had been one of the authors of the Wagner-Steagall Housing Act, a staunch defender of urban renewal, an advocate of architectural and social experimentation. In part, she blamed problems on the recent tendency toward high-rise "islands," or the "tower-in-the-park" concept.[20] But Bauer put the architectural criticism in a social and political context. The fact that these towers cost more than modest FHA houses tended to anger Congress and reduce the cost allowances for public housing even more drastically. High density and monotonous standardization made the projects look harshly institutional, which demeaned the tenants with a charity stigma.

By the 1960s, with rioting in the cities, government reports on urban conditions and housing problems echoed these criticisms. The National Commission on Urban Problems branded public housing not just inadequate but "anti-community," and placed the responsibility on the architects who had advocated high-rise towers.[21] "Perhaps the theories of such architects and city planners as Corbusier also had a share in this influence on height," said the report. "They stressed 'skyscrapers in a park,' and thereby gave some popular acceptance to the idea of high-rise apartments."[22] Once again, middle-class moralists accused residential architecture of causing complex social problems. The reports were perceptive about the faults in public-housing design and suggested viable

By the early 1970s, the elderly had become the favorite clients for new public housing. Because Congress gave higher cost ceilings for elderly units, these buildings often resembled conventional apartment buildings of the period.

alternatives: planning for large families, returning to smaller-scale housing, and scattering sites to integrate subsidized and non-subsidized communities. But they avoided the more political issues of tenant management and selection processes.

Negative response to public housing in the 1950s and 1960s did not destroy the programs but led to another shift in policy and architecture, one that dominates public housing today. The number of elderly persons and their corresponding political power was growing. In 1850, one American in ten was over 64; in 1953, the figure was one in six.[23] "Old folks lobbies" in several states demanded better pensions and living conditions. Congress provided special funds for elderly public housing in 1956, and opened credit to private developers and nonprofit corporations a few years later. It also increased subsidies for elderly public housing, arguing that the higher construction costs reflected the particular needs of elderly persons. While older people were provided with railings and ramps, safety features, clinics, and gardens, the special needs of poor families did not engender the same sympathies or responses. Elderly public housing was often quite attractive and set in good neighborhoods; in short, it did not look like public housing. As legal historian Lawrence Friedman suggests, the popularity of public housing for the elderly is based on the fact that it "taps the only remaining reservoir of poor people who are also white, orderly, and middle-class in behavior. Neighborhoods which will not tolerate a ten-story tower packed with Negro mothers on AFDC might tolerate a tower of sweet but impoverished old folks."[24]

CHAPTER THIRTEEN

THE NEW SUBURBAN EXPANSION AND THE AMERICAN DREAM

We hope to show our diversity and our right to choose. We do not want to have decisions made at the top by one government official that all houses should be built the same way. . . . Is it not far better to be talking about washing machines than machines of war, like rockets? Isn't this the kind of competition you want?

—Vice-President Richard M. Nixon to Soviet Premier Nikita Khrushchev, "Kitchen Debate" at the American model house in Moscow, 1959

DESPITE THEIR OPPOSITION TO "SOCIALISTIC" PUBLIC housing, American house builders and mortgage bankers wanted government support that would take the risk out of investments in conventional residential construction. After some initial disputes, there was little protest about government involvement in this "private-housing" field. The issue was how much authority government should have to regulate the products the builders constructed, the rates the bankers set, and the people who would live in the new housing.

Serious economic problems in housing and an effective builders' lobby brought about the intervention. By 1933, at the peak of the depression, there were one thousand foreclosures per week. Residential construction had plumeted to 93,000 units, down from 937,000 in 1925, and most of these were houses or apartments for the well-to-do. After the inauguration of Franklin Roosevelt, the New Deal government began a major effort to rebuild the construction industry. The landmark National Housing Act of 1934, in addition to establishing a public-housing program, set up the Federal Housing Administration (FHA) to stimulate the moderate-cost private-housing market. The sponsors hoped to devise a program that would insure low-interest, long-term mortgages. At the time, loans were available only for 40–50 percent of the appraised value of a house, repayable in three to five years at interest rates of 5–9 percent. The FHA, on the other hand, provided for loans of up to 80 percent of a home's value, maturities up to twenty years, and amortization at 5–6 percent, payable by small monthly installments. Bankers who agreed to the FHA terms were guaranteed recovery of a certain sum from the government in the event of default.

Many congressmen opposed the program at first, fearing it would effect a regimentation of home-finance and homeownership patterns that would lead to a welfare state. Supporters of the bill made the point that a revived construction and renovation industry could provide thousands of jobs for the unemployed. In addition, FHA guarantees would endow financial institutions with more capital to invest in other sectors of the stagnant economy. With these reassurances to congressional opponents and financial institutions, the government set out to assist the private-housing market.

The first FHA modernization loan was processed in August 1934, when a Cloquet, Minnesota, bank loaned John P. Powers $125 for paint, roof repair, and a water tank. The first FHA-insured mortgage, for a house in Pompton Plains, New Jersey, was approved a few months later. Within a year, four thousand financial institutions—more than 70 percent of the commercial banking resources of the country—had issued

. . . .

The early houses financed by the Federal Housing Administration (FHA), such as this 1939 ranch house in Houston, Texas, were architecturally quite traditional.

nearly seventy-three thousand loans for home improvement under FHA contracts.[1] New construction proceeded more slowly until 1938, when a new staff, more responsive to the needs of moderate-income families, began approving funds for less expensive houses. Although the ceiling remained a $20,000 mortgage, most houses the FHA now financed cost between $6,000 and $8,000.[2] Traditional designs, particularly colonial styles, prevailed, as FHA officials were quite conservative when considering potential resale values.

No sooner had housing begun to rally from the depression than World War II broke out, and construction was curtailed once again. The major focus for housing production was 2 million government-built units for defense workers and their families who migrated to "Arsenals of Democracy" like Los Angeles, Oakland, Atlanta, Detroit, Portland, and Dallas.[3] The Lanham Act of 1940, which provided the first funds for war housing, also allocated money for other home-related services. Several million Rosie-the-Riveters, most of them married with small children, had jobs in aircraft and munitions factories. New federally financed child-care centers were created for the children of some 10 percent of these working mothers, though this federal money was not supposed to set a precedent. A government report stated: "Child care never before had been considered to be a public responsibility, and the committee's approval was predicated exclusively on a war-connected emergency need."[4]

When 6 million men and women were discharged from the armed forces in 1945, and another 4 million in 1946, many of the 20 million women who had been employed during the war found themselves dismissed or demoted in order to ensure jobs for returning GIs.[5] If jobs were scarce, housing was even scarcer. Two and a half million reunited families and recently married couples had to double up with relatives. What had been temporary defense housing and Quonset hut offices now became emergency homes. Senate investigations found hundreds of thousands of veterans living in garages, trailers, barns, and even chicken coops. (The FHA offered modernization loans for those chicken coops and featured suggestions for redecorating them in special "women's page" supplements to their technical bulletins.) The most conservative reports from the government's National Housing Agency estimated that the country needed at least 5 million new units immediately and a total of 12.5 million over the next decade.[6]

Anticipating the sudden and vast demand for postwar housing, the Veterans Administration (VA) had created a veterans' mortgage guarantee program in 1944. This was a major part of the package of benefits that came to be known as the GI Bill of Rights. Administered under the FHA, the VA housing program enabled veterans to borrow the entire appraised value of a house without a down payment. The problem was the housing crisis, which meant that veterans had to wait until housing was built, and then take out mortgages on what was available at the prices the builders set.

• •

A 1949 editorial cartoon from *The Chicago Sun-Times* suggests the fears that the prolonged postwar housing shortage would have a damaging effect on the birth rate and on family stability.

A Republican Congress was elected in 1947, after a campaign that had asked "Had Enough?" about wartime controls on prices and commodities. New legislators joined Representative Jesse P. Wolcott and Senators Harry Cain and Harry Byrd in support of the real-estate lobby's crusade for a "free market" in residential building and real estate.[7] The lobbyists assured Congress that the housing shortage would disappear once the market began to function normally again. The housing stock would be improved naturally by the "trickle-down" phenomenon, as families buying better new houses sold their homes to the class below.

In response to this pressure, in 1947 Congress allowed a 15 percent "voluntary" rent increase and removed the Housing Expediter's power to enforce regulations. It also defeated a move to make VA and FHA appraisers civil servants, which would have cut down on bribery and the hiring of appraisers who were lenient about builders' standards and their costs. Wage and price controls were abandoned. The National Associaton of Real Estate Boards succeeded in extending income-tax benefits for owner-occupants, although the 1951 tax laws were even more remunerative. Savings and loan institutions also won favorable tax benefits.

Research in new building technology as a means of stimulating housing production had widespread support. Prefabrication seemed a promising route toward lower costs and greater numbers of units. With government funding, new materials had been tried out during the war years and had proved successful: "stressed skin" plywood panels for walls, laminated wood roofs, welded-steel roof trusses, steel-frame wall panels with "clapboards" of painted aluminum, "predecorated" gypsum-board ceilings, were all produced in factories. The companies that had developed the new materials demanded that government continue its support. When Congress moved to cut off funds for this research in 1948, Senator Joseph R. McCarthy, as vice-chairman of a joint housing committee, became the principal advocate of continued government funding. The Lustron Company, a major manufacturer of prefabricated houses, paid McCarthy a $10,000 "fee" for a rough draft of an article, never published, expressing such support. McCarthy's endorsement resulted in a total of $22.5 million in government loans to Lustron over the next three years. According to the president of the firm, congressmen like McCarthy backed the subsidy because Lustron's goals " 'sound like free enterprise.' "[8]

Support for prefabrication research was one instance of recurring government belief in dramatic technological solutions for complex housing problems. People expected too much too soon from innovative technologies. The firms of the war years could not gear up quickly enough or produce enough units to meet postwar needs. Also, prices were too high. For example, Lustron's most economical model cost $9,000, apart from land and installation fees. Yet, with government support and public enthusiasm, Lustron and National Homes became well-established businesses, doing a large volume of work and shipping preassembled houses across the country. U.S. Steel built two hundred model prefab houses

Prefabricated houses were the rage in the early 1950s. National Homes built model houses in several locations, and people waited in line for hours to examine them.

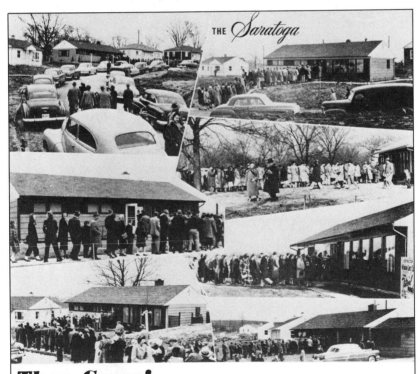

in 1955, including a "bride's house" for the national home builders' convention, co-sponsored by *The House Beautiful* magazine, that was demonstrated by a "model bride" in a blue negligee.[9]

Prefabrication, however, did not solve the postwar housing shortage, which continued to worsen. Only 1.5 million new units were added to the country's housing stock in the two years after the war ended, during which time more than 1.4 million new families had been formed annually.[10] In 1949, the government responded with a new housing act, which guaranteed builders and bankers more substantial profits on large residential developments; and the following year more than 1 million new units were started.

The authors of the Housing Act of 1949 declared their objective to be "the realization as soon as feasible of the goal of a decent home and a suitable living environment for every American family." While the suburban middle-income family received disproportionately the most assistance, the act did set up a range of programs for other populations. For instance, by raising its financial guidelines, the FHA now attracted builders to the lucrative enterprise of providing urban apartments. Under Section 608, the multifamily division of the Housing Act, the government underwrote 711,000 living units in apartment buildings, an aggregate of $5.4 billion over the next eight years.[11] However, much of the construction was shoddy, some of it even dangerous, as builders crowded as many "efficiency units" as possible into poorly built structures. Few of the new apartment buildings provided units large enough for families, and many building managers prohibited children. FHA Section 608 officials did not protest, since they too believed that the suburbs were the appropriate environment for families with children. President Harry Truman celebrated that suburban family ideal when, in an extemporaneous talk on housing, he told participants at the 1948 White House Conference on Family Life that "children and dogs are as necessary to the welfare of this country as is Wall Street and the railroads."[12] Government officials did not see the Housing Act of 1949 as a way to help families in the cities, since they associated healthy family life with nonurban settings.

Section 608 was really written to encourage builders, who were permitted to inflate their cost estimates, land prices, and fees. Apartment builders did not even need to risk capital investments, as they were able to reap their profits even before construction began. Within a year, 70 percent of the apartments built in the United States had FHA 608 insurance.[13] Scandals about excessive profits being gleaned under this program became so frequent that the Senate finally initiated an investigation in 1956. The committee found that 80 percent of the builders had "mortgaged out"; that is, they had borrowed much more than their costs and had walked away with windfall profits, commonly of 25 percent, which added up to $500 million of the taxpayers' money.[14] The program was curtailed, and its replacement had such stringent regulations that few builders applied. The supply of rental housing for urban middle-income people subsequently dwindled, while the proportion of single-family suburban houses being constructed grew even more rapidly than before.

Scandals and indictments also plagued suburban construction as VA appraisers passed on houses and entire developments with faulty sewer lines, no street paving, and jerry-built construction. In contrast, the FHA tried to control design and construction of suburban homes in an effort to achieve "neighborhood stability." The agency endorsed zoning to prevent multifamily dwellings and insisted that no single-family residence could have facilities that would allow it to be used as a shop, office, preschool, or rental unit.

In FHA terms, "neighborhood character" depended primarily on overt policies of ethnic and racial segregation. An FHA technical bulletin on *Planning Profitable Neighborhoods* advised developers to concentrate on a particular market, based on age, income, and race. The agency refused to underwrite houses in areas threatened by "Negro invasion." In the cities, it "red-lined" huge sections that were "changing" and refused to guarantee mortgage loans in those areas, claiming that the influx of blacks made the loans bad risks. In turn, banks and savings and loan associations refused to issue private loans and mortgages in red-lined neighborhoods. These policies played a critical role in the deterioration of stable, working-class communities like Detroit's Lower East Side and North Philadelphia, since rents were increased and services were cut when there was almost no opportunity for selling these houses.

In the suburbs, the FHA encouraged the use of restrictive covenants to ensure neighborhood homogeneity and to prevent any future problems of racial violence or declining property values. The 1947 manual openly stated: "If a mixture of user groups is found to exist, it must be determined whether the mixture will render the neighborhood less desirable to present and prospective occupants. Protective covenants are essential to the sound development of proposed residential areas, since they regulate the use of the land and provide a basis for the development of harmonious, attractive neighborhoods."[15] The National Association for the Advancement of Colored People (NAACP) charged that the FHA was "fostering black ghettos" through urban red-lining and suburban discrimination; but it could do nothing to alter the situation.[16] The federal government already lagged behind the courts. The director of the Housing and Home Finance Administration, Raymond Foley, waited two years after the 1948 Supreme Court decision outlawing restrictive covenants before announcing that the FHA would no longer issue mortgages in restricted neighborhoods. Until 1968, FHA officials still accepted unwritten agreements and existing "traditions" of segregation.

The FHA preferred controlled, segregated subdivisions in suburban areas to more complex and diverse urban development. It was in the suburbs that the postwar housing boom—actually a post–1949 boom—took place, altering huge expanses on the periphery of every large American city. Commuting to work from residential suburbs became the accepted way of life as federal funds for highway construction increased, culminating in the Federal-Aid Highway Act of 1956, which provided for forty-one thousand miles of limited access highways to link all the major cities.[17] By 1957, the FHA had financed 4.5 million suburban homes, with insurance totaling $29.5 billion; this represented about 30 percent of the new homes built in any one year.[18] With assurances from the federal government and long lines of people eager to buy single-family suburban homes, large builders and small began producing as many homes as they could.

This pattern signified a major change from the suburbs of the 1920s. In those days, developers or subdividers purchased large areas of undeveloped land. They platted future lots, installed streets and sewers, and then usually sold all or most of the land to small builders, who took a few blocks, or to individual clients, who hired their own builder or architect. In the 1950s, generous government-financing programs made it much more profitable for the developer to build the houses as well; this often resulted in subdivisions of three or four hundred almost identical tract houses. In Kaiser's Panorama City, California, there were three thousand uniform houses; in Frank Sharp's Oak Forest near Houston, there were five thousand; in the American Community Builders' Park Forest project outside Chicago—the FHA's largest project—there were eight thousand.[19]

Not all postwar developers put up miles of monotonous, poor-quality tract housing. Some tried to provide variety and innovative features, and a few hired architects to design their basic models. A typical contract with a builder gave the architect a retainer fee of $1,000 and $100 for each house that was built from his plans.[20] The architectural journals endorsed these collaborations, proudly declaring that the influence of professional architects would be the salvation of mass building. California builder Joseph Eichler hired the Los Angeles firm of Jones & Emmons and the San Francisco firm of Anshen & Allen to design several hundred prototypes for northern California suburbs.[21] These dwellings had flat shed roofs with exposed beam ceilings that continued outside to form wide overhangs. Large picture windows opened onto a spacious patio or atrium at the back of the house, which became the main entrance. Two-car garages dominated the front façades.

Most architects looked down on the average builder's aesthetic taste,

· ·

The California builder Joseph Eichler hired the San Francisco architectural firm of Anshen & Allen to design this model house with picture windows and an atrium, which was then constructed by the thousands in subdivisions all over the state.

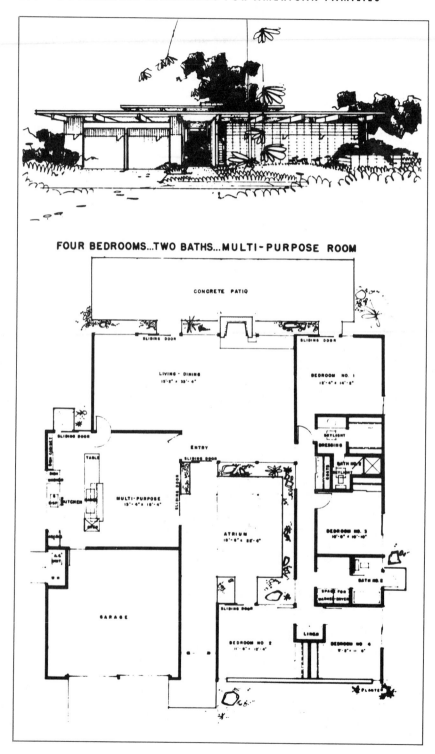

FOUR BEDROOMS...TWO BATHS...MULTI-PURPOSE ROOM

as well as his cost controls; and they scorned the cautious, conservative FHA design guidelines as well. For instance, FHA evaluators were instructed to lower the rating score of houses with conspicuously modern designs because they were not considered a sound investment. An agency pamphlet expressed doubt whether the modern style of flat roofs and plain, asymmetrical façades would prove to be more than a fad. Colonial Revival, Cape Cod, Tudor, Spanish, or a safe contemporary look like the ranch house was preferable. Even noted architects like Frank Lloyd Wright had their work rejected because of a low rating in the "Adjustment for Conformity" category. In November 1955, *House Beautiful,* devoting an entire issue to Wright's earlier prairie houses and a few more recent expensive residences, declared that his houses were the quintessence of American life, the legacy of the Declaration of Independence. But Wright's efforts to develop prefabricated "Usonian" houses for a moderate-income community did not win FHA approval.[22]

The popular ranch style combined the low-pitched roofs, deep eaves, and strong horizontal lines of Wright's early prairie houses with more traditional elements like clapboards, shutters, and a wide front porch. The word "ranch" evoked a rambling dwelling to most postwar buyers, which perhaps explains the great popularity of the design. In reality, most ranch-style houses of the 1950s had less square footage than the average house of the 1920s; but housewives saw an end to their countless trips up and down the stairs, and husbands liked the look of spaciousness, with fewer walls between rooms and a view of the backyard. *Parents' Magazine,* in an article promoting the magazine's own series of model homes, praised the 1950s "built-to-sell" ranch houses, basing their endorsement on the results of market surveys and statistics. "Contemporary design," declared the magazine's architectural consultant, "has recaptured a homey character as appealing as earlier American styles. The new architecture is, of course, an expression of the house plan itself and our new ways of life. Rambling, unsymmetrical plans cannot possibly result in formal, stylized exteriors."[23]

Levitt and Sons, the most important name in postwar suburban development, stayed with traditional styling but used modern construction techniques. In the years between 1947 and 1951, the company built 17,450 houses in Levittown, Long Island, converting a potato field into

· ·

(Opposite, left) Anshen & Allen's floor plan for Eichler Homes zoned social activities around the "multipurpose room," the livingdining area, the backyard patio, and a private atrium.

a community of 75,000 people. By 1950 the company's factory was producing one four-room house every sixteen minutes.[24] William J. Levitt, president of the firm, was easily the largest developer in the country. When sales opened in March 1949 for the new houses to be built that year, the firm signed fourteen hundred contracts in one day on the basis of their reputation and one model house. Their 1949 model had two bedrooms, a dining alcove off the living room, and a potentially expandable attic, providing seven hundred square feet of living space on a lot sixty feet by one hundred feet. Each year the model house had special "built-in" features, a promotional phrase that Levitt originated in 1947. In 1949, those features included a refrigerator, washing machine, and white picket fence. The next year's attraction was a television set embedded in the wall, thereby making it eligible for financing on the

. . . .

The 1949 model house at Levittown, New York, reproduced in *Life* magazine, helped William Levitt become the nation's largest home builder. He based the prototype on conventional residential styles, special "built-in" extras, and extremely low costs.

mortgage. Community features, especially the first of nine public swimming pools, also attracted buyers to Levittown. Abraham Levitt, the founder of the firm, supervised the landscaping and the planting of grass, shrubs, and forty thousand fruit trees.

The Levitts contained construction costs by hiring nonunion labor and setting up a mass-production system. Precut lumber, pipes, and copper coils for the radiant-heated concrete slabs came from the Levitt factory in Roslyn, Long Island. Trucks carried the materials to the site, where each worker, paid for piecework, did one job over and over every day. The firm did little advertising and employed only six salesmen; numerous articles on their success and extremely low costs assured the Levitts of more than enough clients.

Expanding into Pennsylvania and New Jersey in the early 1950s, Levitt and Sons continued to top the list of the country's big builders. As *Fortune* magazine reported in 1952, a few years after each new model appeared, Levitt's built-in features often became commonplace in homes offered by other builders. Across the country, radiant-heated concrete slabs replaced basements; double-glazed sliding windows and doors in a light, aluminum frame opened onto patios; three-way fireplaces in the center of an open plan—a device the Levitts borrowed from Frank Lloyd Wright—could be found in thousands of developers' houses; and the carport replaced the garage to cut costs. The Levitts were also responsible for moving the kitchen to the front of the house so that the living room could open onto the patio and backyard.

These architectural changes reflected something more than the builders' larger scale and desire to reduce expenses. Social scientists studied the "average family" in the suburbs, and psychologists published "livability studies" that correlated the domestic environment with statistics on crime and family stability. Architects like Richard Neutra and Eero Saarinen endorsed such "scientific analyses" of family activities and values. Many merchant-builders also carried out their own surveys of potential buyers. Young couples who moved out to the suburbs hoped to find the "dream house" and the "dream life" they had thought about so often during the war. With extensive research about the most prevalent domestic fantasies, builders tried to provide what the majority of surveyed families wanted.

The *Saturday Evening Post* reported in 1945 that only 14 percent of the population it had polled were willing to live in an apartment or a "used house."[25] The postwar buyers wanted a new house, with modern floor plan, up-to-date materials, and the latest appliances. *McCall's* magazine announced that its readers looked forward to the prospect of solar heating in their dream houses—although air conditioning, which began to be marketed on a mass scale around 1950, would soon seem more enticing. Buyers wanted a big picture window or sliding glass doors to make the house seem larger and more open. Preferably, the glass wall was in the back, facing the "outdoor living room," where so many activities associated with suburban living took place. Here was the barbeque pit, the Junglegym, the flower garden, the well-mowed lawn (thanks to a power mower, which became a status symbol even when the yard had just enough space in which the machine could be turned around). All these joys represented what one study of suburban communities called the "healthy, happy ways of using up surplus energy."[26]

A mother could watch her children outside through the picture window or, inside, with the popular open floor-plan. This visibility was based on a new premise of zoned planning in the home. The "activity area" of living room, dining area, and kitchen had few walls, providing as much space and togetherness as possible. The living room had a built-in radio and hi-fi unit that could be heard throughout the activity area. Built-in storage shelves and cabinets filled an entire wall in every room. Within carefully established dictates of taste, each family sought to give a vivid impression of "something different." Color and texture were signs of decorator aesthetics, so the housewife juxtaposed printed slipcovers with the pine-paneled walls of a traditional living room, or positioned a sectional sofa in front of the exposed stone fireplace in a more contemporary décor. Like her "handyman" husband, she took part in the do-it-yourself fad of painting furniture and laying brightly patterned linoleum floors.

In "economy houses" (650 square feet, by FHA standards), builders made the kitchen a little larger and omitted the dining area. Salesmen evoked the old-fashioned farmhouse kitchen as they explained why the rooms had been combined. Slightly larger houses had a tiny dining alcove at the end of the living room, separated from the kitchen by a storage wall with a pass-through opening, an open counter, or accordion folding doors. Sometimes between the kitchen and living room there was a breakfast bar or snack bar with tall stools. Informal meals were the trend, and a separate dining room would have added a few thousand dollars to the base price of a tract house.

In contrast to this openness, the bedroom, or "quiet zone," had walls and doors. With the vogue for split-level houses in the 1950s, builders put bedrooms on a different half-level up or down from the living space. The parents' bedroom and bath might be isolated from a zoned "children's area," either by a split-level design or an H-shaped plan. The bathroom was fitted with gadgets, even in a moderate-priced house, because surveys showed that clothes chutes, linen closets, sun lamps, or fancy cabinets around the sink boosted sales. Larger architect-designed houses often had an "adult" suite of rooms, which included the living room, a bath, and a "master bedroom," which opened onto its own private atrium. In marriage guides like *Women Today* (1953) and *Building a Successful Marriage* (1948), the attentive wife was advised to give her husband a place apart from the children.

Even in moderate-cost houses, two new rooms often appeared. One was the utility room, a space for the new automatic washer and, if the family could afford it, a dryer. The utility room was next to the kitchen, forming a utility core in order to reduce plumbing costs. It opened onto the backyard, so that children could leave their dirty clothes by the washing machine, and housewives who did not have dryers could get to the backyard clothes-tree easily.

In the suburban houses of the late 1940s and 1950s, attention to children's needs—some would say the creation of children's needs—produced a special place for their activities. First labeled the don't-say-no space or the multipurpose room, it was later called the family room in a 1947 *Parent's Magazine* model house. Sometimes no more than an extension of the kitchen, the family room was usually accessible from the outside through a sliding glass door. It had a linoleum floor for dancing, a table for bridge games, and comfortable furniture for the new family pastime of watching television. In 1946, the FCC authorized four hundred television stations, and antennas went up on the first eight thousand rooftops across the country.[27] Although the family room most often served as a place where children could do as they pleased in the midst of clutter and noise, it was also an architectural expression of family togetherness.

Dr. Benjamin Spock's *Common Sense Book of Baby and Child Care* (1946) emphasized that the good mother should be constantly attentive to her child's changing physical and emotional needs. "How lucky you are to be able to be natural and flexible," he told his readers, explaining why the strict schedules their mothers had followed were harmful to a child's development.[28] Now it was expected that the mother be a constant companion and gentle teacher. Since in the early 1950s few young families had a second car for the mother's use, and most new subdivisions had neither parks nor playgrounds, preschool children were home with their attentive mothers all day.

As suburban families multiplied, many sociologists and psychiatrists became concerned about the effect of suburban life on the families who lived there—and on society as a whole. *The Organization Man* (1955) told of dissatisfied executives and middle-level managers retreating to the suburbs at the end of the day, where they faced more pressures to conform. Women, living in a world almost totally devoid of men, had little to say to their husbands. "Domination by the little woman" extended from the family to the larger community and portended dangerous results, according to social scientists.[29] The uniformity of suburbs, with people of almost exactly the same age, background, and income, seemed to deny individuality. "Mass-produced, standardized housing breeds standardized individuals, too—especially among youngsters," warned psychologist Sidonie Gruenberg in *The New York Times Magazine*.[30] David Riesman's *The Lonely Crowd* (1950) captured the sense of conformity, sadness, and isolation of modern suburban life.

There was, in fact, a definite sociological pattern to the household that moved out to the suburbs in the late 1940s and 1950s. With an average age of thirty-one in 1950, they were younger than the central-city population. There were few single, widowed, or divorced adults, and few elderly ones. Young children abounded, and their numbers increased more rapidly, for the fertility rate in the suburbs was higher than it was in the cities. Only 9 percent of suburban women worked in 1950, compared to 27 percent for the population as a whole.[31] While the average level of education was higher, there were an increasing number of working-class suburbs, and even a number of fast-growing factory suburbs like Skokie, Illinois, and Milpitas, California.

Herbert J. Gans countered the charges of listless personalities and tyrannical conformity with his book on *The Levittowners* (1967). After two years of living in that largely middle-income community, talking in the backyard as well as in the living room, Gans acknowledged the boredom of women tied to their homes, the loneliness of women cut off from family in the cities. However, Gans would not condemn suburbs as escapist retreats; rather, he contended that homeownership gave many of the residents of Levittown a great sense of pride, "a public symbol of achievement, 'something to show for all your years of living,'" one neighbor had declared.[32] The suburban environment was also important to many women, even though daily life was often harder for them. The overwhelming majority of women with whom Gans talked had wanted to come to the suburbs in order to secure more room and more privacy for their families, which gave them great satisfaction in their roles as wives and mothers.

A few critics tried to promote changes in the government's policies for the suburbs. Journalist John Keats's bitter novel *The Crack in the Picture Window* (1957), which ridiculed the suburban life of John and Mary Drone, also sought to explain why the problems existed. Keats attacked the builders, the bankers, and the federal agencies he held responsible for the VA-financed catastrophe of the postwar period. Planner Catherine Bauer advocated an approach to suburban planning that introduced diversity of ages and socioeconomic groups rather than one strait-jacket idea of "the average family" living up to "the American standard of living." The 1948 White House Conference on Family Life stressed the need for such "mixing" in suburban communities, calling for a balance between old and young, rich and poor, though it side-stepped racial and ethnic integration. Yet the actual policies of the government, and the notions of sound investments shared by most builders and bankers, created a suburban world characterized by unimaginative planning, steep housing costs, inadequate services, class and racial segregation: a world that simply could not be blamed on the suburbanites themselves.

To begin with, the families who moved to the suburbs had been priced out of the market for decent city apartments. Furthermore, they sincerely cared about their children and doubted their own judgment about the best way to raise them. The arguments that brought them to the suburbs unilaterally condemned the city as a dangerous place for children and played on the insecurity of an entire generation of parents. Like the critics who blamed suburban conformity on the uniform dwellings, the suburbanites themselves tended to look for architectural ways to solve problems. In 1956 the Housing and Home Finance Administration held a Women's Housing Congress to solicit ideas about changes in housing policy. One hundred and three women were invited to Washington, all of whom were white, middle-class suburban housewives. They were not satisfied with the housing choices available to them, and posed their problems in psychological as well as economic terms. One woman contended that the house took its toll on parents, especially mothers. "Fewer would go to our mental wards and divorce courts," she declared, "if they had one room, even a small one, just for themselves . . . peace and quiet without the television and radio."[33]

Once again, ordinary Americans, echoing those with some authority, gave what sounded like a parody of the idea that domestic architecture determined the course of society and the state of the individual family. The architecture of the postwar suburbs was symptomatic of other problems, but it did not by itself cause those problems. One has only to consider the stifled frustration of women in the suburbs, their isolation from work opportunities and from contact with other adults; the limited experiences available to children and teenagers; or the emphasis on the man's role as the distant provider who should spend his time at home "improving the property." The setting for these psycho-sociological distortions was supposedly a "pure," "safe" suburb. Seemingly necessary restrictions were imposed by builders and by the FHA, who encouraged class, racial, and religious segregation under the guise of neighborhood planning. Their promise of architectural refinement and protection from external dangers fell on willing ears. To many Americans, the suburban house seemed the only way to provide a good family life. This was what the government, the builders, the bankers, and the magazines told them, and many believed it—or felt they had to.

The suburban boom of the 1950s and 1960s masked the fact that not all housing demand was being satisfied. Many people—childless couples, urbanites, ethnic families, the poor who could not afford homeownership—wanted some alternative to suburban sprawl. The lack of a national housing policy was especially hard on the lower middle class, since the recession that hit home building at the end of the 1950s was not due to a lack of demand but to the lack of a coherent program for financing and constructing a variety of housing types. From the early 1960s through the late 1970s, builders began to respond to the groups that had been ignored. Two trends—new residential zoning provisions and a sudden enthusiasm for the urbane pleasures of city life—laid the groundwork for the housing patterns of the 1980s.

The defense of urban life derived, in large part, from a group of books that were published or reissued in the early 1960s. The most widely known were Jane Jacobs's *The Death and Life of Great American Cities* (1961), Lewis Mumford's *The Culture of Cities* (1938, 1960) and *The City in History* (1961), and Paul and Percival Goodman's *Communitas: Means of Livelihood and Ways of Life* (1947, 1960). These authors lauded the vitality of urban life, the visual interest, the social contacts, the cultural diversity. They denounced the antiseptic high-rise towers of modern apartment buildings and public-housing projects, branding this kind of architecture antithetical to real urban life. Cities depended on ethnic neighborhoods, familiar landmarks, a mixture of the grand and the small. The authors also concurred that the cities were in trouble. The middle class and the young were abandoning urban centers in favor of the suburbs. Banks and government encouraged the exodus, leaving the cities to the very rich and the very poor.

Even the people who found these books naïve and romantic recognized that there had to be some middle ground between suburban sprawl and urban high-rise, between isolation in the suburbs and anonymity in the cities. The architectural result was a concept called cluster housing. In the mid-1960s, developers suddenly began to support medium-density, multifamily housing, much of it designed by architects. The favored approach was to group apartments or townhouses close together on a site, and then landscape the remaining space for common use. Residents walked along footpaths lined with benches and trees to small playgrounds or parking lots. Prestigious communities featured tennis courts, swimming pools, or artificial lakes in the communal space. De-

· ·

Reston, Virginia, was one successful example of the shift toward townhouses and communal social spaces—with a special emphasis on natural settings such as lakes and wooded areas—in the housing developments of the late 1960s.

signers tried to re-create the varied skyline and broad range of public activities described in the recent books on urban life. They also looked to Italian hill towns and New England villages as models. This was a step toward more urbanized residential communities, although each development tended to be self-consciously quaint and cloistered.

In the decade between 1963 and 1973, nearly 20 million new dwelling units were built in the United States, more than in any previous decade. Enthusiasm for denser housing developments and a new concept of the planned residential community led to a notable decline in conventional single-family housing. By the mid–1960s, builders in many metropolitan areas put up more multifamily houses than single-family residences.[34] The prospective buyer or renter found a plethora of developments aimed at young singles or retirement villages for the elderly. In turn, the government sponsored thousands of low-income and moderate-income projects, giving churches, unions, and nonprofit groups below-market interest rates.

Local governments often granted private developers special zoning privileges if they built cluster housing, or what came to be known as Planned Unit Developments (PUDs). They relaxed regulations covering setbacks from lot lines, distances between houses, width of streets, densities, and mixing of residential and commercial uses. Environmental organizations praised PUDs, since the developers protected existing trees, hillsides, and natural amenities as part of their package. But it was only the very large developers who could afford to prepare the extensive preliminary reports and site plans the zoning commissions required for PUD applications, and risk that their proposal would be turned down. For them, not the smaller builders, municipal governments relaxed the rigid specifications for residential communities.

The books praising urban life, the continuing murmurs of criticism about suburban monotony, and the developers' interest in reaching new markets did bring forth a new residential pattern. Builders, local zoning boards, and government housing agencies readily accepted cluster housing. In a period of abundance, new kinds of communities provided alternatives to the high-rise and the detached suburban house. But little effort was made to help existing urban neighborhoods or to alter the prevailing pattern in the suburbs. In 1962, for instance, the government spent $820 million to subsidize housing for the poor; in that same year, it spent approximately $2.9 billion simply on homeowners' tax deductions, most of which went to the suburbs.[35]

In the early 1970s, both the middle-class private market and federal housing programs declined sharply once again. Inflation cut into the number of private housing starts; and in 1973, President Nixon issued a moratorium on government funds for low-income and moderate-income housing. By mid-decade, there were television specials and news-paper stories on "the housing crisis" that portrayed cluster housing as the necessary but less-than-desirable solution for young families who could not afford good suburban homes. It was not seen as a positive, realistic approach to economic constraints, energy problems, or demo-graphic change. Instead, townhouses and trailers and cooperative build-ings were consistently presented as inadequate, makeshift substitutes for detached suburban dwellings. The new housing alternatives were posed as a threat to the postwar suburban ideal, as evidence of the average builder's chicanery and the failure of government housing programs; but they were seldom connected to a vision of cultural pluralism, different kinds of family life, and more diverse communities. These architectural experiments had an alarming social dimension for many middle-class Americans. Although dense, multi-use communities clearly represented changes in "the traditional American way of life," they did not, as yet, suggest the idea that people themselves could direct those changes.

CHAPTER FOURTEEN

RESERVING HOMES AND PROMOTING CHANGE

> I've spent a lot of time working in the area of civil rights and voter registration. But now my productivity is direct; my work results in houses, something I can see. Now I'm building houses for people who need them.
>
> —Arthur Pless, crew coordinator for Koinonia Partners, a nonprofit housing corporation in Americus, Georgia

AMERICANS IN THE 1980S ARE FACING YET ANOTHER housing crisis. It derives from the rising cost of homes and financing for homeownership, the shortage of rental units, the effects of an energy shortage, and severe unemployment. It also reflects changing patterns of social life. In 1980, for example, only 13 percent of all American households consisted of a working father, a stay-at-home mother, and one or more children. The growing number of working women; the larger proportion of elderly people; a continuing increase in single-person households; a significant gay presence in many cities; violence in public housing; the middle-class return to the cities and a resulting displacement of the urban poor, have become indisputable facts. There is a consistent social dimension to these issues and to rampant housing speculation, since social trends and economic constraints come together with a painful impact on the housing market. Historically, two out of three new houses in the United States went to first-time home buyers, and the third to a current homeowner who needed more space or could afford more status. The situation is the opposite today: two of those houses go to people who are "trading up," buying what they hope is a better investment than their present home.[1] What this fact means socially was bluntly suggested at a recent home builders' convention when the head of a real-estate consulting firm declared: "We're selling 90 percent of the houses to 15 percent of the people. The ones who can't afford it [sic], can't afford anything."

The overwhelming majority of Americans cannot afford to buy a home today, whether it is a condominium, a townhouse, or a detached dwelling. The president of the National Association of Home Builders estimated in 1980 that only 8 percent of all potential buyers had sufficient income to purchase a home.[2] In 1974, the average price of a single-family home was $37,800. Six years later, that house was selling for over $70,000—an increase of almost 100 percent. The real cost of housing to the purchaser is, of course, much higher, with interest rates more than double what they were in the late 1960s, so the total rise in housing costs far outweighs salary increases. Moreover, the costs of gasoline, electricity, and heating fuel have made home maintenance uncomfortably expensive, especially for elevator apartment buildings and sprawling ranch houses in commuter suburbs. Both renters and home-owners are paying a larger and larger portion of their income for a place to live.

The people who have been excluded from the housing market, relegated to its edges or forced to sacrifice too much in order to buy, are now a population large enough and vocal enough to constitute a political force. A decent home and a desirable neighborhood are worth fighting about, and the spectrum of potential fighters extends from working-class women in ethnic neighborhoods to retired middle-class couples in the suburbs, from professionals who are single parents to poor families, from wealthy suburbanites to backwoods rural dwellers. In New York, black ministers wage a "crusade" against the housing shortage by sponsoring housing renovations in Harlem. Sessions of the San Francisco Board of Supervisors are packed with real-estate lobbyists, retired longshoremen now living in run-down residential hotels, and young community organizers who want to protect those hotels from the speculators. The Suburban Action Institute recently challenged a Union Carbide effort to relocate from New York City to Danbury, Connecticut, when a study revealed that only half the employees could afford to live near there. A local housing-development corporation in Appalachian Kentucky repairs leaking roofs, dangerous underpinnings, and substandard plumbing in rural homes, while providing jobs for former miners, many of whom suffer from black lung disease.

The current housing dilemmas cannot be solved by new financing schemes or more efficient housing prototypes—although both of these are necessary. The displacement of the poor, the unavailability of rental property, the high costs of land and financing, the wasteful energy expenditures, the stigma of public housing, are not isolated problems to be remedied by piecemeal government action or private enterprise. At issue are basic changes in how Americans live, as well as where they live. Like the earlier junctures in American housing, today's situation encompasses redefinitions of family life, class relations, and political power.

Of course, some architectural considerations are exigent, together with government policies of financial support, tax benefits, and building-code reforms, at national and local levels. In the cities and the suburbs, smaller dwellings, clustered closer together and featuring energy-conserving systems, are an inevitable new model for the American home. Already there is government and foundation funding for rehabilitation by low-income neighborhood groups; private banks lend to young profes-

. . . .

The East Kentucky Housing Development Corporation trains retired coal miners to build and repair houses for themselves and their neighbors in rural Appalachia.

sionals who are renovating urban row houses, since they now recognize that such investments are profitable. Some suburbs will become urbanized as zoning regulations are eased; the result will be a closer mixture of houses, businesses, hotels, and services. But other marginal suburbs will deteriorate as they become the next available sites for the poor minorities, which are being displaced from the inner cities. (Professor Franz Schurmann and members of the Third Century American Project predict that these areas will be converted into the kind of *bidonvilles* that ring European and Third World cities, packed with dilapidated houses and makeshift shacks, offering few employment opportunities for the residents.) Older suburbs that try to resist change will find their taxes steadily rising, and their populations in need of expensive health and social services, for these are enclaves with an increasingly elderly median age.[3] Whatever their physical form and social makeup, every kind of suburban development will need political attention and economic investment in the decades to come.

To be sure, technological breakthroughs and cost-cutting measures will continue to have the same appeal they have had in the past. But consider the fate of two such attempts of the 1970s: the stripped-down house and the mobile home. When only one fourth of the population could afford a $35,000 home, builders began promoting the "mini-home," the "compact," the "no-frills" model, with one floor and an unfinished attic. At sizes ranging from nine hundred to twelve hundred square feet, they were one third smaller than conventional tract houses. Builders eliminated appliances, exterior millwork, landscaping, and family rooms. But this approach proved to be a debacle. The cost reductions were inadequate, especially when the familiar signs of domestic comfort and prestige were eliminated. Buyers who could afford suburban homes were not interested in houses that gave them only the basics; they did not want to think about the work that still had to be done in order to get the package they were paying for. And for many, the price of these "mini-homes" was still not low enough.

In 1973, *Forbes* ranked three mobile-home manufacturers among the most profitable American corporations over the previous half-decade. Arthur Decio, chairman of Skyline Homes, the nation's largest producer, gloated: "Some years ago builders just decided to forget about low-income groups. This was our opportunity, and we are trying to make the most of it."[4] But the low-income associations tainted mobile-home courts. Sixty percent of American communities currently ban them from privately owned lots and residential neighborhoods. Three fourths of the

11 million people who live in them cannot afford to own the property their home sits on. Half of the 4 million mobile homes in America are sited in twenty-four thousand parks, surrounded by the high walls required by local codes.[5] While some of these parks are carefully landscaped, many are on land that is undesirable for any other kind of residential property.

The recession of 1973–1974 hurt poor families and the elderly, who comprise the primary mobile-home market. Hundreds of thousands of mobile homes were repossessed, and production dropped dramatically. The industry has not yet recovered. Despite the grave shortage of affordable housing, the mobile-home share of the single-family housing market fell from 37 percent in 1974 to 17 percent in mid–1979.[6] To dispell the idea of mobile homes as "lower-class" squatter settlements, manufacturers have boosted production of "doublewides," in which two single units are joined together to create a house that approaches conventional site-built dwellings in size. But the higher cost of doublewides and the fees for higher-quality parks have narrowed the price differential between mobile homes and other kinds of housing.

The housing of the coming decade will represent new facts of social life as well as economic constraints, but no single new prototype will address all or even most of the issues now before us. Government agencies, builders, manufacturers, and political organizations representing various consumer groups will continue to put forward solutions, each constituency claiming that it represents the shared interests of all. But there are too many different groups demanding better housing, with too many disparate needs. More than ever, American housing, like American society and American families, must be characterized by diversity.

We have yet to reach the point at which our current dilemmas elicit the kind of engaged, idealistic response of previous generations of Americans, who consistently saw housing as a social, political, and cultural device for change. Of course, there were fundamental limitations in the programs of the past, as we have seen; but there was also a sense of possibility. For many people today, the need to make "necessary sacrifices" leads to bitterness and resentment. Accepting a range of housing alternatives or a reasonable policy of energy conservation becomes an imposition. The vision of universal homeownership in the suburbs, the promise of unlimited bounty, the assurances of government agencies and private-home builders, especially during the 1950s, now seem false. More people must rent rather than own, and pay too much for that; they must do without various consumer goods because of inflation; pleasure driving must be curtailed because of the cost of gasoline; many couples must postpone beginning a family so they can afford a house first. For these people, it is "the end of the American Dream," a dream that had become intimately associated with cars and large, single-family suburban houses. In reality, it is the demise of postwar suburbia as the quintessential expression of that dream.

The American Dream also evoked an image of the typical American family. The Harvard-MIT Joint Center for Urban Studies estimates that by 1990 the number of households containing unattached individuals—those who have never been married, who are divorced, or who are widowed—will nearly equal the number of households with married couples. In 86 percent of the married couples, both partners will be salaried workers.[7] In social, political, economic, and architectural terms, such demographic data evidence the need to acknowledge changing definitions of the family; and housing will have to adapt to those plural definitions.

Home builders are all too aware of the critical situation, for the recession in that industry has been severe. Although they are cautiously turning toward more diversified markets, they remain unsure about how to convince these groups to invest in new houses. Between 1980 and 1990, 42 million Americans will reach the age of thirty, traditionally the age for settling down and, for several past generations, buying that first house. But what will they be able to afford? And what will they want? Already, in 1980, reports Michael Sumichrast, the National Association of Home Builders' chief economist, almost half of all home buyers have two incomes. For young people who can afford to buy, the detached house in a strictly "bedroom suburb" is no longer their ideal. They want reduced maintenance and convenient social amenities. At the same time, the most lucrative market is the rapidly expanding number of one-person households. But if large suburban houses are not the answer for them either, no one seems entirely sure what is. Still searching for a close "fit" between one type of dwelling and a precise definition of family life, builders are hoping to find a perfect mold that will assure them of a future market.

The 1980 convention of the National Association of Home Builders presented a variety of possible approaches for ensuring a larger future housing market. Participants examined the displays of new products—ranging from woodsman stoves to Jacuzzi whirlpool bathtubs—eager to believe the claims that luxury products would win the class of buyers they sought. Special workshops concentrated on sales techniques, "perceived value" gimmicks and catchy logos. But other sessions addressed the need for more fundamental changes in the housing business. Arthur Solomon of the Harvard-MIT Joint Center for Urban Studies elaborated on the need for builders to provide more low-cost and moderate-cost housing. Members of the Senate Banking, Housing and Urban Affairs Committee discussed legislation and national economic policies that are holding back construction.

George Fulton, senior vice-president of a major real-estate consulting firm, told his audience that the 1980s will be great for the house-building and real-estate business *if* builders adjust to the changes taking place in society. They cannot continue to build for the "traditional" American family, and they will have to regard low-income housing as an opportunity rather than a threat. Builders will have to plan houses for living situations they might not approve of, houses that will accommodate working mothers or single parents, for instance. James A. Autry, editor of several mass-market house-decorating magazines, spoke of new markets as well: the housing demands of gays, divorced mothers, young singles, and elderly persons. The industry, he said, will have to engage in a different kind of political lobbying, working for financing reforms and new zoning laws. Banks, for instance, still discriminate against unmarried couples and working women, on whom builders will be increasingly dependent. For four decades, the real-estate lobby campaigned against public housing and for government support of suburban homeownership. Now builders will have to ally themselves with people whose values are different from their own.

Not all people with housing needs have been waiting around for builders to recognize them. During the 1970s, a grassroots political activism developed in the United States, quite distinct from the politics of the 1960s. Women's groups, tenants' councils, preservation societies, public-housing residents' boards, "no-growth" suburban leagues, and thousands of neighborhood groups were formed. Housing has been a focal point for many of the local groups and a major organizing issue for the nationwide, more politicized coalitions. Jubilee Housing and the Community of Hope in Washington, D.C., and the St. Landry Low-Income Housing Corporation in rural Louisiana, together with the much larger National People's Action and the National Low-Income Housing Coalition, are part of a self-declared progressive movement for the 1980s, a movement that views housing and neighborhood preservation as key political issues. But it would be quite false to suggest that these issues have an inherently liberal or radical impact. Strong pro-family sentiments have also become politicized and carry with them, in addition to anti-ERA, anti-welfare, and pro-tax reform demands, inevitable extensions to housing and community concerns. While some organizations are determined to preserve single-family housing in segregated suburbs, urban working-class neighborhoods have their demands, too. Labels of "right" and "left" do not easily apply.

Like their predecessors in the progressive movement at the turn of the century, many classes of women have become involved in housing politics because they care deeply about their own homes and families. That is what motivated a group of white working-class women from the Williamsburg section of Brooklyn, New York, to form the National Congress of Neighborhood Women. They believed that their loyalty to home, family, church, and community were the values of working-class culture, and that those values had to be defended. The congress first worked under the aegis of Monsignor Geno Baroni, then director of the National Center for Urban Ethnic Affairs in Washington (and later an official at the Department of Housing and Urban Development [HUD]). Within a year, the women had formed their own political base in Williamsburg and had learned the ropes in Washington. The congress won Comprehensive Employment and Training Act (CETA) money for a salaried staff and almost three hundred local community jobs. Thirty-eight women's groups throughout the five boroughs of New York were eventually brought together. They battled against red-lining; they organized credit unions, a college program, a community-controlled day-care center, and a shelter for battered wives. These last two accomplishments are especially noteworthy, since working mothers, divorced women, and wives in bad marriages had once been ostracized in these communities. The home is still the center of these women's lives; and local schools and parish churches continue to be important to them. They are proud of their roles as wives and mothers, but it took political pressure to protect their families and their communities.

Women in suburbia have different problems and less unified representation. Many of them housewives raising families, they are suspicious of the changes going on around them. In addition, there are suburban retired people and young single mothers on Aid to Families with Dependent Children. Years of segregation battles have resulted in separate suburbs for the poor, for minorities, for the young and the old, a tendency that does not seem to have been fundamentally altered in recent years despite individual movements. But certain social trends affect a majority of these families now, notwithstanding the reservations about change.

One of the inevitable transformations in the suburbs of the 1980s involves accommodations for working women. The average suburban woman these days is not "just a housewife." More than half the country's mothers are employed outside the home. Of married women with children under six years of age, 43 percent work, either full-time or part-time. Many of these women live in the suburbs and want to stay there; some of them work to help pay for the house. Over three fourths of American families, including those of blue-collar workers, own their homes; and most of these are suburban houses.[8] A detached suburban house can be quite functional for working women if the suburb has public transportation (which is used by more women than men), supermarkets open after working hours, and nearby day-care facilities. (Most women who work prefer to leave their child in a smaller, more familiar center that is near home rather than take advantage of on-the-job day-care services.) Builders are promoting time-saving conveniences in the home in an effort to cater to two-career couples—architecture continues to be an appealing way to address social conditions—but the larger scale of the community is more relevant for this group. Desirable residential settings are complex environments, larger than the individual dwelling, encompassing shops and offices and services, which help the working mother and often provide her with a job. Job growth in the recently built suburbs now equals or exceeds the national average.[9]

Young people in particular—singles, childless couples, families of many sorts—are moving to new urbanized suburbs, as well as returning to the cities. They are not necessarily staying in the kinds of suburbs where their parents lived. Instead, many of them are choosing to live in clusters of townhouses or apartments, with shared outdoor space and recreational facilities, which compensate for the loss of private space and provide entertainment in non-working hours. There are commercial buildings, small nonpolluting industries, many shops, and public transportation services. For those who favor them, these settings represent modern notions of efficiency and community, much as the earliest American apartment-hotels did.

In existing suburbs, as in the newer developments, changes in zoning laws are essential. Not only does exclusionary zoning still restrict poor and ethnic minorities from moving to most suburbs, but other ordinances restrict the freedom of the middle-class and working-class women who do live there and make commuting time longer for everyone by separating residential and work areas. Most established suburbs insist upon a physical discontinuity between home and work. "Home occupations" are therefore not allowed. Of course, the restrictions do not encompass cooking, sewing, or child care—unless that occupation becomes public and provides a service for more than one family. The majority of use violations are reported by one owner against another, and usually concern work being done in the home, which is seen as a threat to property values and to stable family life. Clearly, such policies restrict the options for both women and men who want to engage in a productive job while they remain at home with their children.

Zoning that limits the possibility of having non-family members rent or occupy part of a single-family house poses another hardship. Such ordinances prohibit more than three unmarried persons from living together; they also make it impossible to rent a bedroom to a student

· ·

The San Francisco–based firm of Fisher-Friedman Associates designed this "urbanized suburb" for the San Diego area. Brittany Village, which opened in 1981, combines a hotel, townhouses, apartments, and commercial area, mixing several different kinds of uses rather than isolating homes from jobs and public life.

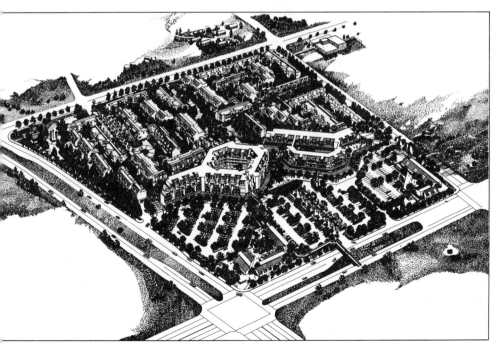

or older person in exchange for watching over the children. The 1974 Supreme Court *Belle Terre* decision defined the characteristics of single-family residential areas, excluding nonrelated persons from living together in such districts. Justice William O. Douglas's description of a residential suburb emphasized isolation in "a quiet place where yards are wide, people few, and motor vehicles restricted . . . in a land-use project addressed to family needs. . . . It is ample to lay out zones where family values, youth values, and the blessings of quiet seclusion and clean air make the area a sanctuary for people."[10] As mortgage payments spiral upwards and an increasing number of wives work, households will want to make some provision for using their homes differently. More families will adapt part of the house as an office for the husband or wife. They already make illegal accommodations, termed "in-law units" in California or "granny apartments" in Chicago, to suggest that the owners are renting to their immediate kin and not violating the zoning ordinances. The day of two-family or three-family houses, and even of planned boarding accommodations, is returning.

People who want residential sanctuaries are also fighting for their ideal of home, family, and property. They want to keep alive the suburbs of the postwar generation, and for a variety of reasons. A "progressive," integrationist, or feminist stance is by no means the most common outcome of housing battles today, nor has it been in the past. In every class of white suburb, as in many white urban working-class areas, the determination to preserve one's neighborhood is a strong force. Sometimes this involves campaigns to improve public schools or to reduce property taxes. Sometimes it simply translates into a firm stand on racial segregation.

No-growth ordinances are a conspicuous means for prohibiting the construction of new multifamily housing developments that might bring in people from a different race or socioeconomic group; they are as well an effort to prevent speculative builders from destroying small towns. Federal and state regulations now require "a reasonable possibility" for a variety of housing choices in a community, but officials are wary about intruding on suburban "home rule." Resistant to change, angry suburbanites in Madison, New Jersey; Petaluma, California; Birmingham, Michigan; and Forest Hills, New York, have recalled elected officials and staged demonstrations in opposition to new housing that would have given them low-income neighbors. As a result of this political threat, the compromise is usually an architectural one: the addition of some higher-density middle-class housing. If these communities cannot openly exclude other groups, they can certainly stand in the doorway.

The pressures on suburban communities arise in part from the difficulty of finding rental property, a situation that was aggravated in many cities during the postwar period. Today, there is a severe shortage of rental units in almost every metropolitan area. The national rental market had a 4.8 percent vacancy rate in late 1979—as tight as it has ever been; in San Francisco, Seattle, and Boston, the situation is even graver.[11] The problem for parents with children, whether the parents themselves are married or not, is especially difficult. According to the Fair Housing for Children Project, 70 percent of the apartment buildings surveyed in Los Angeles would not admit children of any age; another 16 percent had age restrictions.[12] (One landlord charged a pregnant woman an additional $10 for each child—including the one

. . . .

Many suburbanites adamantly defend their residential communities and the way of life these developments evoke for them.

not yet born.) "Fair housing for children" ordinances, like zoning ease-ments in the suburbs, cut across economic and racial lines, to have widespread social and architectural implications.

The large number of single mothers who are poor creates a special set of considerations. Since almost one female-headed family in three lives below the poverty level, compared to about one in eighteen headed by a man, the "feminization of poverty" must be seen as a complex set of problems.[13] An important aspect of those problems concerns housing, and especially urban apartments. HUD found that women heads of households are more urbanized than the general population: 71 percent live in standard metropolitan areas. They are also more likely to rent, and thus to live in multifamily structures. The National Congress of Negro Women found that in one city, 75 percent of female heads of households were renters.[14] These women require programs that address their hous-ing needs, their energy needs, and their social needs in ways that encour-age the recipients to become involved in the development of their urban communities.

Single parents and two-career families with higher incomes are also making a visible impact on the cities. The search for surroundings that are supportive of their way of life has been a major impetus for the resurgence of urban neighborhoods. Though there is not one kind of housing that meets the needs of all working mothers, single or married, several recent studies have found that these women tend to prefer condominiums and apartments to suburban houses. "Basically, we found that women want the more efficient environment," said Donald Roth-blatt, one author of a study on San Jose. "They want fewer demands on their time and they want better supportive services, such as the socializ-ing facilities condominiums often provide, the child-care services that are usually nearer to the city, the lack of yard work and the reduced commuter time."[15] Women are becoming a housing market and a political force because they are entering both the work force and politics in unprecedented numbers.

A coalition of diverse local groups, campaigning under the banner of Neighborhoods First, has tried to address the need for day-care, good schools, safety, and responsible financial investment in housing, both in individual communities and on a legislative level. According to Gail Cincotta, a fifty-year-old mother of six from Chicago who heads Na-tional People's Action, the slogan was a reaction to the fact that concern about the cities had focused for too long on downtown business districts rather than on where people live. Cincotta and others in the citizen lobby staged confrontations with the American Bankers Association when that group met in New Orleans in 1979, challenging the premise that high interest and mortgage rates would combat inflation. They won passage of an anti–red-lining bill; a home mortgage disclosure act, which requires banks to make public where they invest money; and several neighborhood development programs. Speaking before the House Committee on Banking, Currency and Housing in 1976, Cincotta declared that neighborhood groups like hers stood for particular local issues as well as for shared national values. "Grassroots neighborhood organizations," she told the congressmen, "that have accurately predicted the failure and the abuse of governmental programs are the conscience that Jefferson placed his trust in. While these neighborhood organizations exist to foster civic virtue, their voice is seldom heard. They are often categorized as dissidents and outsiders by their own government."[16]

Larger social and political issues are, in fact, brought home to people when they begin campaigning for better housing. According to one recent book on the neighborhood movement:

As the debate has grown, so have the issues. From being denied a $3,000 home improvement loan to the net losses of banks on Real Estate Investment Trusts [REITs] and speculative foreign loans. From that abandoned building on this block to HUD's inability to regulate mortgage bankers. From the home burglary last night to the allocation of funds for the criminal justice system. From an increase in this month's utility bill to fighting the deregulation of the energy industry.[17]

The principal focus of grassroots politics has been housing. But for over eight thousand such groups, according to the National Commission on Neighborhoods, housing is also a vehicle for demanding jobs, safety, and democratic participation in government.[18] For others, it must be said, the critical political issues are protecting segregated neighborhoods and a way of life oriented around family and church.

In the cities, a major aspect of the current housing problem is the reverse filtration, a process for which the British have coined the term "gentrification." Instead of housing passing down to lower-income groups as people buy up, middle-class couples and single people are moving into the older sections of large cities and buying what had been inexpensive dwellings for the poor. In New Orleans, dock workers are evicted from alley dwellings in the Lower Garden district so that enterprising young couples can rehabilitate and rent the houses at their new market value. In Charleston, South Carolina, former slave quarters have become elegant apartments. In Washington, D. C., Boston, Savannah, and other cities, rehabilitated early-nineteenth-century row houses command higher rents than their poor occupants can afford. Displacement was a problem with slum clearance for public housing and with massive urban-renewal projects; but today it is even more pervasive, as middle-class couples, gays, and young professionals who want the social and cultural attractions of city life are forcing out the poor.

Another pressure for city dwellers, especially the poor and the elderly, is the rapid conversion of rental apartment buildings into condominiums, cooperatives, or tourist hotels. The concept of condominiums, quite recent in this country, entered the United States, via Puerto Rico, in the 1960s. It was not until 1968 that all fifty states enacted legislation to authorize condominium ownership; but in 1979 alone, the Senate Subcommittee on Housing and Urban Affairs found that between 130,-000 and 250,000 rental units were taken off the market and converted into condominiums.[19] A number of cities have passed ordinances preventing conversions when vacancy rates fall below a certain threshold, but the speculative profit in "condomania" continues to prevail over such human concerns.

San Franciscans for Affordable Housing was organized to deal with the related problems when developers converted residential hotels for the elderly poor into expensive tourist accommodations. Together with the Gray Panthers (activists for the elderly), the Affordable Housing coalition convinced city supervisers to place a moratorium on such conversions; and there is now a bill under discussion that, if passed, will make the moratorium permanent. A developer will have to find equivalent housing for each tenant—mostly retired union men on fixed incomes—before being allowed to convert, and that will be so difficult that these residents will probably be able to keep their homes.

The New York Times ran a front-page story on the "right to rent" movement in 1979. In twenty-two states, tenants' groups have succeeded in passing ordinances that regulate rental agreements, evictions, relocations, and harassment of renters. The 50,000-member New Jersey Tenants Organization, the now veteran Boston Tenants Union, the city-wide Dallas Tenants Union, and other powerful lobbying groups are evidence of a new political constituency. The New Jersey organization engineered some 130 municipal rent-control laws.[20] In Cambridge, Massachusetts, Urban Planning Aid helped organize tenants in private-market housing, public housing, and FHA-owned property. Rent-control activists in Santa Monica and Santa Barbara, California, mounted precinct-by-precinct campaigns and won strong rent-control boards. The Campaign for Economic Democracy, a powerful force behind the Santa Monica scene, astutely recognized that one of the best ways to build a political base for other changes—a ban on nuclear power, control of energy corporations, increased citizen participation in government—was to begin with housing.

Rehabilitation of existing housing is now a favorite renewal tactic for municipal and federal agencies. It is also a popular organizing technique for reform groups. Thomas Clark, director of the Chicago Rehab Network, a coalition of organizations seeking to spur the redevelopment of housing in neighborhoods throughout the city, asserts: "Once people get organized around housing, other kinds of organization follow. Housing

. . . .

Rehabilitation of existing structures has become a major aspect of public and private housing policies. In Baltimore, HUD's Urban Homesteading program helps poor families purchase and renovate abandoned row houses.

itself touches on so many other aspects of life: economic, social, health."
Most rehab groups are determined to resist displacement while they
demand help for renovating the existing housing in a neighborhood.
"We want our houses improved, but not so much that we won't be able
to live there any more," says an elderly black woman in a Cincinnati
neighborhood. With a commitment to rehabilitation *and* neighborhood
preservation, it is often possible to develop technical and social-service
jobs for some of the residents, and to involve them in other issues,
ranging from mental health to sanitation. The St. Ambrose Housing Aid
Center in Baltimore works in black neighborhoods that have been tar-
geted for middle-income whites. The center raises money to help residents with down payments and repairs. In some cases, a housing cooperative helps families otherwise too poor to buy a house. Self-help rehab
groups have lured private lenders back into previously floundering
working-class communities. They have also had an important impact on
rural areas. Tuskegee's Self-Help Housing Program has helped over two
hundred families build homes in rural Alabama; and other, smaller
groups have organized communities to erect twenty or thirty homes for
residents.

There are now some five thousand self-help housing organizations
around the country, in inner cities and in rural hinterlands.[21] HUD has
recently awarded grants to seventy established groups so that they can
help others get started. Private foundations are also responsive. Drawing
on the successful experience of its president, Franklin Thomas, who
headed the Bedford-Stuyvesant Restoration project in Brooklyn, the
Ford Foundation has formed a new organization, the Local Initiatives
Support Corporation, which will seed grants and technical assistance to
new self-help housing groups.

Public housing, such as it is today, has also undergone a transition
from conspicuous, grand architecture to rehabilitation. Under Urban
Homesteading, which began in 1976 and is the largest of the federally
sponsored rehab programs, HUD purchases single-family homes or multifamily dwellings that have been abandoned and are in need of repair.
These are transferred at no cost to local governments, which then sell
the houses, at nominal cost (usually $1) to homesteaders. The home-
steaders agree to rehabilitate the houses and to occupy them for a
minimum of three consecutive years. The agencies in charge usually
combine "sweat equity" (the homesteader works on the rehabilitation
to make up for the down payment) with on-site training in building

trades. At the end of three years, the residents have full title to the property and skills that might help them get a job.

The other direction public housing has taken is also having an important social impact. In Dallas, New Orleans, Atlanta, and many other cities, housing authorities have decided to build on scattered sites, much as early row house builders did, filling in between existing housing, putting up small numbers at a time, or inserting subsidized housing among conventionally financed dwellings. The policy helps private builders, for the bid usually goes to a local firm that is already constructing some housing. Scattered-site housing can also act as a wedge into segregation patterns. In Chicago, where fights about where to locate public-housing towers became bitter and violent in the 1950s, the courts have appointed a special overseer to ensure that the local authority actively seeks sites for black housing in white neighborhoods. In St. Louis, tenant management groups in two projects helped design eight hundred units of new housing that will be incorporated into a large, downtown residential and commercial development. For public housing to work, it needs both the active involvement of tenants and a commitment to integrate subsidized housing into diverse neighborhoods.

A massive government-funded commitment to build and subsidize housing would be one way to address the current prohibitive cost of housing and, as during the depression of the 1930s, help alleviate high unemployment. But it is unlikely, given the present political climate. What is more probable is that the various organizations and lobbying groups now focusing on housing issues will effect reforms on their own, only some of those in conjunction with the government.

The real changes in housing during the coming decade will involve new ways to use, buy, and sell the kinds of housing that already exist, as well as incentives to encourage builders to provide affordable shelter for diverse groups of people. Architects and builders have been preoccupied with technological innovations in housing production since the Great Depression and continue to concentrate on new construction techniques. At present, though, new housing accounts for only 1.5 percent of the housing stock. The remaining 98.5 percent—valued at $1.5 trillion—is the focus for those who want to change the social life that revolves around housing.[22] Some of this effort will be directed toward urban housing, especially the renovation and recycling of older buildings. But there are already 50 million suburban homes, many in industrial suburbs, many in black suburbs, as well as in conventional middle-class or working-class white residential areas. These dwellings will have to be lived in—and worked out of—differently, in much the same way that new suburban developments will proceed. Some communities need jobs and day-care facilities; others, social services and recreational activities for aging populations; still others, more lenient zoning to allow for multifamily living and commercial buildings. Suburban houses do not have to be used as they were originally intended to be used. Nor is it necessary that the urban tenements of the nineteenth century or the public-housing towers of the 1950s be demolished as inhuman environments. Like rigid land-use regulations in some suburban communities, economic inequalities for the urban poor and the authoritarian social policies of public-housing administrators are more at issue than the architecture itself, as inadequate as much of it is.

In addition to the most pervasive types of housing from the past— row houses, apartment buildings, public housing, rural farmhouses, and especially suburban dwellings—there are other alternatives that have been discarded but deserve a second look. Government-supported self-help housing projects began in the 1930s at Penn Craft, a mining community in western Pennsylvania, where community members built fifty sturdy stone houses before unions and government withdrew support. This time the self-help approach must be continued so that entire communities rather than a few model dwellings can result. Cooperative housing was an important alternative in the 1920s, especially in and around New York City, and all across the country after the Second World War, until the FHA withdrew support in 1950. Alternative forms of property ownership are necessary to supplement the prohibitively expensive norm of privately owned single-family houses. (HUD recently showed some initiative in this area with a program designed to build elderly public housing that the residents could own, at a minimal cost, but only for their lifetime; then HUD would keep up its costs by reselling the property to new temporary owners.) In all likelihood, the high cost of housing today will force many corporations and large institutions— hospitals, universities, and research organizations—to provide housing or at least low-interest mortgages to employees, much as company towns did in the early twentieth century. Churches, unions, and other non-profit groups will need more federal assistance to rehabilitate or build housing and community services for people who are not part of the corporate structure, assistance that earlier limited-dividend corporations once extended.

The recent surge of organizations rallying around housing issues will not necessarily be able to solve housing problems, but they can do something about the ways in which those problems are addressed. Is gentrification the only hope for the cities? Do strictly residential, low-density suburbs serve the needs of most of the population? Is poor-quality housing, whether in the rural South or the industrial Northeast, a sign of passivity and squalor, or can it be a means for community organization and self-improvement, given skills and some financial assistance? These are not isolated problems, yet the focus on only the local level or the special-interest group sometimes tends to be fragmented. Because of the widely held belief that a consensus exists about home and family, each group sees itself alone, outside that consensus. It is this parochial isolation, rather than the issue of housing needs, that weakens the effectiveness of grassroots housing groups.

Americans' housing needs are critically important, in and of themselves. What is also at issue, however, are the recurring ways in which questions about those needs have led many different kinds of people to confront—or avoid—inequality, urban problems, or changing patterns of family life. The choices do raise issues of class, sex, race, and political power, just as they raise more personal feelings about family and friends. A recasting of American housing policies, a diversified way of approaching them, will do more than produce good homes. It can also encourage more men and women to become involved in defining the kinds of cities and communities they want. Whatever lies in the future for American families and community planning, we can be sure that it will be cast in architectural terms and that it will have implications far beyond architecture.

NOTES

FURTHER READING

INDEX

NOTES

PART ONE

CHAPTER ONE

1. Bernard Bailyn, *The New England Merchants in the Seventeenth Century* (Cambridge, Mass.: Harvard University Press, 1955), p. 22.
2. Edward Johnson, *Johnson's Wonder-Working Providence, 1628–1651*, ed. J. Franklin Jameson (New York: Charles Scribner's Sons, 1910), pp. 21–22.
3. Ibid., pp. 113–14.
4. Cited in Perry Miller, *The New England Mind: The Seventeenth Century* (1939; reprint ed., Cambridge, Mass.: Harvard University Press, 1954), p. 416.
5. Cited in Perry Miller, *Errand into the Wilderness* (Cambridge, Mass.: Belknap Press of Harvard University Press, 1956), p. 11.
6. Emmanuel Altham, cited in John Demos, *A Little Commonwealth: Family Life in Plymouth Colony* (New York: Oxford University Press, 1970), p. 26.
7. Richard Baxter sermon, cited in Miller, *The New England Mind*, p. 358.
8. "New England's Plantation" (1630), cited in [Sidney] Fiske Kimball, *Domestic Architecture of the American Colonies and of the Early Republic* (1922; reprint ed., New York: Dover Publications, 1966), p. 10.
9. Cited in Kimball, *Domestic Architecture*, p. 12.
10. Ibid., p. 11.
11. John Cotton, *Christ the Fountaine of Life* (1651), cited in Edmund S. Morgan, *The Puritan Family: Religion & Domestic Relations in Seventeenth-Century New England*, rev. and enl. ed. (New York: Harper & Row, 1966), p. 7.

12. Demos, *A Little Commonwealth*, p. 68.
13. Michael Wigglesworth, *Day of Doom* (1662), cited in Michael Zuckerman, *Peaceable Kingdoms: New England Towns in the Eighteenth Century* (New York: Alfred A. Knopf, 1970), p. 74.
14. Miller, *The New England Mind*, p. 42.
15. Anne Bradstreet, "To My Dear and Loving Husband," cited in Perry Miller and Thomas H. Johnson, eds., *The Puritans*, 2 vols. (New York: Harper & Row, 1963), 2: 573.
16. *The Diary of Samuel Sewall, 1674–1729*, cited in Abbott Lowell Cummings, *The Framed Houses of Massachusetts Bay, 1625–1725* (Cambridge, Mass.: Harvard University Press, 1979), p. 192.
17. The phrase is from Edmund S. Morgan, *Visible Saints: The History of a Puritan Idea* (Ithaca: Cornell University Press, 1963), p. 66. Also see Miller, *The New England Mind* on Puritan literalism.

PART TWO

1. Adams diary, cited in David Flaherty, "Law and the Enforcement of Morals in Early America," *Perspectives in American History* 5 (1971): 247.
2. Hector St. John de Crévecoeur, *Letters from an American Farmer* (1782; reprint ed., New York: E.P. Dutton & Co., 1957), p. 36.
3. Jackson Turner Main, *The Social Structure of Revolutionary America* (Princeton: Princeton University Press, 1965), pp. 41–47.

CHAPTER TWO

1. James Fenimore Cooper, *Home as Found* (1838; reprint ed., New York: D. Appleton, 1907), p. 23.
2. *The Writings and Speeches of Daniel Webster*, 18 vols. (Boston: Little, Brown, 1903), 13: 74.
3. Review of James Gallier's *The American Builder's General Price Book and Estimator* in the *North American Review* 43 (October 1843): 384.
4. "On the Architecture of America," *American Museum* 8 (October 1790): 176, cited in Neil Harris, *The Artist in American Society: The Formative Years, 1790–1860* (New York: George Braziller, 1966), p. 44.
5. The phrase is from the radical intellectual Philip Freneau. See Esmond Wright, *Fabric of Freedom, 1763–1800*, rev. ed., American Century Series (New York: Hill and Wang, 1978); Robert N. Bellah, *The Broken Covenant* (New York: Seabury Press, 1975); and Perry Miller, *The Life of the Mind in America from the Revolution to the Civil War* (New York: Harcourt, Brace & World, 1965).
6. Edmund Willis, "Social Origins and Political Leadership in New York City from the Revolution to 1815" (Ph.D. diss., University of California, Berkeley, 1967), p. 113.
7. Sam Bass Warner, Jr., *The Private City: Philadelphia in Three Periods of Its Growth* (Philadelphia: University of Pennsylvania Press, 1968), p. 9; Betsy Blackmar, "Re-Walking the 'Walking City': Housing and Property Relations in New York City, 1780–1840," *Radical History Review* 21 (Fall 1979): 137; Allan Kulikoff, "The Progress of Inequality in Revolutionary Boston," in *Many Pasts: Readings in Ameri-*

can Social History, vol. 1, *1600–1876,* ed. Herbert Gutman and Gregory Kealey (Englewood Cliffs, N.J.: Prentice-Hall, 1973), pp. 133–62. In New York, the proportion of property owners among voters declined from 29.6 percent in 1795 to 19.5 percent in 1815. A similar pattern was seen in other cities.

8. Asher Benjamin, *The American Builder's Companion* (Boston: Etheridge and Bliss, 1806), p. 67.

9. *Autobiography of James Gallier, Architect* (1864; reprint ed., New York: Da Capo Press, 1973), p. 18; William Ross, "Street Houses of the City of New York," *The Architectural Magazine,* London, 1835; reprinted in the *Architectural Record* 9 (July 1899): 53.

10. Frances Trollope, *Domestic Manners of the Americans* (1832; reprint ed., London: Folio Society, 1974), p. 338.

11. Frances Wright, *Views of Society and Manners in America,* ed. Paul R. Baker (1821; reprint ed., Cambridge, Mass.: Belknap Press of Harvard University Press, 1963), p. 252.

12. *Ladies' Companion* 6 (November 1836): 1.

13. Ross, "Street Houses," p. 54.

14. James Fenimore Cooper, *Notions of the Americans; Picked up by a Travelling Bachelor,* 2 vols. (1828; reprint ed., New York: Frederick Ungar, 1963), 1: 143.

CHAPTER THREE

1. Leslie Howard Owens, *This Species of Property: Slave Life and Culture in the Old South* (New York: Oxford University Press, 1976), p. 8.

2. Kenneth M. Stampp, *The Peculiar Institution: Slavery in the Ante-Bellum South* (New York: Random House, 1956), pp. 29–31; Owens, *This Species of Property,* pp. 7–9.

3. Interview with Bailey Cunningham in *Weevils in the Wheat: Interviews with Virginia Ex-Slaves,* ed. Charles L. Perdue et al. (Bloomington: Indiana University Press, 1980), p. 82.

4. Frederick Law Olmsted, *A Journey in the Seaboard Slave States, with Remarks on the Economy* (1856; reprint ed., New York: Negro Universities Press, 1968), p. 1.

5. Writers' Program. Georgia. *Drums and Shadows: Survival Studies among the Georgia Coastal Negroes* (Athens: University of Georgia Press, 1940), p. 179, cited in John Michael Vlach, *The Afro-American Tradition in Decorative Arts* (Cleveland: The Cleveland Museum of Art, 1978), p. 136.

6. Louis Hughes, *Thirty Years a Slave* (1897; reprint ed., New York: Negro Universities Press, 1969), p. 25.

7. John Brown, *Slave Life in Georgia* (London: W. M. Watts, 1855), p. 158.

8. John W. Blassingame, *The Slave Community: Plantation Life in the Antebellum South* (New York: Oxford University Press, 1972), p. 91.

9. Nehemiah Adams, *A South-Side View of Slavery; or, Three Months at the South in 1854* (Boston: T. R. Marvin and B. B. Mussey & Co., 1854), p. 85.

10. Frances A. Kemble, *Journal of a Residence on a Georgian Plantation in 1838–1839,* ed. John A. Scott (1863; reprint ed., New York: New American Library, 1975), pp. 23–34, 63–64, 214–16.

11. Owens, *This Species of Property,* p. 138.

12. Frederick Douglass, *Narrative of the Life of Frederick Douglass, An American Slave,*

Written by Himself (1845; reprint ed., New York: New American Library, 1968), p. 50.

13. Richard C. Wade, *Slavery in the Cities: The South, 1820–1860* (New York: Oxford University Press, 1964), pp. 17–20.

14. Ibid., p. 58.

15. W. E. B. DuBois, *The Souls of Black Folk* (1903; reprint ed., Greenwich, Conn.: Fawcett Publications, 1961), p. 106.

CHAPTER FOUR

1. Alexis de Tocqueville, *Democracy in America,* trans. George Lawrence (1835; reprint ed., Garden City, N.Y.: Anchor Books, 1966), p. 278.

2. *Address to the People of the United States* (New York: Van Winkle, Wiley, & Co., 1817), p. 264, cited in Thomas Bender, *Toward an Urban Vision: Ideas and Institutions in Nineteenth-Century America* (Lexington: University Press of Kentucky, 1975), p. 19.

3. George S. White, *Memoir of Samuel Slater* (Philadelphia: G. S. White, 1836), p. 264.

4. Peter J. Coleman, *The Transformation of Rhode Island, 1790–1860* (Providence: Brown University Press, 1963), p. 234.

5. Anthony F. C. Wallace, *Rockdale: The Growth of an American Village in the Early Industrial Revolution* (New York: Alfred A. Knopf, 1978), pp. 38–39.

6. Timothy Dwight, *Travels in New-England and New York,* ed. Barbara Miller Soloman, 4 vols. (1821–33; reprint ed., Cambridge, Mass.: Belknap Press of Harvard University Press, 1969), 3: 275–76, 392.

7. White, *Memoirs,* p. 118. Also see the reports by Alexander Hamilton and Tench Coxe, making the same argument, noted in Edith Abbott, *Women in Industry* (New York: D. Appleton & Co., 1913), p. 52.

8. White, *Memoirs,* p. 263.

9. Ibid., p. 127.

10. Alan Dawley, *Class and Community: The Industrial Revolution in Lynn,* Harvard Studies in Urban History (Cambridge, Mass.: Harvard University Press, 1976), p. 51.

11. Melvin Thomas Copeland, *The Cotton Manufacturing Industry of the United States* (Cambridge: Harvard University Press, 1912), p. 11; Elizabeth Faulkner Baker, *Technology and Woman's Work* (New York: Columbia University Press, 1964), pp. 9, 23.

12. Cited in Thomas Dublin, *Women at Work: The Transformation of Work and Community in Lowell, Massachusetts, 1826–1860* (New York: Columbia University Press, 1979), p. 37.

13. Dublin, *Women at Work,* pp. 26–27.

14. Ibid., p. 57.

15. Harriet Martineau, *Society in America* (1837; reprint ed., Garden City, N.Y.: Anchor Books, Doubleday & Co., 1962), p. 240.

16. Henry A. Miles, *Lowell As It Was and As It Is* (Lowell, Mass.: Powers and Bagley, 1845), p. 128.

17. "The Spirit of Discontent," *Lowell Offering* 1 (1841): 111–14, cited in Benita Eisler, ed., *The Lowell Offering* (Philadelphia: J. B. Lippincott, 1977), pp. 161–62.

18. From the *Voice of Industry,* May 7, 1847, cited in Helen Sumner, *History of*

Women in Industry in the United States: Bureau of Labor Report on Conditions of Woman and Child Wage-Earners (1910; reprint ed., New York: Arno Press, 1974), p. 102.

19. *Lawrence American*, 1856, cited in Donald Cole, *Immigrant City: Lawrence, Massachusetts, 1845–1921* (Chapel Hill: University of North Carolina Press, 1973), pp. 28–29.

20. Josiah Curtis, "Brief Remarks on Hygiene of Massachusetts," *Transactions of the American Medical Association*, 1849, p. 36, cited in John P. Coolidge, *Mill and Mansion: A Study of Architecture and Society in Lowell, Massachusetts, 1820–1865*, Columbia Studies in American Culture, no. 10 (1942; reprint ed., New York: Russell, 1967), p. 188, note 53.

CHAPTER FIVE

1. Thomas Jefferson, *Notes on the State of Virginia* (1785; reprint ed., New York: W. W. Norton & Co., 1972), p. 418.

2. James Fenimore Cooper, *Home as Found* (1838; reprint ed., New York: D. Appleton, 1902), pp. 125–30.

3. See Bernard Wishy, *The Child and the Republic* (Philadelphia: University of Pennsylvania Press, 1968); Anne L. Kuhn, *The Mother's Role in Childhood Education: New England Concepts, 1830–1860* (New Haven: Yale University Press, 1947); Daniel Calhoun, *The Intelligence of a People* (Princeton: Princeton University Press, 1974), pp. 132–305; Philip J. Greven, Jr., *The Protestant Temperament: Patterns of Child-Rearing, Religious Experience and the Self in Early America* (New York: Alfred A. Knopf, 1977); and Barbara M. Cross, *Horace Bushnell: Minister to a Changing America* (Chicago: University of Chicago Press, 1958).

4. Lydia Sigourney, *The Western Home and Other Poems* (Philadelphia: Parry & MacMillan, 1854), p. 31.

5. Henry David Thoreau, *Walden; or, Life in the Woods* (1854; reprint ed., Garden City, N.Y.: Doubleday & Co., 1960), p. 207.

6. George L. Hersey, "Godey's Choice," *Journal of the Society of Architectural Historians* 18 (October 1959): 104. Also see Ruth E. Findley, *The Lady of Godey's: Sarah Josepha Hale* (Philadelphia: J. P. Lippincott, 1931) and Isabelle Webb Entrekin, *Sarah Josepha Hale and Godey's Lady's Magazine* (Philadelphia: J. P. Lippincott, 1946).

7. Andrew Jackson Downing, *The Architecture of Country Houses* (1850; reprint ed., New York: Dover Publications, 1969), p. 262.

8. Ibid., pp. ixx–xx, 269–70.

9. Andrew Jackson Downing, *Rural Essays* (1854; reprint ed., New York: Da Capo Press, 1974), pp. 13, 202.

10. Timothy Dwight, *Travels in New-England and New York*, 4 vols. (1821–22; reprint ed., Cambridge: Harvard University Press, 1969), 4: 73.

11. Nathaniel Willis, *The Rag-Bag, A Collection of Ephemera* (New York: Charles Scribner, 1855), p. 36.

12. Nathaniel Willis, *Out-Doors at Idlewild, or, the Shaping of a Home on the Banks of the Hudson* (New York: Charles Scribner, 1855), p. 447.

13. *Homes of American Authors* (1853), p. 124, cited in Kirk Jeffrey, Jr., "Family History: The Middle-Class American Family in the Urban Context, 1830–1870" (Ph.D. diss., Stanford University, 1971), p. 72.

14. Daniel Harrison Jacques, *The House: A Pocket-Manual of Rural Architecture* (New York: Fowler & Wells, 1859), p. 29.

15. Ralph Waldo Emerson, *The American Scholar* (1837), in *Selections from Ralph Waldo Emerson*, ed. Stephen E. Whicher (Boston: Houghton Mifflin, 1957), p. 78.

16. Gervase Wheeler, *Homes for the People in Suburb and Country* (New York: Charles Scribner, 1855), pp. 25–26.

CHAPTER SIX

1. Sam Bass Warner, Jr., *Streetcar Suburbs: The Process of Growth in Boston, 1870–1900* (Cambridge, Mass.: Harvard University Press, 1978), pp. 26, 120; Daniel D. Luria, "Wealth, Capital, and Power: The Social Meaning of Home Ownership," *Journal of Interdisciplinary History* 7 (Autumn 1976): 261–82.

2. Robert M. Fogelson, *The Fragmented Metropolis: Los Angeles, 1850–1930* (Cambridge, Mass.: Harvard University Press, 1967), p. 139.

3. Gwendolyn Wright, *Moralism and the Model Home: Domestic Architecture and Cultural Conflict in Chicago, 1873–1913* (Chicago: University of Chicago Press, 1980), pp. 41–44, which contains a more extended discussion of Victorian domestic imagery.

4. H. Morton Bodfish, *History of Building and Loan in the United States* (Chicago: United States Building and Loan League, 1931), pp. 80–83. Also see W. A. Linn, "Building and Loan Associations," *Scribner's Magazine* 5 (June 1889): 700–13.

5. Clarence Cook, *The House Beautiful* (New York: Scribner, Armstrong & Co., 1878), p. 19.

6. Arthur Meier Schlesinger, *The Rise of the City, 1878–1898* (Chicago: Quadrangle Books, 1961), p. 92.

7. James M. Guinn, *Historical and Biographical Record of Los Angeles and Vicinity* (1901), p. 268, cited in Glenn S. Dumke, *The Boom of the Eighties in Southern California* (San Marino, Cal.: Huntington Library, 1944, 1966), p. 201.

8. Edward C. Bruce, "Our Architectural Future," *Cosmopolitan* 16 (September 1875): 311.

9. George Palliser, *Palliser's New Cottage Homes and Details* (New York: Palliser, Palliser & Co., 1887), unpaginated.

10. Mrs. M. E. W. Sherwood, "The Mission of Household Art," *Appleton's Journal* 15 (February 5, 1876): 179.

11. "A Further Notion or Two about Domestic Bliss," *Appleton's Journal* 3 (March 19, 1870): 329.

12. Schlesinger, *The Rise of the City*, pp. 171–72.

13. Thomas E. Hill, *Right and Wrong, Contrasted* (Chicago: Hill Standard Book Co., 1884), p. 47.

14. Harriet Prescott Spofford, *Art Decoration as Applied to Furniture* (New York: Harper & Bros., 1877), p. 222.

15. "Forty Years Ago and Now," *Harper's Bazaar* 13 (August 1880): 514.

16. David M. Katzman, *Seven Days a Week: Women and Domestic Service in Industrializing America* (New York: Oxford University Press, 1978), pp. 44–59, 66, 286.

17. Paul H. Jacobson, *American Marriage and Divorce* (New York: Rinehart, 1959), p. 131.

18. Ella Rodman Church, "City Interiors," *Godey's Lady's Magazine* 108 (May 1884):

488. Also see Joel Benton, "The Physiogamy of the House," *Appleton's Journal*, n. s. 1 (October 18, 1876): 363–67.

19. Eugene C. Gardner, *Home Interiors: Leaves from an Architect's Diary* (Boston: James R. Osgood, 1878), p. 209.

CHAPTER SEVEN

1. Paul S. Boyer, *Urban Masses and Moral Order in America, 1820–1920* (Cambridge, Mass.: Harvard University Press, 1978), p. 98.

2. Josiah Strong, *Our Country, Its Possible Future and Its Present Crisis* (1885; reprint ed., Cambridge, Mass.: Harvard University Press, 1963), p. 177.

3. Ernest Flagg, "The New York Tenement-House Evil and Its Cure," *Scribner's Magazine* 16 (July 1894): 117; reprinted in Robert A. Woods et. al., *The Poor in Great Cities: Their Problems and What Is Being Done to Solve Them* (New York: Charles Scribner's Sons, 1895).

4. James Ford, *Slums and Housing, With Special References to New York City, History, Conditions, Policy*, 2 vols. (1936; reprint ed., Westport, Conn.: Negro Universities Press, 1972), 1: 120.

5. Charles Dickens, *American Notes for General Circulation* (1842; reprint ed., Gloucester, Mass.: Peter Smith, 1968), pp. 109–110.

6. *New York Times*, February 18, 1900, p. 23; cited in Roy Lubove, *The Progressives and the Slums: Tenement House Reform in New York City, 1890–1917* (Pittsburgh: University of Pittsburgh Press, 1962), p. 106.

7. *Chicago Herald*, July 17, 1887, cited in Humbert S. Nelli, *Italians in Chicago, 1880–1930: A Study in Ethnic Mobility* (New York: Oxford University Press, 1970), p. 11.

8. Ford, *Slums and Housing*, 1: 187; Marcus T. Reynolds, *The Housing of the Poor in American Cities* (1893; reprint ed., College Park, Md.: McGrath Publishing Co., 1969), p. 32.

9. Roger Starr, "The New York Apartment House," in *Concepts, Critiques and Comments*, ed. Bern Dibner and Murray Rubien (Norwalk, Conn.: Burndy Library, 1976), p. 304.

10. Lawrence Veiller, *City Life* (Washington, D.C.: American Academy of Political and Social Sciences, 1905), p. 59.

11. *Historical Statistics of the United States*, 2 vols. (Washington, D.C.: U.S. Government Printing Office, 1975): 1, Series D-583, p. 144.

12. Cited in Ellen Richards, *The Cost of Shelter* (New York: John Wiley, 1905), p. 7. Richards noted the need for a compromise between this lack of privacy and the excessive privatism of the suburbs.

13. Testimonial before a 1901 Congressional committee, cited in U. S. Department of Labor, *How American Buying Habits Change* (Washington, D.C.: U.S. Government Printing Office, ca. 1915).

14. Robert Treat Paine, "Housing Conditions in Boston," *Annals of the American Academy of Political and Social Sciences* 9 (July 1902): 121–136; P. Griffin, "Model Cottages at Homewood," *Municipal Affairs* 3 (March 1899): 132–38.

15. Charles Richmond Henderson, *Proceedings of the Lake Placid Conference on Home Economics*, 1902, cited in Ellen Richards, *Euthenics: The Science of the Controllable Environment* (Boston: Whitcomb & Barrows, 1910), p. 159.

16. *Report of the Committee on Tenement Houses of the Citizens Association of Chicago, 1884* (Chicago: The Citizens Association, 1884), pp. 19–20.
17. Albion Fellows Bacon, *What Bad Housing Means to the Community* (Boston: American Unitarian Association, n.d.), p. 8.
18. Robert H. Bremner, *From the Depths: The Discovery of Poverty in the United States* (New York: New York University Press, 1956), p. 52.
19. Albion Fellows Bacon, *Beauty for Ashes* (New York: Dodd, Mead & Co., 1914), p. 54.
20. Isabel F. Hyams, "The Louisa May Alcott Club," *Proceedings of the Second Annual Conference on Home Economics, Lake Placid, New York, 1902*, p. 18.
21. U. S. Commissioner of Labor, *The Slums of Baltimore, Chicago, New York and Philadelphia* (Washington, D.C.: U.S. Government Printing Office, 1894), pp. 12–13.
22. Jacob G. Schmidlapp, *Low-Priced Housing for Wage Earners* (New York: National Housing Association, 1916), p. 10.
23. Roy Lubove, "I. N. Phelps Stokes: Tenement Architect, Economist, Planner," *Journal of the Society of Architectural Historians* 23 (May 1964): 75–87; Thomas Lee Philpott, *The Slum and the Ghetto: Neighborhood Deterioration and Middle-Class Reform, Chicago, 1880–1930*, The Urban Life in America Series (New York: Oxford University Press, 1978), p. 95.
24. *Reports of the President's Homes Commission* (Washington D.C.: U.S. Government Printing Office, 1909), p. 110, cited in Lizabeth A. Cohen, "Embellishing a Life of Labor: An Interpretation of the Material Culture of American Working-Class Homes, 1885–1915" (Unpublished paper, Department of History, University of California, Berkeley, 1979).
25. Edith Abbott, assisted by Sophonisba P. Breckinridge, *The Tenements of Chicago, 1908–1935* (Chicago: University of Chicago Press, 1936), p. 112.

CHAPTER EIGHT

1. C. O. Loring, "Stuyvesant Apartments," *American Builder* 2 (December 1869): 232–33.
2. "Editor's Table," *Appleton's Journal* 15 (February 5, 1876): 183; *Boston Street Directory*, 1878; cited in Douglass Shand Tucci, *Built in Boston: City and Suburb, 1800–1950* (Boston: New York Graphic Society, 1978), p. 103; Harold M. Mayer and Richard C. Wade, with the assistance of Glen E. Holt, *Chicago: Growth of a Metropolis* (Chicago: University of Chicago Press, 1969), p. 144; Bessie Louise Pierce, *A History of Chicago*, 3 vols. (Chicago: University of Chicago Press, 1975), 3: 57.
3. A New York newspaper, fall 1872, clipping in the Lienau Collection, Avery Library, Columbia University Library.
4. James Richardson, "The New Houses of New York: A Study in Flats," *Scribner's Monthly* 8 (May 1874): 75.
5. *American Architect and Building News* 3 (February 9, 1878): 45.
6. "The Women's Hotel," *Harper's Weekly* 22 (April 13, 1878): 294.
7. *Carpentry and Building* 27 (April 1905): 105.
8. "Editor's Table," p. 183.
9. Everett N. Blanke, "The Cliff Dwellers of New York," *Cosmopolitan* 15 (July 1893): 354–62.

10. "New Apartment-Houses in New York," *American Architect and Building News* 5 (May 31, 1878): 175.
11. Charlotte Perkins Gilman, "The Passing of the Home in Great American Cities," *Cosmopolitan* 38 (December 1904): 138.
12. John Pickering Putnam, *Architecture Under Nationalism* (Boston: Nationalist Educational Association, 1890), p. 13.
13. Hubert, Pirsson & Hoddick, "New York Flats and French Flats," *Architectural Record* 36 (July/September 1892): 55–64.
14. Edith Wharton, *The Age of Innocence* (1920; reprint ed., New York: Charles Scribner's Sons, 1968), pp. 28–29.
15. Reverend Henry F. Cope, "The Conservation of the Modern Home," in *The Child Welfare Manual*, 2 vols. (New York: The University Society, 1915), 1: 21.
16. "Apartment Hotels in New York City," *Architectural Record* 13 (January 1903): 90.
17. Ibid.; Walter B. Chambers, "The Duplex Apartment House," *Architectural Record* 29 (April 1911): 327.
18. Bernard J. Newman, "Shall We Encourage or Discourage the Apartment House," in *Housing Problems in America: Proceedings of the Sixth National Conference on Housing, New York, 1917*, pp. 153–66, cited in Tucci, *Built in Boston*, pp. 215–16. Newman was a professor, specializing in housing studies, at the University of Pennsylvania.
19. Mayer and Wade, *Chicago*, p. 324; Robert M. Fogelson, *The Fragmented Metropolis: Los Angeles, 1850–1930*, Joint Center for Urban Studies Publications (Cambridge: Harvard University Press, 1967), p. 151.
20. Letter cited in George Walter Fiske, *The Changing Family: Social and Religious Aspects of the Modern Family* (New York: Harper and Brothers Publishers, 1928), p. 68.

PART FOUR

1. Orison Swett Marden, *Woman and Home* (New York: Thomas Y. Crowell, 1915), p. 305.

CHAPTER NINE

1. "House Decoration and Furnishing," *The House and Home*, ed. Lyman Abbott, 2 vols. (New York: Charles Scribner's Sons, 1896), 1: 157.
2. Paul V. Betters, *The Bureau of Home Economics* (Washington, D. C.: The Brookings Institute, 1930), p. 5; Isabel Bevier and Susannah Usher, *The Home Economics Movement* (Boston: Whitcomb and Barrows, 1906), pp. 34–36.
3. William Hard, *The Women of Tomorrow* (New York: Baker & Taylor, 1911), p. 128.
4. Ellen H. Richards, *The Cost of Shelter* (New York: John Wiley, 1905), p. 78; Isabel Bevier, "The Comfortable House," *The House Beautiful* 15 (January 1904): 128; Helen Campbell, *Household Economics* (New York: G.P. Putnam's Sons, 1898), pp. 89–94.
5. Mabel Tuke Priestman, *Artistic Houses* (Chicago: A. C. McClurg, 1910), p. 6.
6. Helen Campbell, "Household Furnishings," *Architectural Record* 6 (October/December 1896): 101.

7. This was the title of a course Talbot offered in the Department of Sociology and then in the Department of Household Administration. See my *Moralism and the Model Home: Domestic Architecture and Cultural Conflict in Chicago, 1873–1913* (Chicago: University of Chicago Press, 1980) for a full description of the domestic science and housing reform movement in that city.

8. "The Craftsman House," designed by E. G. W. Dietrich and Gustav Stickley, *The Craftsman* 4 (May 1903): 84–92.

9. Gustav Stickley, *More Craftsman Houses* (New York: The Craftsman Publishing Co., 1912), p. 1.

10. Edward Bok, *The Americanization of Edward Bok* (New York: Charles Scribner's Sons, 1924), pp. 249–50.

11. Charles Keeler, *The Simple Home* (San Francisco: The Tomoye Press, 1904), p. 5.

12. "Modern American Homes," *National Builder* 55 (January 1913): 51.

13. "The Tendency in Home Architecture," *Carpentry and Building* 22 (June 1900): 165.

14. Isabell McDougall, "An Ideal Kitchen," *The House Beautiful* 13 (December 1902): 27.

15. L. Eugene Robinson, *Domestic Architecture* (New York: Macmillan Co., 1917), p. 126.

16. Henry Demarest Lloyd, "In New Applications of Democracy," *Congregationalist* 85 (January 5, 1901): 5.

17. Mrs. W. N. Shaw, "Science in the Household," in *Household Administration: Its Place in the Higher Education of Women,* ed. Alice Ravenhill and Catherine J. Schiff (New York: Henry Holt & Co., 1911), p. 74.

18. Linda Gordon, *Woman's Body, Woman's Right: A Social History of Birth Control in America* (New York: Viking Press Grossman Publishers, 1976), p. 154.

19. Harold U. Faulkner, *The Quest for Social Justice, 1898–1914* (Chicago: Quadrangle Books, 1971), pp. 194–95.

20. David M. Katzman, *Seven Days a Week: Women and Domestic Service in Industrializing America* (New York: Oxford University Press, 1978), pp. 55–57, 126.

21. Mary I. Wood, *The History of the General Federation of Women's Clubs* (New York: General Federation of Women's Clubs, 1912), pp. 249–50.

22. *Harper's Bazaar* 45 (1911): 57, cited in Daniel T. Rodgers, *The Work Ethic in Industrial America, 1850–1920* (Chicago: University of Chicago Press, 1978), p. 195.

23. "Beaux-Arts: The Community Problem Solved," *Bungalow* (Seattle) 2 (July 1913): 13–29; Una N. Hopkins, "A Picturesque Court of 30 Bungalows: A Community Idea for Women," *Ladies' Home Journal* 30 (April 1913): 99. Laura Chase graciously allowed me to read her unpublished paper, "Gardens and Slums: Bungalow Courts and House Courts in Los Angeles, 1910–1930" (Department of City Planning, University of California, Los Angeles, 1977).

24. *Thirteenth Census of the United States Taken in the Year 1910,* vol. 1, Table 6, pp. 1300–01.

25. Katherine G. Busbey, *Home Life in America* (New York: Macmillan Co., 1907), p. 373; Joy Wheeler Dow, *American Renaissance* (New York: William T. Comstock, 1904), p. 41.

26. Grosvenor Atterbury, "Model Towns in America," *Scribner's Magazine* 52 (July 1912): 26.

CHAPTER TEN

1. See William H. Tolman, *Industrial Betterment* (New York: Social Science Press, 1900) and *Social Engineering: A Record of Things Done by American Industrialists Employing Upwards of One and One-Half Million of People,* with an introduction by Andrew Carnegie (New York: McGraw-Hill, 1909).

2. John H. Patterson to Seth Low, then president of the NCF, 1912, cited in James Weinstein, *The Corporate Ideal in the Liberal State, 1900–1918* (Boston: Beacon Press, 1968), p. 19.

3. Daniel Nelson, *Managers and Workers: Origins of the New Factory System in the United States, 1880–1920* (Madison: University of Wisconsin Press, 1975), p. 111.

4. Josiah Strong, "What Social Service Means: A Clearing House of Experience in Social and Industrial Betterment," *Craftsman* 9 (February 1906): 621.

5. George H. Miller, "Kaulton, Alabama: A Southern Pine Manufacturing Town Built Along Model Lines," in *Homes for Workmen* (New Orleans: Southern Pine Association, 1919), p. 10.

6. W. Jett Lauck and Edgar Sydenstricker, *Conditions of Labor in American Industries* (New York: Funk & Wagnalls, 1917), pp. 229–30; Leifur Magnusson, "Housing by Employers in the United States," *Monthly Review of the U. S. Bureau of Labor Statistics* (November 1917), reprinted in *Homes for Workmen,* p. 39.

7. Graham Taylor, *Satellite Cities: A Study of Industrial Suburbs* (1915; reprint ed., New York: Arno Press, 1970), pp. 8–10, 168.

8. Thomas Dublin, *Women at Work* (New York: Columbia University Press, 1979), p. 20; *Camp and Plant* 1 (December 14, 1901): 1; Georges Benoit-Lévy, *Cités-Jardins d'Amérique* (Paris: Henri Jouvé, 1905), p. 72; *Homes for Workmen,* p. 135.

9. *Homes for Workmen,* pp. 11, 173.

10. Ibid., pp. 10–11.

11. From Pullman's testimony before the U. S. Strike Commission of 1894, cited in J. Seymour Currey, *Chicago: Its History and Its Builders,* 3 vols. (Chicago: S. J. Clarke, 1918), 3: 205.

12. Richard T. Ely, "Pullman: A Social Study," *Harper's Monthly* 70 (February 1885): 452–66; George Schelling, *Chicago Tribune* (March 22, 1886), cited in Stanley Buder, *Pullman* (New York: Oxford University Press, 1967), p. 140.

13. Ida M. Tarbell, *New Ideals in Business* (New York: Macmillan Co., 1916), p. 154.

14. *Industrial Housing* (Bay City, Mich.: The Aladdin Company, 1918), p. 31.

15. R. S. Whiting, *Housing and Industry* (Chicago: National Lumber Manufacturers Association, 1918); Alfred Lief, *The Firestone Story* (New York: Whittlesey House, 1951), pp. 79–83; Hugh Allen, *The House of Goodyear* (Cleveland: Corday & Gross, 1943), p. 296.

16. Nelson, *Managers and Workers,* p. 146.

17. Magnusson, "Housing," p. 46.

18. "Housing by Employers in the United States," *Bulletin of the U. S. Bureau of Labor Statistics* 263 (October 1920): 11.

19. Winthrop A. Hamlin, *Low-Cost Cottage Construction in America* (Cambridge: Harvard University Social Museum, 1917); G. W. W. Hanger, "Housing of the Working People in the United States by Employers," *Bulletin of the U. S. Bureau of Labor Statistics* 54 (1904); Robert C. Chapin, *The Standard of Living Among Workingmen's Families in New York City* (New York: Charities Publication Com-

mittee, 1909), p. 63; Frank Hatch Streightoff, *The Standard of Living Among the Industrial People of America* (Boston: Houghton Mifflin, 1911), pp. 78–85.

20. Margaret Byington, *Homestead: The Households of a Mill Town* (1910; reprint ed., Pittsburgh: University of Pittsburgh Center for International Studies, 1974), pp. 135–44.
21. Ibid., p. 145.
22. Hamlin, *Low-Cost Construction*, p. 29.
23. "The Colorado Coal Mines," *The Tenants Weekly* 1 (July 27, 1914): 1–4.

CHAPTER ELEVEN

1. Edith Elmer Wood, *The Housing of the Unskilled Wage Earner* (New York: Macmillan Co., 1919), p. 7.
2. *Fourteenth Census of the United States, Taken in the Year 1920*, vol. 2, chap. 14; also see Amos H. Hawley, *The Changing Shape of Metropolitan America: Deconcentration Since 1920* (Glencoe, Ill.: Free Press, 1956) and R. D. McKenzie, *The Metropolitan Community* (New York: McGraw-Hill, 1933).
3. Arthur Gleason, "The Lack of Houses," *Nation* 110 (April 17, 1920): 511; *The Better Homes Manual*, ed. Blanche Halbert (Chicago: University of Chicago Press, 1931), p. 53; H. Van dervoort Walsh, *The Construction of the Small House* (New York: Charles Scribner's Sons, 1923), p. 2.
4. Charles N. Glaab, "Metropolis and Suburb: The Changing American City," in *Change and Continuity in Twentieth Century America: The 1920's*, ed. John Braeman, Robert H. Bremner, and David Brody (Columbus: Ohio State University Press, 1968), p. 404.
5. Lewis Mumford, "The Wilderness of Suburbia," *New Republic* 28 (September 7, 1921): 44–45; Christine Frederick, "Is Suburban Living a Delusion?" *Outlook* 148 (February 22, 1928): 290.
6. "The Second New York Own-Your-Home Exposition," *Building Age* (June 1920): 50; National Small House Competition, *Home Builder's Plan Book* (New York: Building Plan Holding Corporation, 1921); Pearl Janet Davies, *Real Estate in American History* (Washington, D.C.: Public Affairs Press, 1958), pp. 137–39; Edith Elmer Wood, *Recent Trends in American Housing* (New York: Macmillan Co., 1931), pp. 246–50; *Plans and Elevations of Houses for Settlers* (Sacramento: California State Printing Office, 1920); Edward L. Rada, *The Cal-Vet Program: A Study of State-Financed Housing in California* (Los Angeles: UCLA Real Estate Research Program, 1962); Roy Lubove, *Community Planning in the 1920's: The Contribution of the Regional Planning Association of America* (Pittsburgh: University of Pittsburgh Press, 1963), pp. 24–25.
7. James Ford, "Better Homes in America," in *The Better Homes Manual*, p. 743.
8. *Guidebook for Better Homes Campaigns, 1929* (Washington, D.C.: Better Homes in America, Inc., 1928), p. 41.
9. "Help for Home-Building America," *Independent* 117 (August 14, 1926): 181; *Tentative Report of the Committee on Home Information Services and Centers of the President's Conference on Home Building and Home Ownership* (Washington, D.C.: U. S. Government Printing Office, 1931), p. 66.
10. *Festival Journal: Amalgamated Cooperative Community, 1927–1947* (New York: Amalgamated Clothing Workers of America, 1947); "The Clothing Workers' Union," *Life* 25 (June 28, 1948): 79–87.

11. John M. Gries and Thomas M. Curran, "Choosing a Home Financing Agency," in *The Better Homes Manual*, pp. 23–43.
12. Leo Grebler, David Blank, and Louis Winnick, *Capital Formation in Residential Real Estate* (Princeton: Princeton University Press, 1956), p. 333.
13. John Nolen, *New Towns for Old* (Boston: Marshall Jones, 1927), p. 107.
14. Rollin L. McNitt, "Architectural Control Under the Police Power," *Community Builder* 1 (January 1928): 26–28.
15. "Portrait of a Salesman: Jesse Clyde Nichols," *National Real Estate Journal* 40 (February 1939): 20.
16. *Mariemont, the New Town, "A National Exemplar"* (Cincinnati: The Mariemont Corporation, 1925), p. 19, cited in John Loretz Hancock, "John Nolen, and the American City Planning Movement: A History of Culture Change and Community Response, 1900–1940" (Ph.D. diss., University of Pennsylvania, 1964), p. 371.
17. John Nolen, "Mariemont, Ohio—A New Town Built to Produce Local Happiness," *The Better Homes Manual*, pp. 735–38.
18. James Ford Papers, Graduate School of Design, Harvard University. I would like to thank Brian Horrigan for this reference.
19. Clarence S. Stein, *Toward New Towns for America* (1957; rev. ed., Cambridge: The M.I.T. Press, 1973), p. 61.
20. *Historical Statistics of the United States* (Washington, D.C.: U. S. Government Printing Office, 1952), p. 223.
21. Edith Louise Allen, *American Housing as Affected by Social and Economic Conditions* (Peoria, Ill.: Manual Arts Press, 1930), p. 148.
22. *Historical Statistics*, p. 420; U. S. Department of Commerce, *Commerce Yearbook for 1928* (Washington, D.C.: U. S. Government Printing Office, 1929), p. 275.
23. *Small Homes of Architectural Distinction: A Book of Suggested Plans Designed by the Architects' Small House Service Bureau*, ed. Robert T. Jones (New York: Harper & Bros., 1929), p. 78.
24. Harwood Hewitt, "A Plea for Distinctive Architecture in Southern California," Allied Architects Association of Los Angeles, *Bulletin* 1 (March 1, 1925), cited in Robert M. Fogelson, *The Fragmented Metropolis: Los Angeles, 1850–1930* (Cambridge: Harvard University Press, 1967), p. 157.
25. Palos Verdes Homes Association Files, cited in Fogelson, *Fragmented Metropolis*, p. 324; also see *The Palos Verdes Protective Restrictions* (Los Angeles: Palos Verdes Homes Association, 1929).
26. Fred Bosselman and David Callies, *The Quiet Revolution in Land Use Control: Report to the Presidential Council on Environmental Quality* (Washington, D.C.: U. S. Government Printing Office, 1971); cited in Leonard J. Downie, Jr., *Mortgage on America* (New York: Praeger, 1974), pp. 89–90.
27. McKenzie, *The Metropolitan Community*, pp. 299–301.

CHAPTER TWELVE

1. Josephine C. Brown, *Public Relief, 1929–1939* (New York: Henry Holt, 1940), pp. 145–46; William E. Leuchtenburg, *Franklin D. Roosevelt and the New Deal, 1932–1940*, The New American Nation Series (New York: Harper & Row, 1963), p. 134.
2. Lead advertisements that appeared in many cities, cited in Richard O. Davies,

Housing Reform During the Truman Administration (Columbia: University of Missouri Press, 1966), p. 127.

3. Edith Elmer Wood, *Introduction to Housing: Facts and Principles* (Washington, D.C.: U. S. Housing Authority, 1939), pp. 84, 90.

4. Blair Bolles, "Resettling America," *American Mercury* 39 (November 1936): 338.

5. Paul K. Conkin, *Tomorrow a New World: The New Deal Community Program* (Ithaca: Cornell University Press, 1959), p. 6.

6. Arthur S. Link and William B. Catton, *American Epoch: A History of the United States Since 1900*, 3 vols. (New York: Alfred A. Knopf, 1973), vol. 2 (1921–1945): 164.

7. Robert Moore Fisher, *Twenty Years of Public Housing: Economic Aspects of the Federal Program* (New York: Harper & Bros., 1959), pp. 82–91.

8. Louise D. Sherman, "Life in a Public Housing Project," in *Public Housing in America*, ed. M. B. Schnapper (New York: H. W. Wilson, 1939), p. 92.

9. Ibid., p. 99; also see accounts in *Public Housing Progress*, a publication of the National Public Housing Conference.

10. Cited in the *Journal of Housing* 2 (October 1945): 173.

11. Timothy McDonnell, *The Wagner Housing Act* (Chicago: Loyola University Press, 1957), p. 189.

12. Charles J. Stokes, "A Theory of Slums," *Land Economics* 38 (1962): 187, describing tenements as way stations for immigrants' acculturation, cited in Lawrence M. Friedman, *Government and Slum Housing*, Rand McNally Political Science Series (Chicago: Rand McNally, 1968), p. 8.

13. *Congressional Record* 81 (August 4, 1937), cited in Friedman, *Government and Slum Housing*, pp. 112–13.

14. Herbert J. Gans, *The Urban Villagers: Group and Class in the Life of Italian-Americans* (New York: Free Press of Glencoe, 1962), p. 21.

15. Martin Mayer, *The Builders: Houses, People, Neighborhoods, Governments, Money* (New York: W. W. Norton, 1978), p. 120.

16. James Ford, *Slums and Housing*, 2 vols. (1936; reprint ed., Greenwood, Conn.: Negro Universities Press, 1972), 2: 772.

17. Address before the American Public Works Association, reprinted as "Realities of Urban Redevelopment" in the *Journal of Housing* 3 (December 1945–January 1946): 12–14.

18. Lee Rainwater, *Behind Ghetto Walls: Black Families in a Federal Slum* (Chicago: Aldine, 1970), p. 12.

19. William Moore, Jr., *The Vertical Ghetto: Everyday Life in an Urban Project* (New York: Random House, 1969), p. 27.

20. Catherine Bauer, "The Dreary Deadlock of Public Housing," *Architectural Forum* 106 (May 1957): 140–42.

21. National Commission on Urban Problems, *More than Shelter: Social Needs in Low- and Moderate-Income Housing*, Research Report, no. 8, ed. George Schermer Associates (Washington, D.C.: U.S. Government Printing Office, 1968), p. 58.

22. *Building the American City, Report of the National Commission on Urban Problems* (Washington, D.C.: U.S. Government Printing Office, 1968), p. 123.

23. David Hackett Fischer, *Growing Old in America* (New York: Oxford University Press, 1978), p. 145.

24. Lawrence M. Friedman, "Public Housing and the Poor," in *Housing Urban Amer-*

ica, ed. Jon Pynoos, Robert Schafer, and Chester W. Hartman (Chicago: Aldine, 1973), p. 454.

CHAPTER THIRTEEN

1. *The FHA Story in Summary* (Washington, D.C.: U. S. Government Printing Office, 1959), pp. 9–11.
2. FHA Archives, National Archives, Washington, D. C.
3. National Housing Agency, *Housing for War and the Job Ahead* (Washington, D.C.: U. S. Government Printing Office, 1944); National Housing Agency, *Fourth Annual Report,* (Washington, D.C.: U. S. Government Printing Office, 1945), p. 3.
4. William H. Chafe, *The American Woman* (New York: Oxford University Press, 1972), p. 137; Federal Works Agency, *Annual Report,* 1946, p. 27, cited in Howard Dratch, "The Politics of Child Care in the 1940s," *Science and Society* 38 (Spring 1974): 176–77.
5. Chafe, *American Woman,* p. 148.
6. Cited in Richard O. Davies, *Housing Reform during the Truman Administration* (Columbia: University of Missouri Press, 1966), p. 25.
7. Press release, June 30, 1947, cited in Davies, *Housing Reform,* pp. 66–67.
8. "The Factory-built House Is Here, but Not the Answer to the $33 Million Question: How to Get It to Market?" *Architectural Forum* 90 (May 1949): 109.
9. "Prefabricated Promotion," *House and Home* 7 (April 1955): 57.
10. Paul F. Wendt, *Housing Policy—The Search for Solutions,* Institute of Business and Economic Research Publications (Berkeley: University of California Press, 1963), p. 164.
11. *This Is the FHA* (Washington, D.C.: U. S. Government Printing Office, 1957), p. 13.
12. "Housing Gets No. 1 Spot at Family Life Conference," *The Christian Science Monitor,* May 14, 1948, reprinted in *Journal of Housing* 5 (May 1948): 125.
13. "FHA's Impact on the Financing and Design of Apartments," *Architectural Forum* 92 (January 1950): 97.
14. Leonard Downie, Jr., *Mortgage on America* (New York: Praeger, 1974), p. 59; "Middle-Income Housing: The Big City's Big Problem," *Time* 104 (September 16, 1957): 70; Martin Mayer, *The Builders* (New York: W. W. Norton, 1978), p. 124.
15. Federal Housing Administration, *Underwriting Manual,* January 1947, cited in Charels Abrams, "The Segregation Threat in Housing," in *Two-Thirds of a Nation: A Housing Program,* ed. Nathan Straus (New York: Alfred A. Knopf, 1952), pp. 219–23.
16. "Equality in Housing," *New Republic* 121 (December 19, 1949): 8.
17. Sam Bass Warner, Jr., *The Urban Wilderness: A History of the American City* (New York: Harper & Row, 1972), p. 43.
18. "Federal Housing Activities," *Housing Almanac* (Washington, D.C.: National Association of Home Builders, 1957), pp. 35–49.
19. "Built-in Salesmanship," *Architectural Forum* 90 (April 1949): 118; "A New Method of Merchant Building," *Architectural Forum* 91 (September 1949): 75–80; "Park Forest Moves into '52," *House and Home* 1 (March 1952): 115.
20. "The Architect's New Frontier: The Volume-built House," *House and Home* 4 (July 1953): 91.

21. Joseph Eichler, *Eichler Homes Designed for Better Living* (Palo Alto, Cal.: Eichler Homes, 1951), p. 41.
22. "Usonian Homes," *Journal of Housing* 10 (October 1953): 319–20, 344.
23. William H. Scheick, AIA, "What's Happened to Housing in the Last 30 Years," *Parents' Magazine* 31 (October 1956): 94–95.
24. "Levitt's Progress," *Fortune* 46 (October 1952): 155; Wolfgang Langewiesche, "Everybody Can Own a House," *The House Beautiful* 96 (November 1956): 227–35.
25. *Urban Housing Survey* (Philadelphia: Curtis Publishing Company, 1945), p. 11.
26. James Dahir, *Communities for Better Living* (New York: Harper & Co., 1950), unpaginated.
27. *Historical Statistics of the United States* (Washington, D.C.: U. S. Government Printing Office, 1952), p. 796; Mary and George Catlin, *Building Your New House* (New York: Current Books, 1946), p. 141.
28. Benjamin Spock, M.D., *Common Sense Book of Baby and Child Care*, pp. 51–52, cited in Nancy Pottishman Weiss, "Mother, the Invention of Necessity: Dr. Benjamin Spock's *Baby and Child Care*," *American Quarterly* 29 (Winter 1977): 524.
29. Dr. Henry A. Davidson, "Living atop a Civic Mushroom," *Newsweek* 49 (April 1, 1957): 36–42; reprinted in *City and Suburban Housing*, ed. Poyntz Tyler (New York: H. W. Wilson, 1957), p. 155, expresses this position.
30. Sidonie M. Gruenberg, "Homogenized Children of New Suburbia," *The New York Times Magazine* (September 19, 1954): 14.
31. Ernest R. Mowrer, "The Family in Suburbia," in *The Suburban Community*, ed. William M. Dobriner (New York: G. P. Putnam's Sons, 1958), p. 158.
32. Herbert J. Gans, *The Levittowners: Ways of Life and Politics in a New Suburban Community* (New York: Pantheon, 1967), p. 277.
33. "These Women Are Talking About You," *House and Home* 9 (June 1956): 140.
34. Donald Sullivan, "Housing in the 1970's," in *The Story of Housing*, ed. Gertrude Sipperly Fish (New York: Macmillan for the Federal National Mortgage Association, 1979), p. 385; "Housing: Rising," *Time* 80 (November 30, 1962): 85.
35. Alvin Schorr, *Explorations in Social Policy* (New York: Basic Books, 1968), pp. 272–87; Downie, *Mortgage on America*, p. 52, makes a similar point.

CHAPTER FOURTEEN

1. George Sternlieb and James W. Hughes, "The Post-Shelter Society," *The Public Interest* 57 (Fall 1979): 47.
2. "NAHB Goes on Offensive in '80," *Los Angeles Times*, January 27, 1980.
3. "Suburbs Growing Grayer," *Aging* 309 (July/August 1980): 42–43.
4. "Trailers: The Business," *Southern Exposure* 8 (Spring 1980): 19.
5. Ibid., p. 20.
6. Ibid., p. 19.
7. *The Nation's Families: 1960–1990* (Cambridge: MIT-Harvard Joint Center for Urban Studies, 1980).
8. Ibid.; Merrill Butler, speech before the National Association of Home Builders Convention, January 26, 1980. In 1975, 77 percent of union members owned their homes. [*Survey of AFL-CIO Members Housing 1975* (Washington, D.C.: AFL-CIO, 1975), p. 16, cited in Dolores Hayden, "What Would a Non-Sexist City Be Like? Speculations on Housing, Urban Design, and Human Work," *Signs: Journal*

of Women in Culture and Society supplement to volume 5, *Women in the American Cities* (Spring 1980): S171.]

9. J. S. Coyle, "Job Meccas for the '80s," *Money* 7 (May 1978): 40–47.

10. *Village of Belle Terre v. Boraas,* 1974 (416 U.S. 9), cited in Constance Perin, *Everything in Its Place: Social Order and Land Use in America* (Princeton: Princeton University Press, 1977), p. 48.

11. Peter Dreier, "The Politics of Rent Control," *Working Papers for a New Society* 6 (March/April 1979): 55–63.

12. *Fair Housing for Children Project Newsletter* (Winter 1979). A 1982 California law now prevents such discrimination.

13. *Critical Choices for the 80's: Twelfth Report of the National Advisory Council on Economic Opportunity* (Washington, D.C.: U.S. Government Printing Office, 1980), p. 147.

14. *Women Heads of Households* (Washington, D.C.: U.S. Department of Housing and Urban Development, 1980), pp. 1–3; National Congress of Negro Women report, cited in Gerda Wekerle, "A Woman's Place Is in the City," *Signs* 5 (Spring 1980, Supplement)

15. "New Ideal for the Modern Woman," *San Francisco Chronicle,* December 4, 1979. The publication based on this research is Donald Rothblatt, Jo Sprague, and Daniel Garr, *The Suburban Environment and Women* (New York: Praeger, 1979); also see Jacob M. Duker, "Housewife and Working-wife Families: A Housing Comparison," *Land Economics* 46 (February 1970): 138–45; Susan Saegert and Gary Winkel, "The Home: A Critical Problem for Changing Sex Roles," in *New Space for Women*, ed. Gerda R. Wekerle, Rebecca Peterson, and David Morley (Boulder, Colorado: Westview Press, 1980); and Wekerle, "A Woman's Place Is in the City," and Hayden, "What Would a Non-Sexist City Look Like?"

16. Statement of Gail Cincotta, chairperson of the National Peoples's Action, in *The Rebirth of the American City: Hearings before the Committee on Banking, Currency and Housing,* U. S. House of Representatives, 1976 (Washington, D.C.: U.S. Government Printing Office, 1976), p. 584.

17. Ted Wusocki et al., *Neighborhoods First: From the '70s into the '80s* (Chicago: National Training and Information Center, 1977), p. 4.

18. Janice Perlman, "Grassroots Empowerment and Government Response," *Social Policy* 10 (September–October 1979): 16.

19. John Atlas and Peter Dreier, "The Housing Crisis and the Tenants' Revolt," *Social Policy* 10 (January–February 1980): 20; also see Daniel Lauber, "Condominium Conversions—The Number Prompts Controls to Protect the Poor and Elderly," *Journal of Housing* 37 (April 1980): 201–09.

20. Dreier, "The Politics of Rent Control," pp. 55–63.

21. "Who, in Fact, Rebuilds Neighborhoods?" *The New York Times,* June 4, 1980.

22. Martin Mayer, *The Builders* (New York: W. W. Norton, 1978), pp. 5–6.

FURTHER READING

CHAPTER ONE

The books of Perry Miller are the classic texts on Puritanism and its continuing influence on Americans. See, in particular, *The New England Mind*, 2 vols. (1939; reprint ed., Cambridge, Mass., 1954), *Errand into the Wilderness* (Cambridge, Mass., 1956), *Nature's Nation* (Cambridge, Mass., 1967), and *The Life of the Mind in America, from the Revolution to the Civil War; Books One Through Three* (New York, 1965). Robert N. Bellah, *The Broken Covenant* (New York, 1975) provocatively demonstrates the continued heritage of Puritan thought and imagination for present-day Americans.

Other useful books on Puritanism include Kai T. Erikson, *Wayward Puritans: A Study in the Sociology of Deviance* (New York, 1966); Edmund S. Morgan, *Visible Saints: The History of a Puritan Idea* (New York, 1963); Samuel Eliot Morison, *Builders of the Bay Colony* (Boston, 1930); Bernard Bailyn, *Education in the Forming of American Society: Needs and Opportunities for Study* (Chapel Hill, 1960) and *The New England Merchants in the Seventeenth Century* (Cambridge, Mass., 1955); and David E. Stannard, *The Puritan Way of Death: A Study in Religion, Culture, and Social Change* (New York, 1977).

Works on town planning begin with Sumner Chilton Powell, *Puritan Village: The Formation of a New England Town* (Middletown, Conn., 1963) and Carl Bridenbaugh, *Cities in the Wilderness: The First Century of Urban Life in America, 1625–1742* (New York, 1938). Also see Anthony N. B. Garvan, *Architecture and Town Planning in Colonial Connecticut* (New Haven, 1951); Sylvia Doughty Fries, *The Urban Idea in Colonial America* (Philadelphia, 1977); Darrett Bruce

Rutman, *Winthrop's Boston: Portrait of a Puritan Town, 1630–1649* (Chapel Hill, 1965); Michael Zuckerman, *Peaceable Kingdoms: New England Towns in the Eighteenth Century* (New York, 1970); Kenneth A. Lockridge, *A New England Town: The First Hundred Years, Dedham, Massachusetts, 1636–1736* (New York, 1970); William Haller, *The Puritan Frontier: Town Planning in New England Colonial Development, 1630–1660* (New York, 1951); and John Archer, "Puritan Town Planning in New Haven," *Journal of the Society of Architectural Historians* 34 (1975).

On Puritan architecture, see [Sidney] Fiske Kimball, *Domestic Architecture of the American Colonies and Early Republic* (New York, 1922, 1966); James J. F. Deetz, *In Small Things Forgotten: The Archaeology of Early American Life* (Garden City, N.Y., 1977); and William H. Pierson, Jr., *American Buildings and Their Architects: The Colonial and Neo-Classical Styles* (Garden City, N.Y., 1976). An outstanding, highly detailed new work is Abbott Lowell Cummings, *The Framed Houses of Massachusetts Bay, 1625–1725* (Cambridge, Mass., 1979). On general cultural life, see Louis B. Wright, *The Cultural Life of the American Colonies, 1607–1763* (New York, 1957) and Carl Bridenbaugh, *The Colonial Craftsman* (Chicago, 1950).

Two books stand out on the colonial New England family: Edmund S. Morgan, *The Puritan Family* (New York, 1944, 1966) and John Demos, *A Little Commonwealth: Family Life in Plymouth Colony* (New York, 1970). Also see Sandford Fleming, *Children and Puritanism* (New Haven, 1933); Philip J. Greven, Jr., *Four Generations: Population, Land, and Family in Colonial Andover, Massachusetts* (Ithaca, N.Y., 1970); Elizabeth Anthony Dexter, *Colonial Women of Affairs* (Boston, 1911); and the less scholarly texts of Alice Morse Earle, *Home Life in Colonial Days* (1898; reprint ed., Middle Village, N.Y., 1975) and *Child Life in Colonial Days* (1899; reprint ed., New York, 1967).

CHAPTER TWO

A number of local histories deal with the row house in some detail, although the focus has predominantly been on the architect-designed upper-class dwelling. The most extensive study is Charles Lockwood, *Bricks & Brownstones: The New York Row House, 1783–1929; An Architectural and Social History* (New York, 1972). Jacob Landy, *The Architecture of Minard Lafever* (New York, 1970) surveys the career of a prominent New York builder. Montgomery Schuyler, "The Small City House in New York," *Architectural Record* 8 (1899) is also helpful.

Boston has received considerable attention in Bainbridge Bunting, *Houses of Boston's Back Bay: An Architectural History, 1840–1917* (Cambridge, Mass., 1967); Walter Muir Whitehill, *Boston: A Topographical History* (New York, 1959); Carl J. Weinhardt, Jr., "The Domestic Architecture of Beacon Hill, 1800–1850," *Proceedings of the Bostonian Society* (1958); Walter Firey, *Land Use in Central Boston* (Cambridge, Mass., 1947); Harold Kirker and James Kirker, *Bulfinch's Boston, 1787–1817* (New York, 1964); and Walter Kilham, *Boston after Bulfinch* (Cambridge, Mass., 1946).

On Philadelphia, see Grant Miles Simon, "Houses and Early Life in Philadelphia," *Proceedings of the American Philosophical Society* 43 (1953); Margaret B. Tinkcom, "Southwark, A River Community: Its Shape and Substance," *Proceedings of the American Philosophical Society* 114 (1970); Kenneth Ames, "Robert Mills and the Philadelphia Row House," *Journal of the Society of Architectural Historians* 27 (1968); and William John Murtagh, "The Philadelphia Row House," *Journal of the Society of Architectural Historians* 16 (1957).

Two books on Washington, D. C., are useful: Constance McLaughlin Green, *Washington, vol. 1, Village and Capital, 1800–1878* (Princeton, 1962) and Daniel D. Reiff, *Washington Architecture, 1791–1861: Problems in Development* (Washington, D.C., 1971). On Baltimore, see Robert I. Alexander, "Baltimore Row Houses of the Early Nineteenth Century," *American Studies* 16 (1975). Richard C. Wade, *The Urban Frontier: The Rise of Western Cities, 1790–1830* (Cambridge, Mass., 1959) and John W. Reps, *Cities of the American West* (Princeton, 1979) cover the western cities.

David P. Handlin, "New England Architects in New York, 1820–1840," *American Quarterly* 19 (1967) connects architectural and social history. Howard B. Rock, *Artisans of the New Republic: The Tradesmen of New York City in the Age of Jefferson* (New York, 1979) discusses political as well as social conditions. Charles E. Peterson, ed., *Building Early America* (Randor, Pa., 1976) contains much useful material on construction. Alan Gowans, *Images of American Living: Four Centuries of Architecture and Furniture as Cultural Expression* (Philadelphia, 1964) considers both style and cultural symbolism in architecture. Neil Harris, *The Artist in American Society* (New York, 1966) and Lillian B. Miller, *Patrons and Patriotism* (Chicago, 1966) analyze early republican reactions to each of the arts. Also see William Dunlap, *History of the Rise and Progress of the Arts of Design in the United States,* ed. Alexander Wyckoff, 3 vols. (1834; reprint ed., New York, 1965).

Economics of urban housing receive careful attention in Betsy Blackmar, "Re-Walking the 'Walking City': Housing and Property Relations in New York City, 1780–1840," *Radical History Review* 21 (1979); Allan Kulikoff, "The Progress of Inequality in Revolutionary Boston," in *Many Pasts: Readings in American Social History,* ed. Herbert G. Gutman and Gregory S. Kealey (Englewood Cliffs, N.J., 1973); James E. Vance, Jr., "Housing the Worker: The Employment Linkage as a Force in Urban Structure," *Economic Geography* 42 (1966); Sam Bass Warner, Jr., *The Private City: Philadelphia in Three Periods of Its Growth* (Philadelphia, 1968); Stephen Thernstrom, *Poverty and Progress* (New York, 1970); Peter R. Knights, *The Plain People of Boston, 1830–1860* (New York, 1973); and Allan R. Pred, *Spatial Dynamics of Urban Industrial Growth, 1800–1914* (Cambridge, Mass., 1966).

CHAPTER THREE

Several recent books have brought forth new interpretations of the slave experience. The most notable are Herbert G. Gutman, *The Black Family in Slavery and Freedom, 1750–1925* (New York, 1976); Lawrence W. Levine, *Black Culture and Black Consciousness: Afro-American Folk Thought from Slavery to Freedom* (New York, 1977); Eugene D. Genovese, *Roll, Jordan, Roll: The World the Slaves Made* (New York, 1974); Leon F. Litwack, *Been in the Storm So Long: The Aftermath of Slavery* (New York, 1979); and Nathan Irvin Huggins, *Black Odyssey: The Afro-American Ordeal in Slavery* (New York, 1977). Other useful texts are Leslie Howard Owens, *This Species of Property: Slave Life and Culture in the Old South* (New York, 1976) and John W. Blassingame, *The Slave Community: Plantation Life in the Antebellum South* (New York, 1972). Kenneth M. Stampp, *The Peculiar Institution: Slavery in the Ante-Bellum South* (New York, 1956); John Hope Franklin, *From Slavery to Freedom: A History of Negro Americans* (New York, 1956, 1978); and Winthrop D. Jordan, *White over Black: American Attitudes toward the Negro* (New York, 1955, 1977) remain important works. David Brion Davis's *The Problem of Slavery in Western Culture* (Ithaca, N.Y., 1966) and *The Problem of Slavery in the Age of Revolution, 1770–1823* (Ithaca, N.Y., 1975) probe the cultural background of pro-slavery and anti-slavery beliefs with unusual erudition and understanding, offering important comparisons with non-American societies.

Slave narratives also give a rich, textured description. The most comprehensive of those collected in the 1930s is George P. Rawick's multi-volume series for the Federal Writers Project, *The American Slave: A Composite Autobiography* (Westport, Conn., 1971–1978). Among the one-volume collections are Benjamin A. Botkin, *Lay My Burden Down* (Chicago, 1945, 1979); Gilbert Osofsky, *Puttin' on Ole Massa* (New York, 1969); Robert S. Starobin, *Blacks in Bondage: Letters from American Slaves* (New York, 1974); Gerda Lerner, *Black Women in White America* (New York, 1973); and *Weevils in the Wheat: Interviews with Virginia Ex-Slaves*, ed. Charles L. Perdue, Jr., et al. (Bloomington, Ind., 1980).

Architecture in West Africa has received scant attention. However, Susan Denyer, *African Traditional Architecture* (New York, 1978) is exemplary. Also see Labelle Prussin, *Architecture in Northern Ghana* (Los Angeles, 1969) and "An Introduction to Indigenous African Architecture," *Journal of the Society of Architectural Historians* 33 (1974); and Richard W. Hull, *African Cities and Towns before the European Conquest* (New York, 1976). Major studies of the slave trade include Philip D. Curtin, *The Atlantic Slave Trade* (Madison, Wis., 1969) and Daniel P. Mannix in collaboration with Malcom Cowley, *Black Cargoes: A History of the Atlantic Slave Trade, 1518–1865* (New York, 1965).

Scholarship on slavery in the Caribbean is extensive; it is of special interest, since many slaves in the American Deep South spent years in Jamaica or Haiti before being shipped to the United States. See, in particular, Orlando Patterson, *The Sociology of Slavery* (London, 1967); Jerome S. Handler and Frederick W. Lange, *Plantation Slavery in Barbados* (Cambridge, Mass., 1978); Gabriel Debien, "Les cases des esclaves des plantations," *Conjonction* 101 (1966); and Sidney Mintz and Richard Price, *An Anthropological Approach to the Afro-American Past* (Philadelphia, 1976).

The work on urban blacks offers a detailed portrait, especially Richard C. Wade, *Slavery in the Cities: The South, 1820–1860* (New York, 1964); Robert S. Starobin, *Industrial Slavery in the Old South* (New York, 1976); Ira Berlin, *Slaves Without Masters: The Free Negro in the Antebellum South* (New York, 1974); and John W. Blassingame, *Black New Orleans, 1860–1880* (Chicago, 1973).

Finally, several works deal specifically with architecture and construction of the slave quarters. John Michael Vlach, *The Afro-American Tradition in the Decorative Arts* (Cleveland, 1978) covers numerous forms of material culture. George McDaniel, "Preserving the People's History: Traditional Black Material Culture in Nineteenth and Twentieth Century Southern Maryland" (Ph.D. diss., Duke University, 1979) makes a strong case for the importance of construction skills among the slaves. Carl Anthony, "The Big House and the Slave Quarters," *Landscape* 20–21 (1976) treats architecture in too deterministic a fashion but offers several interesting insights. Charles H. Fairbanks, "The Kingsley Slave Cabins in Duval County, Florida, 1968," *The Conference on Historic Site Archaeology Papers*, vol. 7 (1972) provides a more thorough, if less interpretive, approach.

CHAPTER FOUR

The origins of American industrialism are, once again, receiving considerable attention from scholars. Anthony F. C. Wallace, *Rockdale: The Growth of an American Village in the Early Industrial Revolution* (New York, 1978), a study of life in a Pennsylvania mill town, is a remarkable synthesis of cultural history, anthropology, technological information, and biography. Alan Dawley, *Class and Community: The Industrial Revolution in Lynn* (Cambridge, Mass., 1976) presents the political and social conflicts in this Massachusetts shoe-making town. Donald Cole, *Immigrant City: Lawrence, Massachusetts, 1845–1921* (Chapel Hill, 1973); John Borden Armstrong, *Factory under the Elms: A History of Harrisville, New Hampshire, 1774–1969* (Cambridge, Mass., 1969); Jeannette Mirsky and Allan Nevins, *The World of Eli Whitney* (New York, 1952); Peter Coleman, *The Transformation of Rhode Island, 1790–1860* (Providence, 1963); and Tamara K. Hareven and Randolph Langenback, *Amoskeag: Life and Work in an American Factory-City* (New York, 1978) give detailed accounts of other manufacturing towns. Henry-Russell Hitchcock's section on these towns in his *Rhode Island Architecture* (1939; reprint ed., New York, 1968) has several illustrations.

Most attention has been focused on Lowell and the factory girls. Thomas Dublin, *Women at Work: The Transformation of Work and Community in Lowell, Massachusetts, 1826–1860* (New York, 1979) analyzes the bonds of friendship and protest. Eric Foner, *The Factory Girls* (Urbana, Ill., 1977) and Benita Eisler, *The Lowell Offering* (Philadelphia, 1977) present first-hand accounts. Also see the autobiographies of Lucy Larcom, *A New England Girlhood* (Boston, 1889) and Harriet Hanson Robinson, *Loom and Spindle* (New York, 1898). Elizabeth Faulkner Baker, *Technology and Women's Work* (New York, 1964) gives a brief picture. Thomas Bender, *Toward an Urban Vision* (Lexington, Ky., 1975) considers the role of Lowell in the new nation. Caroline F. Ware, *The Early New England Cotton Manufacture* (New York, 1931, 1966) and Edith Abbott, *Women in Industry* (New York, 1913) remain excellent surveys. Gerda Lerner, "The Lady and the Mill Girl: Changes in the Status of Women in the Age of Jackson," *Mid-Continent American Studies Journal* 10 (1969) is a clear-headed comparison of two opposite roles for American women.

More technical accounts of architecture and mill operations are also valuable. John P. Coolidge, *Mill and Mansion: A Study of Architecture and Society in Lowell, Massachusetts, 1820–1865* (New York, 1942, 1967) is exemplary for its synthesis of architectural and social history. Steve Dunwell's well-illustrated *The Run of the Mill* (Boston, 1979) gives many useful details about textile production.

CHAPTER FIVE

Recent work in women's history provides important material on home life and the ideology of domesticity in the early nineteenth century. Among the best work is Ann Douglas, *The Feminization of American Culture* (New York, 1977); Carl N. Degler, *At Odds: Women & the Family in America, from the Revolution to the Present* (New York, 1980); Kathryn Kish Sklar, *Catharine Beecher: A Study in American Domesticity* (New Haven, 1973); Nancy F. Cott, *The Bonds of Womanhood: "Women's Sphere" in New England, 1780–1835* (New Haven, 1977); and Dolores Hayden, "Catharine Beecher and the Politics of Housework," in *Women in American Architecture*, ed. Susana Torre (New York, 1977).

Henry Nash Smith, *Virgin Land* (New York, 1959) and Leo Marx, *The Machine in the Garden* (New York, 1964) provide literary and cultural analyses. F. O. Matthiessen, *American Renaissance* (New York, 1941, 1969) remains a classic of American scholarship and insight.

On architecture, David Handlin, *The American Home: Architecture and Society,*

1815–1915 (Boston, 1979) is a lively, informed study of social history through domestic design. Vincent J. Scully, Jr., *The Shingle Style and the Stick Style* (New Haven, 1971); Clifford E. Clark, Jr., "Domestic Architecture as an Index to Social History: The Romantic Revival and the Cult of Domesticity in America, 1840–1890," *Journal of Interdisciplinary History* 7 (1976); Manfredo Tafuri, *Architecture and Utopia: Design and Capitalist Development,* trans. Barbara La Penta (Cambridge, Mass., 1976); and James Early, *Romanticism and American Architecture* (New York, 1965) offer interpretive analyses. More formalistic studies include Alma de C. McArdle and Deirdre Bartlett McArdle, *Carpenter Gothic* (New York, 1978); Wayne Andrews, *American Gothic* (New York, 1975); William H. Pierson, Jr., *American Buildings and Their Architects: The Colonial and Neo-Classical Styles* (New York, 1976); and Hugh S. Morrison, *American Architecture from the First Colonial Settlements to the National Period* (New York, 1952). An excellent specialized study is Talbot F. Hamlin, *Greek Revival Architecture in America* (New York, 1944, 1964). Henry Lionel Williams and Ottalie K. Williams, *A Guide to Old American Houses, 1700–1900* (New York, 1962) points up regional differences. On builders' guides, see Clay Lancaster, "Builders' Guides and Plan Books and American Architecture," *The Magazine of Art* 41 (1948) and Henry-Russell Hitchcock, Jr., *American Architectural Books: A List of Books, Portfolios, and Pamphlets on Architecture and Related Subjects Published in America before 1895* (Minneapolis, 1962). Reprints of major nineteenth-century domestic guides, in particular Catharine Beecher and Harriet Beecher Stowe's *The American Woman's Home* and the works of Andrew Jackson Downing, Calvert Vaux, and other architects or builders, give extremely detailed descriptions of houses and domestic ideology.

Finally, several books on the West note architectural conditions. Julie Roy Jeffrey, *Frontier Women* (New York, 1979) shows that domesticity was, indeed, many women's main concern. Richard A. Bartlett, *The New Country* (New York, 1974) presents a general social history, while books such as Kathleen Neils Conzen, *Immigrant Milwaukee, 1836–1860* (Cambridge, Mass., 1976) concentrate on individual cities. Pierce Lewis analyzes the presistence and varying paths of housing styles across the frontier in "Common Houses, Cultural Spoor," *Landscape* 19 (1975). James Brinckerhoff Jackson's essays in *Landscapes* (Boston, 1970), collected from this journal *(Landscape),* delight as well as inform. Dolores Hayden, *Seven American Utopias: The Architecture of Communitarian Socialism: 1790–1975* (Cambridge, Mass., 1976) analyzes the role of architecture and planning in the pre–Civil War communitarian experiments. Richard Lingeman, *Small Town America: A Narrative History, 1620–the Present* (New York, 1980) brings together a wide variety of positive and negative descriptions.

CHAPTER SIX

There are now a number of books dealing with the social and architectural history of the late nineteenth century. Lewis Mumford, *The Brown Decades: A Study of the Arts of America, 1865–1895* (New York, 1931, 1971) is a classic study that was the first to offer a positive reading of this "Awkward Age." John Brinckerhoff Jackson, *American Space: The Centennial Years, 1865–1876* (New York, 1972) compares the rural and urban landscapes of various regions. Herwin Schafer, *Nineteenth Century Modern: The Functional Tradition in Victorian Design* (New York, 1970) looks beneath the surface of Victorian ornament. My own earlier book, *Moralism and the Model Home: Domestic Architecture and Cultural Conflict in Chicago, 1873–1913* (Chicago, 1980) contrasts the designs and social goals of architects, builders, building workers, and reform groups.

The major studies of architecture during this period include Vincent J. Scully, Jr., *The Shingle Style and the Stick Style* (New Haven, 1971); Mark Girouard, *Sweetness and Light: The "Queen Anne" Movement, 1860–1900* (New York, 1977); and the more popular book by John Maass, *The Victorian Home in America* (New York, 1972). On the influence of a major English art critic, see Roger B. Stein, *John Ruskin and Aesthetic Thought in America, 1840–1900* (Cambridge, Mass., 1967).

For historical background, see Arthur Meier Schlesinger, *The Rise of the City, 1878–1898* (Chicago, 1961) and Edgar Martin, *The Standard of Living in 1860* (Chicago, 1942). On domesticity, relevant recent works include David M. Katzman, *Seven Days a Week: Women and Domestic Service in Industrializing America* (New York, 1978) and the chapter on interior decorator Candace Wheeler in Madeleine B. Stern, *We the Women: Career Firsts of Nineteenth-Century America* (New York, 1974).

On the evolution of an important form of building finance, see H. Morton Bodfish, *History of the Building and Loan Associations in the United States* (Chicago, 1931). The larger-scale builders and subdividers are the subject of Anne Bloomfield, "The Real Estate Associates: A Land and Housing Developer of the 1870s in San Francisco," *Journal of the Society of Architectural Historians* 37 (1978) and Roger D. Simon, "The City Building Process: Housing and Services in New Milwaukee Neighborhoods, 1880–1910," *Transactions of the American Philosophical Society* 68 (1978). On sanitary engineers, see Mary N. Stone, "The Plumbing Paradox: American Attitudes toward Late-Nineteenth-Century Domestic Sanitary Arrangements," *Winterthur Portfolio* 14 (1979); John Duffy, *A History of Public Health in New York City*, 2 vols. (New York, 1968–1974); and Stanley K. Schurtz and Clay McShane, "To Engineer the Metropolis: Sewers, Sanitation, and City Planning in Late-Nineteenth-Century America," *Journal of American History* 65 (1978).

Material on individual cities sometimes goes beyond the guidebook stage, especially in Robert M. Fogelson, *The Fragmented Metropolis, Los Angeles, 1850–1930* (Cambridge, Mass., 1967); and Richard R. Brettell, *Historic Denver: The Architects and the Architecture, 1858–1893* (Denver, 1978). Sam Bass Warner, Jr., *Streetcar Suburbs: The Process of Growth in Boston, 1870–1900* (Cambridge, Mass., 1978) remains the best example of urban and social history through architecture. On suburban planning in general during this period, see John W. Reps, *The Making of Urban America* (Princeton, 1965); Jon C. Teaford, *City and Suburb: The Political Fragmentation of Metropolitan America, 1850–1970* (Baltimore, 1979); and Christopher Tunnard, "The Romantic Suburb in America," *The Magazine of Art* 40 (1947). Adna Weber, "Suburban Annexations," *North American Review* 146 (1898) is representative of the period's enthusiasm.

CHAPTER SEVEN

Recent books of interviews with former immigrants give vivid portraits of their experiences: Eli Ginzberg and Hyman Berman, *The American Worker in the Twentieth Century: A History through Autobiographies* (New York, 1963); Sydelle Kramer and Jenny Masur, *Jewish Grandmothers* (Boston, 1976); Daniel M. Brownstone et al., *Island of Hope, Island of Tears* (New York, 1979). Other histories of working-class people's experience that stress home life as well as political activity include Virginia Yans-McLaughlin, *Family and Community: Italian Immigrants in Buffalo, 1880–1930* (Ithaca,

N.Y., 1977); Joseph Barton, *Peasants and Strangers: Italians, Roumanians, and Slavs in an American City, 1880–1950* (Cambridge, Mass., 1975); and Oscar Handlin, *Boston's Immigrants, 1790–1880* (New York, 1974), which poses a greater disjunction between old world and new than the other books. Herbert G. Gutman's compelling *Work, Culture and Society in Industrializing America: Essays in American Working-Class and Social History* (New York, 1976) is a passionately written and important overview of immigrant workers' lives.

Accounts of individual cities include Allen F. Davis and Mark H. Haller, *The Peoples of Philadelphia: A History of Ethnic Groups and Lower-Class Life, 1790–1940* (Philadelphia, 1972); John Bodner, *Immigration and Industrialization: Ethnicity in an American Mill Town, 1870–1940* (Pittsburgh, 1977); and Devereux Bowly, Jr., *The Poorhouse: Subsidized Housing in Chicago, 1895–1976* (Carbondale, Ill., 1978). New York has received the most attention, beginning with James Ford, *Slums and Housing,* 2 vols. (1936; reprint ed., Westport, Conn., 1972), and more recently in such books as Moses Rischin, *The Promised City: New York's Jews, 1870–1914* (Cambridge, Mass., 1962); Anthony Jackson, *A Place Called Home: A History of Low-Cost Housing in Manhattan* (Cambridge, Mass., 1976); Roy Lubove, *The Progressives and the Slums: Tenement House Reform in New York City, 1890–1917* (Pittsburgh, 1962); and Gordon Atkins, *Health, Housing, and Poverty in New York City, 1865–1898* (Ann Arbor, 1947).

Studies concentrating on the history of urban blacks include Allan H. Spear, *Black Chicago: The Making of a Negro Ghetto, 1890–1920* (Chicago, 1967); Gilbert Osofsky, *Harlem: The Making of a Ghetto, Negro New York, 1890–1930* (New York, 1968); W. E. B. DuBois, *The Philadelphia Negro* (1899; reprint ed., New York, 1968); and *Housing Conditions among Negroes in Harlem* (New York, 1915), a study of the National League on Urban Conditions among Negroes.

Special attention to the home lives of working-class women is found in Barbara Mayer Wertheimer, *We Were There: The Story of Working Women in America* (New York, 1977); Susan Estabrook Kennedy, *If All We Did Was to Weep at Home: A History of White Working-Class Women in America* (Bloomington, Ind., 1979); and Rosalyn Baxandall, Linda Gordon, and Susan Reverby, *America's Working Women: A Documentary History, 1600 to the Present* (New York, 1976).

On the settlements, see Thomas Lee Philpott, *The Slum and the Ghetto: Neighborhood Deterioration and Middle-Class Reform, Chicago, 1880–1930* (New York, 1978); Allen F. Davis, *Spearheads to Reform: The Settlement House, the Social Settlements and the Progressive Movement* (New York, 1967); and Paul Boyer, *Urban Masses and Moral Order in America, 1820–1920* (Cambridge, Mass., 1978). Autobiographies and accounts by the reformers include Mary K. Simkovitch, *The City Worker's World in America* (New York, 1917); Jacob Riis, *How the Other Half Lives: Studies among the Tenements of New York* (1890; reprint ed., New York, 1971); Lillian D. Wald, *The House on Henry Street* (1915; reprint ed., New York, 1971); Robert Hunter, *Tenement Conditions in Chicago* (Chicago, 1901) and *Poverty* (1904; reprint ed., New York, 1965); Association for the Improvement of the Condition of the Poor, *Housing Conditions in Baltimore* (1907; reprint ed., New York, 1974); and Albion Fellows Bacon, *Beauty for Ashes* (New York, 1914). Eugenie Ladner Birch and Deborah S. Gardner detail women's involvement in "Impatient Crusaders: Women and Low-Income Housing Reform in Britain and America, 1865–1975," *Women & History* 1 (1980).

Histories of housing reform include *The Urban Community: Housing and Planning in the Progressive Era,* ed. Roy Lubove (Englewood Cliffs, N.J., 1967); Kenneth Frampton, "The Evolution of Housing Concepts, 1870–1970," *Lotus International* 10 (1975); David Ward, "The Emergence of Central Immigrant Ghettos in American Cities, 1840–1920," *Annals of the Association of American Geographers* 38 (1968); Peter Marcuse, "Housing in Early City Planning," *Journal of Urban History* 6 (1980); and the classic work by Robert W. De Forest and Lawrence Veiller, *The Tenement House Problem,* 2 vols. (New York, 1903). Kathleen Neils Conzen provides an interpretive bibliography in "Immigrants, Immigrant Neighborhoods, and Ethnic Identity: Historical Issues," *Journal of American History* 66 (1979).

CHAPTER EIGHT

There is as yet no adequate history of apartment houses in the United States, although a few authors have recently given it some attention. See Dolores Hayden, *The Grand Domestic Revolution: A History of Feminist Designs for American Homes, Neighborhoods, and Cities* (Cambridge, Mass., 1981); David P. Handlin, *The American Home* (Boston, 1878); Douglas Shand Tucci, *Built in Boston: City & Suburb* (Boston, 1978); Carl W. Condit, *The Chicago School of Architecture* (Chicago, 1964); Robert A. M. Stern, "With Rhetoric: The New York Apartment House," *Via* 14 (1980); Richard Plunz, *Housing Form in New York City, 1850–1950* (Paris, 1980); and *Housing Form and Public Policy in the United States,* ed. Richard Plunz (New York, 1980). Andrew Alpern, *Apartments for the Affluent: A Historical Survey of Buildings in New York* (New York, 1975) relies almost exclusively on photographs and floor plans. Deborah S. Gardner, "The Architecture of Commercial Capitalism: John Kellum and the Development of New York, 1840–1875" (Ph. D. diss., Columbia University, 1979) contains a chapter on the Working Women's Hotel. Barbara K. Silvergold, "Richard Morris Hunt and the Importation of Beaux-Arts Architecture to the United States" (Ph. D. diss., University of California, Berkeley, 1974) discusses the Stuyvesant Flats. Stephen Birmingham, *Life at the Dakota* (New York, 1979) gives a good close-up of social life and technological innovations at one of New York's most famous buildings.

The earlier material on apartments that is most available includes E. Idell Zeisloft, *The New Metropolis* (New York, 1899); Russell Sturgis, "Apartment House" in his *Dictionary of Architecture and Building* (New York, 1905); John Pickering Putnam, *Architecture under Nationalism* (Boston, 1890); Sarah Gilman Young, *European Modes of Living, or The Question of Apartment Houses* (New York, 1881); *Apartment Houses of the Metropolis* (New York, 1908); and R. W. Sexton, *American Apartment Houses of Today* (New York, 1926). The articles and books of Charlotte Perkins Gilman adamantly endorse apartment-hotels, especially "The Passing of the Home in Great American Cities," *Cosmopolitan* 38 (1904) and *Women and Economics* (1898; reprint ed., New York, 1966). Also see William Hutchins, "New York Hotels," *Architectural Record* 12 (1902); Everett Blanke, "The Cliff-Dwellers of New York," *Cosmopolitan* 15 (1893); "The New Homes of New York: A Study of Flats," *Scribner's Monthly* 8 (1874); and the numerous illustrations and articles in architectural journals.

CHAPTER NINE

Several books on the architectural side of progressivism are worth pursuing for their illustrations, as much as for their texts. Mark L. Peisch, *The Chicago School* (New York,

1964); H. Allen Brooks, *The Prairie School* (New York, 1964); Grant C. Manson, *Frank Lloyd Wright to 1910* (New York, 1958); Esther McCoy, *Five California Architects* (New York, 1975); *Bay Area Houses*, ed. Sally Woodbridge (New York, 1976); and William H. Jordy, *American Buildings and Their Architects*, vol. 3, *Progressive and Academic Ideals at the Turn of the Twentieth Century* (Garden City, N.J., 1972) all place houses in a social context.

The arts-and-crafts movement has attracted special interest, although most present-day enthusiasts discount the industrial propaganda. See *The Arts and Crafts Movement in America*, ed. Robert Judson Clark (Princeton, 1972); John Freeman, *The Forgotten Rebel: Gustav Stickley and His Craftsman Mission Furniture* (Watkins Glen, N.Y., 1966); and *California Design 1910*, ed. Timothy J. Anderson, Eudorah M. Moore, and Robert W. Winter (Pasadena, Cal., 1974). The earlier work of Oscar Lovell Triggs, *Some Chapters in the History of the Arts and Crafts Movement* (Chicago, 1902) and *The New Industrialism* (Chicago, 1902) captures the mood of the time. There are also several reprints of house designs from *The Craftsman* now available.

The bungalow phenomenon is considered in Clay Lancaster, "The American Bungalow," *Art Bulletin* 40 (1958); M. H. Lazear, "The Evolution of the Bungalow," *The House Beautiful* 36 (1914); Henry H. Saylor, *Bungalows* (Philadelphia, 1911); and other pattern books and bungalow magazines of the period. On the bungalow court, see Peter Wight, "Bungalow Courts in California," *Western Architect* 28 (1919); Robert Brown, "The California Bungalow in Los Angeles" (Ph. D. diss., University of California, Los Angeles, 1964); and James Tice and Stefanos Poyzoides, "Los Angeles Courts," *Casabella* 412 (1976). See also R. Winter, *The California Bungalow* (Los Angeles, 1980).

On the state of the suburbs, see Dana Bartlett, *The Better City* (Los Angeles, 1907) and the "New Suburb" issue of *Scribner's Magazine* 52 (1912). Mel Scott, *American City Planning Since 1890* (Berkeley, 1971) remains the best overview of the demands for urban and suburban planning.

The domestic-science movement has received special attention in recent years in Barbara Ehrenreich and Deirdre English, *For Her Own Good: 150 Years of the Experts' Advice to Women* (Garden City, N.Y., 1978); Sheila M. Rothman, *Woman's Proper Place: A History of Changing Ideals and Practices, 1870 to the Present* (New York, 1978); and David P. Handlin, "Efficiency and the American Home," *Architectural Association Quarterly* 5 (1973). The texts of the period, especially those of Christine Frederick and Ellen Richards, still deserve attention. Samuel Haber, *Efficiency and Uplift: Scientific Management in the Progressive Era, 1890–1920* (Chicago, 1964) relates the movement to other efficiency campaigns. Heidi I. Hartman, "Capitalism and Women's Work in the Home" (Ph. D. diss., Yale University, 1971) analyzes the industrial backdrop to the private home. Edward Bok, *The Americanization of Edward Bok* (New York, 1924) is the autobiography of the editor of the *Ladies' Home Journal,* and describes his efforts to redirect American taste and domesticity. On women's magazines and home decorating (or "shelter") magazines, see Frank L. Mott, *A History of American Magazines,* 4 vols. (Cambridge, Mass., 1957).

A major study of collective, feminist alternatives to more traditional domestic arrangements is Dolores Hayden, *The Grand Domestic Revolution: A History of Feminist Designs for American Homes, Neighborhoods, and Cities* (Cambridge, Mass.: Harvard University Press, 1981). Hayden demonstrates that many American women and men not only used discussions about housing design to raise questions about prevailing social values, but they also built dwellings and communities to support their ideals.

CHAPTER TEN

The best sources for information on early-twentieth-century industrial towns are still the original reports, especially those issued by the U. S. Bureau of Labor Statistics and the National Housing Association. Privately commissioned reports include *Homes for Workmen* (New Orleans, 1919); William H. Tolman, *Industrial Betterment* (New York, 1900) and *Social Engineering: A Record of Things Done by American Industrialists Employing Upwards of One and One-Half Million of People*, with an introduction by Andrew Carnegie (New York, 1909); E. Wake Cook, *Industrial Betterment* (New York, 1906); Graham Taylor, *Satellite Cities: A Study of Industrial Suburbs* (1915; reprint ed., New York, 1974); Budgett Meakin, *Model Factories and Villages* (Philadelphia, 1906); Edwin Shuey, *Factory People and Their Employers* (New York, 1900); and the Aladdin Company, *Industrial Housing* (Bay City, Mich., 1919). Special attention is given to World War I government-funded housing in R. C. Feld, *Humanizing Industry* (New York, 1920); Clinton MacKenzie, *Industrial Housing* (New York, 1920); and Morris Knowles, *Industrial Housing* (New York, 1920). Georges Benoit-Lévy's report on American industrial garden cities, *Cités-Jardins d'Amérique* (Paris, 1905) is quite detailed. Specialized studies include the National Cash Register Company publications, such as *Nature, the Factory and the Home* (Dayton, 1903); Margaret Byington, *Homestead: The Households of a Mill Town*, (Pittsburgh, 1910) and the other volumes of the Pittsburgh Survey; August Kohn, *Cotton Mills of South Carolina* (Charleston, S. C., 1907); and Harriet L. Herring, *Welfare Work in Mill Villages* (Chapel Hill, 1929), also on southern mill towns.

Two contemporary articles on Gary are John Kimberly Mumford, "This Land of Opportunity: Gary, the City That Rose from a Sandy Waste," *Harper's Weekly* 52 (1908) and Henry B. Fuller, "An Industrial Utopia," *Harper's Weekly* 51 (1907). George H. Miller, "Fairfield, a Town with a Purpose," *American City* 9 (1913); A. T. Luce, "Kincaid, Illinois—Model Mining Town," *American City* 13 (1905); "The New Mining Community of Tyrone, New Mexico," *Architectural Review* 6 (1918); and Leonora B. Ellis, "A Model Factory Town," *Forum* 32 (1901–1902) on Peltzer, South Carolina, are representative accounts.

More recent work on industrial towns includes Robert S. Smith, *Mill on the Dan* (Durham, N. C., 1960); James B. Allen, *The Company Town in the American West* (Norman, Okla., 1966); John Reps, "The Towns the Companies Built," in his *The Making of Urban America* (Princeton, 1965); and Leland Roth, "Three Industrial Towns by McKim, Mead & White," *Journal of the Society of Architectural Historians* 38 (1979), which provides insights about the architect-planner's role in the 1890s. Specialized studies include John S. Garner, "Leclaire, Illinois: A Model Company Town (1890–1934)," *Journal of the Society of Architectural Historians* 30 (1971); Raymond A. Mohl and Neil Betten, "The Failure of Industrial City Planning: Gary, Indiana, 1906–1910," *Journal of the American Institute of City Planners* 38 (1972); and Freeman Champney, *Art and Glory: The Story of Elbert Hubbard* (New York, 1968), on the Roycrofters at East Aurora, New York. On Pullman, see Stanley Buder, *Pullman* (New York, 1967) and Almont Lindsey, *The Pullman Strike* (Chicago, 1942).

Detailed accounts of working people's lives in industrial towns are more difficult to find. See David Brody, *Steelworkers in America* (Cambridge, Mass., 1960); Susan J. Kleinberg, "Technology and Women's Work: The Lives of Working Class Women in Pittsburgh, 1870–1900," *Labor History* 17 (1976); and Corinne Azen Krause, "Urbanization Without Breakdown: Italian, Jewish and Slavic Women in Pittsburgh, 1900 to 1945," *Journal of Urban History* 4 (1978).

CHAPTER ELEVEN

An extensive literature deals with the suburban boom of the 1920s. Louis Pink, *The New Day in Housing* (1928; reprint ed., New York, 1974); volume 2 of the *Supplementary Report of the Urbanism Committee to the National Resources Committee* (Washington, D. C., 1939); and the National Association of Real Estate Boards' *Home Building and Subdivisions* (Chicago, 1925) describe individual developers as well as the larger phenomenon. The *National Real Estate Journal*, the American Civic Association *Bulletins*, and the *Journal of Land and Public Utility Economics* contain numerous articles on subdivisions. Harlan Paul Douglas, *The Suburban Trend* (New York, 1925) is a key work.

Government publications reveal definite goals. See John Gries and James T. Ford, eds., *Publications of the President's Conference on Home Building and Home Ownership*, 11 vols. (Washington, D.C., 1932); the White House Conference on Child Health report on *The Home and the Child* (New York, 1931); J.S. Taylor, *The Division of Building and Housing and Its Services* (Washington, D.C., 1925); and *How To Own Your Home* (Washington, D.C., 1923). Better Homes in America, Inc., sponsored numerous booklets and guides as well as larger texts, including *The Better Homes Manual*, ed. Blanche Halbert (Chicago, 1931). Ellis W. Hawley, "Herbert Hoover, the Commerce Secretariat, and the Vision of an 'Associative State,' 1921–1928," *Journal of American History* 61 (1974) provides an excellent study of Hoover's goals.

Architecture guides of the period suggest the changing ideas of residential design. *The Small Home* and pattern books such as *Small Homes of Architectural Distinction*, ed. Robert T. Jones (New York, 1929) show the work of the Architects' Small House Service Bureau. Robert L. Stevenson, *Homes of Character* (Boston, 1923); G. H. Edgell, *The American Architecture of To-Day* (New York, 1928); Edwin Bont, *The Small Home Primer* (Boston, 1925); Ernest Flagg, *Small Houses* (New York, 1922); Marcia Mead, *Homes of Character* (New York, 1926); and such specialized texts as Rexford Newcomb, *The Spanish House for America* (Philadelphia, 1927) and R. W. Sexton, *Spanish Influence on American Architecture and Decoration* (New York, 1926) inspired many home builders. Recent studies of 1920s architecture include David Gebhard, *George Washington Smith: The Spanish Colonial Revival in California* (Santa Barbara, 1964); Gebhard's "Life in the Dollhouse," in *Bay Area Houses*, ed. Sally Woodbridge (New York, 1976); and Jonathan Lane, "The Period House in the Nineteen-Twenties," *Journal of the Society of Architectural Historians* 20 (1961).

Books on the model suburbs of the 1920s expressed great enthusiasm. The best survey is Clarence S. Stein, *Toward New Towns for America* (New York, 1973). Also see Henry Wright, *Rehousing Urban America* (New York, 1935) and Robert Whitten and Thomas Adams, *Neighborhoods of Small Homes* (Cambridge, Mass., 1931). Union mortgage plans are explored in "Housing Activities of Labor Groups," *Monthly Labor Review* 27 (1928) and in a student paper on the Brotherhood of Sleeping Car Porters by Susan Longley at the University of California at Berkeley. On the co-ops, see Elsie Danenberg, *Get Your Own Home the Co-Operative Way* (New York, 1949); "The House—A Success Story," *Survey Graphic* 37 (1948); and "The Cooperative Plan: One Answer to the Low Cost Housing Problem," *Architectural Forum* 55 (1931). Roy Lubove, *Commu-*

nity Planning in the 1920s (Pittsburgh, 1963) analyzes the many advanced housing ideas of the decade.

Studies of zoning tend to pose the rational side of the enterprise. Theodora Kimball Hubbard and Henry Vincent Hubbard, *Our Cities To-Day and To-Morrow* (Cambridge, Mass., 1929); "The Social Aspects of Zoning," *Survey* 48 (1922); and Thomas Adams and Edward M. Bassett, *Buildings: Their Uses and the Spaces About Them* (New York, 1931) describe the expectations of the zoning pioneers. More recently, Stanislaw J. Makielski, *The Politics of Zoning* (New York, 1960) and Seymour I. Toll, *Zoned America* (New York, 1969) stress the controlling functions.

Volume 6 of *The President's Conference on Home Building and Home Ownership,* entitled *Negro Housing,* has material on segregation. Bessie Averne McClenahan, *The Changing Urban Neighborhood* (Los Angeles, 1929) provides interviews with residents about race and other issues.

Social background on the decade can be found in many books. The most vivid are the classic *Middletown: A Study in Contemporary American Culture,* by Robert Lynd and Helen Merrell Lynd (New York, 1929); Frederick Lewis Allen, *Only Yesterday* (New York, 1959); and Mark Sullivan, *Our Times,* vols. 3 and 4 (New York, 1926–1935). Useful scholarly books include William E. Leuchtenburg, *The Perils of Prosperity* (Chicago, 1958); Preston Slosson, *The Great Crusade and After* (Chicago, 1971); and *Change and Continuity in Twentieth-Century America: The 1920's,* ed. John Braeman, Robert H. Bremner, and David Brody (Columbus, Ohio, 1968), which contains an excellent article on suburbanization by Charles N. Glaab. The most substantial survey of the period remains that of the President's Research Committee on Social Trends, *Recent Social Trends in the United States* (Washington, D.C., 1933).

CHAPTER TWELVE

There is a massive literature on public housing among city planners. Good general sources are Nathaniel S. Keith, *Politics and the Housing Crisis Since 1930* (New York, 1973); David R. Mandelker and Roger Montgomery, *Housing in America* (Indianapolis, 1973); *Housing Urban America,* ed. Jon Pynoos, Robert Schafer, and Chester Hartman (Chicago, 1973); Lawrence M. Friedman, *Government and Slum Housing* (Chicago, 1968); Leonard Freedman, *Public Housing: The Politics of Poverty* (New York, 1969). Robert Moore Fisher, *Twenty Years of Public Housing* (New York, 1959) and Henry Aaron, *Shelter and Subsidies: Who Benefits from Federal Housing Policies?* (Washington, D.C., 1972) are more specifically concerned with economics. Two case studies, Lee Rainwater, *Behind Ghetto Walls* (Chicago, 1971), on Pruitt-Igoe in St. Louis, and Martin Meyerson and Edward Banfield, *Politics, Planning, and the Public Interest* (New York, 1955), on Chicago's fights about public-housing locations, are exemplary accounts. Several books describing public-housing policies for the public are useful: Nathan Straus, *The Seven Myths of Housing* (1944; reprint ed., New York, 1974); Catherine Bauer, *A Citizen's Guide to Public Housing* (Poughkeepsie, N. Y., 1940) and Edith Elmer Wood, *Introduction to Housing* (Washington, D. C., 1939). Bauer's *Modern Housing* (1934; reprint ed., New York, 1974) provides the background to the housing fights of this period. *Public Housing in America,* ed. M. B. Schnapper (New York, 1939) contains both sides of the controversy, with articles and speeches from the real-estate lobby, the government, and the reformers. The USHA's *Public Housing Design* (Washington, D. C., 1946) was published at the end of a period of low-rise buildings and fairly extensive community services.

Books on pre–1937 federally funded housing include Paul Conkin, *Tomorrow a New World: The New Deal Community Program* (Ithaca, N.Y., 1959) and Joseph L. Arnold, *The New Deal in the Suburbs: A History of the Greenbelt Town Program, 1935–1954* (Columbus, Ohio, 1971). On PWA programs, see *Urban Housing: The Story of the PWA Housing Division, 1933–1936* (Washington, D.C., 1936); Michael W. Straus and Talbot Wegg, *Housing Comes of Age* (New York, 1938); and Harold Ickes, *Back to Work: The Story of the PWA* (New York, 1935). Richard Pommer gives an excellent architectural overview in "The Architecture of Urban Housing in the United States during the Early 1930s," *Journal of the Society of Architectural Historians* 37 (1978).

Critiques of urban renewal include the conservative attack by Martin Anderson, *The Federal Bulldozer* (Cambridge, Mass., 1964); more liberal accounts in Scott Greer, *Urban Renewal and American Cities* (Indianapolis, 1965); *Urban Renewal: People, Politics, and Planning*, ed. Jewel Bullush and Murray Hausknecht (New York, 1967); and *Urban Renewal: The Record and the Controversy*, ed. James Q. Wilson (Cambridge, Mass., 1966); and a Marxist analysis by Marc A. Weiss, "Origins and Legacy of Urban Renewal," in *Urban and Regional Planning in an Age of Austerity*, ed. Pierre Clavel, John Forester, and William W. Goldsmith (New York, 1980). Charles Abrams, *Forbidden Neighbors* (New York, 1955) gives a scathing critique of segregation policies.

Elizabeth Coit, "Housing from the Tenant's Viewpoint," *Architectural Record* 89 and 90 (1941, 1942) and "Notes on the Design and Construction of the Dwelling Units for the Lower-Income Family," *The Octagon* 13 (1941) were important recommendations for public-housing design. On Bauer, see Mary Sue Cole, "Catherine Bauer and Public Housing Government, 1926–1936" (Ph. D. diss., George Washington University, 1975).

CHAPTER THIRTEEN

Federal middle-income housing policies have come under attack from many directions. Nathan Straus published *Two-Thirds of a Nation: A Housing Program* (New York, 1952), an insightful critique of intentions and biases by a former administrator. *Fortune* contained many articles on housing problems; "The Industry Capitalism Forgot," 36 (1947), is representative. That magazine also published *The Exploding Metropolis* (New York, 1957) on land-use planning in the cities and the suburbs. More recent work includes Richard O. Davies, *Housing Reform During the Truman Administration* (Columbia, Mo., 1966); Blake McKelvey, *The Emergence of Metropolitan America, 1915–1966* (New Brunswick, N.J., 1968), which is concerned mostly with federal–urban relations; Martin Myerson et al., *Housing, People, and Cities* (New York, 1962); *The Prospective City*, ed. Arthur P. Solomon (Cambridge, Mass., 1980), which discusses problems of taxation and energy; and Kenneth T. Jackson, "Race, Ethnicity, and Real Estate Appraisal: The Home Owners Loan Corporation and the Federal Housing Administration," *Journal of Urban History* 6 (1980) pp. 419–452.

Studies of postwar community planning and neighborhood life include James Dahir, *Communities for Better Living* (New York, 1950); the Urban Land Institute guide, *The Community Builders Handbook*, which has appeared every few years since 1947; and the utopian tract, *Communitas*, by Paul and Percival Goodman (New York, 1947), which continues to be an exciting book to read and ponder.

More strictly social-science accounts of the suburbs are numerous; many were widely read when they first appeared. See, in particular, "Social Policy and Social Research in Housing," a special issue of the *Journal of Social Issues* 7 (1951); *City and Suburban*

Housing, ed. Poyntz Tyler (New York, 1957); *The Suburban Community,* ed. William M. Dobriner (New York, 1958); Robert C. Wood, *Suburbia: Its People and Their Problems* (Boston, 1958); David Riesman, *The Lonely Crowd* (New York, 1958); and William H. Whyte, Jr., *The Organization Man* (New York, 1956). A. C. Spectorsky, *The Exurbanites* (New York, 1955); and John R. Seeley et al., *Crestwood Heights* (New York, 1956) describe upper-middle-class suburbs. See also Bennett M. Berger, *Working Class Suburb* (Berkeley, 1960). Herbert J. Gans's later study of *The Levittowners* (New York, 1967) is a sympathetic presentation of a postwar suburb that had become quite stable. On the situation of the housewife, see Helena Z. Lopata, *Occupation Housewife* (New York, 1971) and Mirra Komarovsky, *Blue-Collar Marriage* (New York, 1962).

Less scholarly comments on the suburbs include Harry Henderson, "The Mass-Produced Suburbs," *Harper's* 107 (1953); Bernard Rudofsky, *Behind the Picture Window* (New York, 1955); and Scott Donaldson, *The Suburban Myth* (New York, 1969), an overview of writings on postwar suburbs that seeks to defend this way of life.

Among the most widely read books on home design during this period were Henry Wright and George Nelson, *Tomorrow's House* (New York, 1945); Frederick Gutheim, *Houses for Family Living* (New York, 1948); Mary Davis Johnson, *McCall's Book of Modern Houses* (New York, 1951); Elizabeth B. Mock, *If You Want to Build a House* (New York, 1946), a treatise promoting modern design commissioned by the Museum of Modern Art; Katherine Morrow Ford and Thomas H. Creighton, *The American House Today* (New York, 1951); and A. Quincy Jones and Frederick E. Emmons, *Builders' Homes for Better Living* (New York, 1957). Robert Woods Kennedy, *The House and the Art of Its Design* (New York, 1953) was a textbook for home economists and architects alike that emphasized environments for family life. Richard Neutra, *Survival Through Design* (New York, 1954); Eero Saarinen, *The City* (New York, 1943); and Frank Lloyd Wright, *Genius and the Mobocracy* (New York, 1949) and *The Natural House* were the quintessential architects' commentaries on housing and suburban life. Kevin Lynch, *Image of the City* (Cambridge, Mass., 1960) was an influential study of reactions to urban environments.

Architectural journals and home magazines were filled with material on the modern dream house. The *Architectural Forum* had a special "Builders' Issue," vol. 90 (1949). Levittown received constant attention. See, among other accounts, "The Most House for the Money," *Fortune* 46 (1952); Eric Larrabee, "The Six Thousand Houses that Levitt Built," *Harper's* 197 (1948); "Nation's Biggest Housebuilder," *Life* 25 (1948); and the chapter on Levittown in Eugene Rachlis and John E. Marquesee, *The Landlords* (New York, 1963). Other pertinent magazines include *Perfect Home, Popular Home, McCall's,* and *Parents' Magazine.*

CHAPTER FOURTEEN

There has been a recent surge of material on housing and families done from many different perspectives. The best of the general books is Martin Mayer, *The Builders: Houses, People, Neighborhoods, Governments, Money* (New York, 1978), which does manage to cover each of those topics well. More historical works include *The Story of Housing,* ed. Gertrude Sipperly Fish (New York, 1979); Anthony Ridley, *At Home: An Illustrated History of Houses and Homes* (London, 1976); Glenn H. Beyer, *Housing and Society* (New York, 1965); Robert A. Liston, *The Ugly Palaces: Housing in America* (New York, 1974); Jan Cohn, *The Palace or the Poorhouse: The American House as a Cultural Symbol* (East Lansing, Mich., 1979); and Jane Davison, *The Fall of a Doll's*

House: Three Generations of American Women and the Houses They Lived In (New York, 1980). For a critical overview of urban development, Sam Bass Warner, Jr., *The Urban Wilderness: A History of the American City* (New York, 1972) is excellent.

Specialized books on the housing crisis, especially in non-market housing, include Chester W. Hartman, *Housing and Social Policy* (Englewood Cliffs, N.J., 1975); *A Decent Home and Environment*, ed. Donald Phares (Cambridge, Mass., 1977); *Housing Urban America*, ed. Jon Pynoos, Robert Schafer, and Chester W. Hartman (Chicago, 1973); Constance Perin, *Everything in Its Place: Social Order and Land Use in America* (Princeton, 1977) on zoning; and a compelling book by Washington, D.C., journalist Leonard Downie, Jr., *Mortgage on America: The Real Cost of Real Estate Speculation* (New York, 1974). On organizing, see *Citizen Participation*, ed. Edgar S. Cahn and Barry A. Passett (New York, 1971); Chester W. Hartman, *Yerba Buena: Land Grab and Community Resistance in San Francisco* (San Francisco, 1974); Robert Cassidy, *Livable Cities: A Grass-Roots Guide to Rebuilding Urban America* (New York, 1980); Stuart Dill McBride, *A Nation of Neighborhoods* (Boston, 1978); Juliet Saltman, *Open Housing: Dynamics of a Social Movement* (New York, 1978); Prentice Bowsher & Jubilee Housing, Inc., *People Who Care: Making Housing Work for the Poor* (Washington, D.C., 1980); Housing Assistance Council, *The Politics of Rural Housing: A Manual for Building Rural Housing Coalitions* (Washington, D.C., 1980); Jerome G. Rose and Robert E. Rothman, *After Mount Laurel: The New Suburban Zoning* (New Brunswick, N.J., 1977); and the special issue of *Social Policy*, vol. 10 (1979).

Recent architectural books cover a wide range. Mary Mix Foley, *The American House* (New York, 1980) has prototypical drawings. Charles Moore, Gerald Allen, and Donlyn Lyndon, *The Place of Houses* (New York, 1974) is concerned with intricate personal spaces. Oscar Newman, *Community of Interest* (Garden City, N.Y., 1980) analyzes ways to humanize institutional-scale housing. Newman's earlier *Defensible Space* (New York, 1973) condemned the danger as well as the monotony of public-housing towers. *The Form of Houses*, ed. Sam Davis (New York 1978) gives a range of viewpoints, from the political to the formalistic. Martin Pawley, *Architecture versus Housing* (New York, 1971) and *Homeownership* (New York, 1979) are provocative refutations of more traditional ways of viewing the home.

The real place to find current material is in magazines and newspapers. In particular, see *Working Papers for a New Society, Shelterforce, Social Policy,* and *Tenant Voice. Southern Exposure* put out an excellent issue on "Building South," vol. 8 (1980). For a range of more popular magazines' coverage of the housing crisis, see W.S. Kowinski, "Suburbia: End of the Golden Age," *The New York Times Magazine,* March 16, 1980; R. M. Williams, "Assault on Fortress Suburbia: How Long Can the Poor Be Kept Out?" *Saturday Review* 6 (1978); and Roger L. Williams, "Our Cities Are Showing Age but also Showing Signs of Fight," *Smithsonian Magazine* 9 (1979) on rehab programs for low-income groups.

On the special situation of women, see Kathleen McCourt, *Working Class Women and Grass Roots Politics* (Bloomington, Ind., 1977); Donald Rothblatt, Jo Sprague, and Daniel Garr, *The Suburban Environment and Women* (New York, 1979); *Women in Architecture: Historical and Contemporary Perspectives,* ed. Susana Torre (New York, 1977); *New Space for Women,* ed. Gerda Wekerle, Rebecca Peterson, and David Morley (Boulder, Colo., 1980); Ronald Lawson and Stephen E. Barton, "Sex Roles in Social Movements: A Case Study of the Tenant Movement in New York City," *Signs: A Journal of Women in Culture and Society* 6 (1980), which analyzes women's involvement in tenant organizations throughout the twentieth century; and the special issue of

Signs entitled *Women in the American Cities* (supplement to volume 5, Spring 1980). A positive view about the family is found in Mary Jo Bane. *Here to Stay: American Families in the Twentieth Century* (New York, 1976) and *Changing Images of the Family*, ed. Virginia Tufte and Barbara Meyerhoff (New Haven, 1979). Two important critical works are Jacques Donzelot, *The Policing of Families*, trans. Robert Hurley (New York, 1979); and Michel Foucault, *The History of Sexuality, vol. 1: An Introduction*, trans. Robert Hurley (New York, 1978).

INDEX